THE AUTHORS have been rowing correspondents and commentators throughout Jurgen Grobler's two lives. They met when Hugh Matheson was rowing in the national squad in the early 1970s and Chris Dodd was chasing the squad round the regatta circuit on behalf of the *Guardian*. In one capacity or another, they have witnessed all of Grobler's World and Olympic performances. When Dodd's *Guardian* colleague Charlie Burgess was appointed sports editor of the new *Independent* newspaper in 1986 and sought a rowing specialist, Dodd recommended Matheson who had recently retired as a competitor.

HUGH MATHESON's rowing career began when he fell into the Thames, aged thirteen, alongside the rafts at Eton. He thrived on the challenge of rowing, loved the adrenalin of racing and was hooked. Ten years on he was rowing in the British coxed four at the Munich Olympics, off the pace and finishing tenth.

Following a silver medal in the Montreal Olympic Games and a year off adapting to an unexpected inheritance in Sherwood Forest, Matheson bought a single sculling boat and found that he preferred to be solely responsible for his failures and successes. Having no one else to blame and no one else to claim the glory was the drug, although it left few excuses for a lamentable sixth place after a boat-stopping entanglement with a lane marker in the final of the single sculls in the Moscow Olympics of 1980.

At the Atlanta Olympics ten years later, Matheson became a summariser for Eurosport, an all-sports subscription television channel. This is his first book.

CHRIS DODD has written about rowing in newspapers, magazines and books since the coming of Janoušek in 1970. His introduction to rowing was as a schoolboy cox at Clifton College, having no talent for cricket. He progressed to the stroke seat of his school's second eight, a crew that satisfyingly beat the first eight in a challenge race at the end of the season. He stopped rowing after his first term at Nottingham University to edit the student newspaper, which led to a career on the *Guardian* in 1965.

As a *Guardian* staffer, his main job was layout, design and section editing in the features department, but he also worked on the sport and city pages.

He began writing about rowing at weekends in 1970, covering Boat Races and Henley regattas. He covered his first world championships in 1974 to witness Matheson's eight win a silver medal, and his first Olympics in 1984 to see Steve Redgrave launch his golden Olympic career in Los Angeles.

Dodd was the founding editor of Britain's *Regatta* magazine and FISA's *World Rowing* magazine.

In 1994 Dodd turned freelance when his off-the-wall scheme to set up the River & Rowing Museum in Henley-on-Thames became a reality. He was responsible for creating the rowing collection and library and curating special exhibitions.

Dodd is a board member of the Friends of Rowing History and has contributed to history symposia at the River & Rowing Museum and Mystic Seaport. From 1994 he continued as rowing correspondent at the *Guardian* until moving to the *Independent* in 2004.

This is his tenth book (for book details see www.doddsworld.org)

BOOKS BY CHRISTOPHER DODD

Henley Royal Regatta (1981)

The Oxford and Cambridge Boat Race (1983)

Boating (1983)

The Story of World Rowing (1992)

Battle of the Blues (Ed, 2004)

Water Boiling Aft (2006)

Pieces of Eight (2012)

Bonnie Brave Boat Rowers (2014)

Unto the Tideway Born (2015)

MORE POWER

The Story of Jurgen Grobler: The most
successful Olympic coach of all time.

Hugh Matheson & Christopher Dodd

ONE PLACE. MANY STORIES

HQ
An imprint of HarperCollins*Publishers* Ltd
1 London Bridge Street
London SE1 9GF

This edition 2018

1
First published in Great Britain by
HQ, an imprint of HarperCollins*Publishers* Ltd 2018

A catalogue record for this book is
available from the British Library.

ISBN: 978-0-00-821780-8 (HB)
ISBN: 978-0-00-821782-2 (TPB)

Printed and bound in Great Britain by
CPI Group (UK) Ltd, Croydon, CR0 4YY

MIX
Paper from
responsible sources
FSC™ C007454

For Bohumil 'Bob' Janoušek who changed the face of British rowing and put Britain's oarsmen back on the medal podium during his tenure as chief coach from 1970–76.

Contents

Preface

'Neil, you are a world champion. Now go and derig the boat.'
— JURGEN GROBLER

As *More Power* went to press, Jurgen Grobler was at the start of his eighth Olympiad as Britain's chief rowing coach for men, the first year of the four-year cycle that began as the Olympic flame died in Rio's stadium and will end four years later in Japan when he pilots a voyage to the Tokyo Olympics of 2020. In each of the previous seven Games, crews under his personal coaching have won gold medals, including two in Rio in 2016. At most of the world championships in non-Olympic years, his crews have also won gold medals. The pressure has never been greater for a man in his seventies who began his sensational run of successes in a previous life.

Grobler was brought up in Magdeburg, East Germany, studied at the hothouse of sporting achievement, Leipzig University, and produced Olympic golds in three Games for the country until the Berlin Wall collapsed in 1989, thawing the Cold War and leading to a new, united Germany. His forty-year Olympic career compares with no other in the history of sport.

From Munich when he was 26 to Rio when he was 70, his athletes

9

have gathered medals on the podium while he has stood nearby with joy and fulfilment on his face. But behind the tears in his eyes, his next campaign is beginning to take shape.

For the few engaged in full-time sport to the millions who watch and dream, the prize-giving and medal-kissing rituals – ceremonies with oldies in blazers and the winners swollen with muscular pride – are as glamorous as anything offered in life. Those peaks are reached only by doing a life term in grim physical exhaustion inspired solely by fear of failure. That's where Jurgen has lived six days a week for fifty years since the very beginning of his life in rowing at the German College of Physical Culture in Leipzig when he was preparing to climb the podium. Fifteen thousand days, perhaps, of anxiety and expertise, of working through simple solutions to complex problems, always alert for weakness in his athletes and in himself.

His job has offered extreme stress every day since he left school, and the matrix of his economic, political and social life has been as crisis-ridden as anyone's who has avoided living through a war. When he signed on to become a rowing coach in East Germany, it was an elite profession in a country which had chosen sport as its means of expression to avoid admitting that it was an expendable buffer of the Soviet Union, which in turn was suffering a bad reaction to the strain of its own contradictions.

He was one in a population of fifteen million, many of whom thought the grass was greener on the other side of the concrete wall that had been built 'for the protection' of the people, but where they were shot if they did not agree that they were happier where they were.

Countries like East Germany have always depended on State Security and on police, sometimes secret, sometimes public, but always brutal. Every citizen, Jurgen not excepted, has to determine the degree of collaboration he will offer to live the life that suits him and his family. There is discretion in each person's decision: you can choose to help the state and thrive, or you can offer less and get back much less. No one could treat the GDR with lofty humour and get away with it. Even the elites of the communist party, the SED – the equivalents of Eton, Oxford and a Tory cabinet in Britain – could not crack a joke and survive.

When the GDR suddenly fell apart in 1989, choices had to be made and opportunities grasped. Jurgen brought his family to live in Henley-on-Thames when he was hired to coach the world's best oarsmen of the time, Steve Redgrave and Matt Pinsent. By fate, luck or design, he exchanged the world's richest but now defunct rowing country for one destined – with his significant help – to rise to the top of the performance table.

This is his story.

I

1972
The Munich Olympiad

'Grobler understood that collaboration with the other key elements
would bring the results the state required.'
— KLAUS FILTER

Three-quarters of the way through the final of the single-sculls event
at the Munich Olympics in 1972, German political and sporting history was poised on the needle of a stopwatch. West German Udo
Hild was holding bronze-medal place by 0.02 of a second ahead of the
young, blond East German, Wolfgang Güldenpfennig. At the 1500-
metre mark, with 500 metres of the 2000-metre course left to decide,
the question was not only which German was the faster sculler, but
also which half of the nation had chosen the right path to prosperity
and prestige from the ruins of the Second World War. As it happened,
Güldenpfennig, the scion of Magdeburg, powered on to take third
place by nearly four seconds from the fading Hild.

This result was vindication for a training programme designed
not only to place the Magdeburger ahead of the West German, but to
put East Germany, at worst, third on the Olympic medal table behind
the United States, the world's richest nation with a population of 210
million, and the Soviet Union with 260 million people. East Germany

at the time had sixteen million and a wealth ranking at least twenty years behind its western neighbour.

Güldenpfennig's trainer was Jürgen Grobler, a 26-year-old assistant coach born and raised in Magdeburg. He had been a clever opportunist to identify Güldenpfennig and take him through national trials to the Olympic podium. He was an interpreter of a method and practice of rowing that informed the entire national effort, a practice that brought East Germany a harvest of sixty-six medals in 1972 – exactly two-thirds of the total won by the table-toppers, the Soviet Union. Grobler had a deeply researched and tested system on which to lean: East Germany's thrust to pile up medals at the 1972 Games in Munich was a national one-party-state sponsored effort, aimed particularly at the hated Federal Republic where Munich was the capital of Bavaria.

East Germany, the Deutsche Demokratische Republik, grew out of the post-war Soviet occupation zone and derived its authority from the Socialist Unity Party, or SED, and its Politbüro. It began its life as a separate nation in the buffer zone between East and West during the Cold War in 1949, when Jürgen Grobler was a three-year-old growing up in Magdeburg, a town almost completely destroyed by Allied bombers in 1945. It controlled every aspect of his life for the next forty years until it crumbled after its border crossings were thrown open and its people tore down the hated Berlin Wall in November 1989.

Team GDR, as the state would have been branded in the twenty-first century, had done well in the XIX Olympiad held in Mexico City, where a new rowing course was built at Xochimilco at an altitude of 2200 metres above sea level. Mexico was the first Games in which the two Germanys fielded separate teams, and what distinguished East Germany from all its competitors was the analysis to which the Mexico experience was submitted. The training programmes used since Tokyo in 1964 and the benefits and hazards of altitude training in particular were reassessed ruthlessly, and the 'right' approach was hammered out at a conference hosted by Manfred Ewald, the president of the German Gymnastics and Sports Federation, the body created to lead the impoverished nation to prestige on the international stage. Sport was a branch, or at least the principal lever, of foreign policy in the Politbüro's grand plan of 1959, and the Politbüro now had evidence that it was working. Rowing was established at all fifteen high-performance centres to give selected athletes the environment and support necessary to achieve the great things expected of them. The sportsclub at Magdeburg was in addition to the two nineteenth-century rowing clubs in the town that enjoyed good stretches of water on the Elbe for training and racing.

Ewald set the standard of achievement: 'The objective in Munich can only be to defend the third position won in Mexico and thus to place ahead of West Germany.' The federation decided that it should refine the number of disciplines in which East Germany could excel and concentrate the effort on eighteen summer sports. Among other excluded sports were basketball and modern pentathlon. In the case of basketball, there was no domestic league to match the Americans and, therefore, no realistic chance of a gold medal. As for modern pentathlon, one-fifth of the points come from a show-jumping competition on a horse picked at random from a paddock of similarly trained animals. Too much is left to chance for a state interested only in winning.

Rowing made the cut, and fifty million East German marks (£12 million at 1977 rates) was pushed into the 1972 Olympiad. By then rowing was a reliable source of medals, and Grobler, aged 23 in 1969 when the Munich plans were laid, was still studying sports science at Leipzig. When he graduated in 1970, he went straight into a post as assistant coach in his hometown.

Dr Peter Schwanitz, who describes himself as a biomechanics

specialist, came to know Grobler at that time in Berlin when Schwanitz was demonstrating boat testing at a training programme for elite coaches. Dr Theo Koerner, the head trainer of the East German rowing association DRSV, led the programme and promoted Grobler, enabling him and Sportclub Magdeburg to prosper.

Schwanitz says of Grobler today that he 'was always very interested in the science of training', science which encompassed all the specialisms that constitute a full understanding of how a human can move a boat over the required 2000 metres. Whenever a coach deconstructs a race, he or she will look at the split times for each quarter of the course and measure how these vary from perfectly even splits. In Munich, Hild's race showed 102 seconds for the first 500, 109.7 seconds for the second, 114 seconds for the third and, in spite of the need for a final sprint, 115 seconds for the last 500. Alongside him, Wolfgang Güldenpfennig began more slowly at 103 seconds and gave away a further second (or one boat length in a single scull) to 1000 metres in under 111 seconds. He pulled all of Hild's lead back to draw level at the 1500-metre mark in 112 seconds and left him wallowing in his wake in fourth place by covering the last 500 in fewer than 109 seconds.

Seen from the grandstand, Güldenpfennig held on to a place in the middle of the pack of scullers from the start and then sculled at a more even pace for the next three-quarters of the race, clocking successively 110, 112, 108.67 seconds for each 500 metres. Hild was quicker to the first and second marks before going progressively more slowly over the second half. While far from perfect, Güldenpfennig was demonstrating the superb endurance and racing nous that marked all the great East German crews of that era, and it was Grobler who had developed that ability in his 20-year-old club mate.

Hild's race pattern of a quick first half followed by a slow second was standard practice for western nations, and even for other Eastern

European states where full-time training should have resulted in greater endurance. The gold-medal winner in Munich, the Russian Yury Malyshev, took eleven seconds longer over the second half. The silver medallist Alberto Demiddi from Argentina was just over ten seconds slower and Hild, as we have seen, was seventeen seconds slower. Güldenpfennig dropped only 7.5 seconds.

Güldenpfennig's preparation brought him far closer than everyone else to the even-paced splits ideal, and his trainer could claim some of the credit. However, the same pattern becomes evident when analysis is applied to all the East German medal-winning crews in Munich. The Germans were doing something consistently and well. The training programme designed by Dr Koerner was applied across all the performance centres. So Grobler would have started with a paper in his hand that told him exactly how much work was to be done, and at what pace, in each of thirteen sessions a week. The key was to equip him to test his charge on a daily basis to measure improvement and detect overtraining before it became apparent to anyone, including the athlete.

The East German trainers employed the 'super-compensation cycle', which is now universal. The athlete is pushed harder and harder for about six weeks of continuous training with no respite and builds up 'residual fatigue' so that the recovery between sessions is compromised. Then, when the bottom has been reached and the standard measures are well off the pace, the trainer's foot is lifted from the pedal and light work is allowed for a number of days. The leap in recovery is marked by sharply improved measurements and, if the system is applied properly, the athlete soon rises above his previous best. Once the improvement is secured, the cycle is repeated with another sustained period of increasingly hard work until the bottom of the graph is reached again and the pressure is relieved to allow another rise, to a new peak.

Some of the East Germans were light years ahead of every other nation in the application of science to measure improvement and to detect decline in the performance of an individual in otherwise full health. This is the application of good science that Schwanitz recognised in Grobler. It was a safeguard against overtraining, and sometimes a complete collapse, that can result when a trainer uses unsophisticated measures to assess how deeply the hard work part of the cycle has bitten into the athlete's performance, or if he is insensitive to a change in demeanour. Klaus Filter – who, as the leader of the team that developed the GDR fleet of competition boats, knew all the coaches – says that some of the Navy and Army coaches would measure only the number of strokes to the minute and number of kilometres covered to decide that the training had been successful. It was Grobler's job to ensure that Magdeburg athletes were trained better and more wisely in order to beat the Navy and Army clubs by applying his sophisticated knowledge acquired at the university in Leipzig.

The other ingredient of training athletes better than any rivals was provision of support to enable them to accept the punishing regime. They were offered better accommodation in the high-performance centres than they would ever be likely to find at home. Their diet was enhanced well above the norm – the standard training of an international rower requires consumption of about 6500 calories a day for a man, in the proportion 50 per cent carbohydrates, 30 per cent fats and 20 per cent protein. These amounts were made available in SC Magdeburg, where Jürgen Grobler worked, by two club cooks with no one else to cater for.

Additionally, the scientists searched for any other medical cushion that would enable the bodies they trained to absorb more work without breaking down. In 1962 the East German state pharmacological research and development enterprise, Jenapharm, had isolated an anabolic steroid that it called Oral Turinabol. It was made available for therapeutic use in 1965. Within a year, testing for its effectiveness and for the appropriate dosage for athletes had begun. Once it was approved by the medical team it was made available to the coaches. It was the coaches' decision, not the medical team's, to use it to assist athletes. Men and, more controversially, women were dosed in time for the 1968 Olympics in Mexico City.

Oral Turinabol – a synthetic version of testosterone, the hormone that is known to increase muscle mass and bone density – was the 'little blue pill' on the breakfast tray of all East Germans training in sports that require either explosive or endurance strength. The athletes had to be seen to take the pill by the coach. The pills could not be taken home or even out of the room because of the secrecy surrounding the whole programme. The pills were described as 'support' and the athletes were not told of their content. Indeed, most experiments involved a control group that took a blue placebo.

Güldenpfennig was in the programme and his training intensity would have taken account of the assistance given by the drug. Grobler understood – better than many of his less curious colleagues – what was in the blue pill and will have measured its benefit and reported his findings to the medical commission, run directly by Manfred Ewald, through the Sport Medical Service and its deputy director and chief physician. At the Mexico Olympics in 1968 when Grobler was still studying in Leipzig, testing of competitors for illegal doping was rudimentary and the list of banned substances was short and unso-phisticated. Few were discovered to be abusing performance drugs, but the divisions of opinion around the ethical questions posed by their use were becoming clear. The rights and wrongs of this matter were the subject of every coaching and training conference.

Without doubt, the physiological effect of added testosterone and the methodology to establish the most beneficial dose will have been part of the curriculum that Grobler followed. The bulk of the research work at PhD level in the adaptation to sport of therapeutic drugs was carried out in the German College of Physical Culture in Leipzig. There, too, the research studied the damaging side effects and the point at which more damage than benefit was being felt, and when an athlete should be dropped from the programme.

The institute where Grobler was a student was the mothership of the East German sports doping programme, working to orders from the Politbüro. He and his classmates will not have been allowed to graduate without a deep understanding of the development of sports doping at that time. But, unlike almost every other person considering the problem elsewhere in the world, their freedom of expression, and even of thought, was strictly controlled. They had no choice. Even the option of a dignified resignation and exit from their career path was denied. If Grobler or any of his contemporaries had resigned over the state-sponsored doping regime, the quality of life for them and their families would have been compromised deeply and quickly. They could have been convicted and imprisoned for open conflict with the 'vanguard of the people' or its representative on earth, the Politbüro. More likely, they would have found that housing and work were denied them.

The authorities' adverse reaction to a coach or athlete who bucked the system and refused the drugs is the explanation offered by Grobler himself on the few occasions when he has been challenged on his record of compliance with the regime. His mantra has been 'You have to understand the system at that time. There was no room for disagreement.'

What is rarely admitted – probably because it sounds foolish to readers in a liberal western democracy – is that most of the population of East Germany were part of the collective consciousness expressed as 'We are the state'. On the opening page of *Das Rudern*, the detailed rowing textbook published in 1977, the first paragraph ends:

'The principal objectives of the sport of rowing in the GDR are: 1. The achievement of high performances in competitive rowing for men, women and youths, based on a wide membership, on a comprehensive and systematic basic training, and on a party and class-conscious education of the oarsman into a socialist sports personality.'

The third paragraph ends:

'In addition, general or specific work in the sport of rowing is carried out in the German College of Physical Culture, in the various Sport Science Committees, in obligatory student sports, in schools, in the National People's Army, and in the People's Police, in agreement with the goals of the DRSV.'

These 'socialist sports personalities' were all willing and 'conscious' members of an elite in East German society that earned its privileges by working harder than anyone else to achieve the aims of the state in beating all contenders. They were the 'vanguard of the people' who represented the state abroad.

Already by 1972, only twenty-three years after the state came into existence and in only its second Olympic Games competing as a separate nation, the under-performance of its socialist economy was impossible to hide. For one thing, the Soviet Union had dismantled much of its satellite's industry. For another, freedom of movement between East and West, difficult since 1945, was blocked completely in 1963 when the already robust frontier to the West was doubled in strength and the walled section through the divided city of Berlin was built. But during this Cold War, television had come to almost every household on both sides of the border, and so East Germans were reminded daily of the gulf in living standards.

In late August 1972 the sun shone on teams arriving in Munich and reflected off the revolutionary acrylic panels in the roof of the main stadium. Everything from the accommodation in the athlete village, to the U-Bahn underground system, to the rowing course at Oberschleißheim – built for the occasion at cost of DM7 million – seemed on the cutting edge of modernist architecture and design. It felt, and was, superior to any Olympic venue in the modern era. It pushed the boundaries of experience in the same way as, it was hoped, the competitions would push the boundaries of human physical achievement.

Into this showcase of expectation and glamour came a drably uniformed rowing team, picked not for their joy in taking part but for their probability of winning medals. There were seven events for men and none for women. A full team comprised twenty-six people, including three coxes. The East German team met the standard it had been set from above by winning a medal in each event. Güldenpfennig won bronze in the single sculls, while Hans-Joachim Böhmer and Hans-Ulrich Schmied also took bronze in the double sculls. East Germany won gold in the coxless pair with the youthful Siegfried Brietzke and Wolfgang Mager, and in the coxed pair with Wolfgang Gunkel and Jörg Lucke, steered by Klaus-Dieter Neubert. They won the coxless fours with arguably their best boat and most reliable medal bet, but lost the coxed fours to the West Germans who had put all their talent into the only boat they could see as a 'banker'.

In the grand finale, the eights, East Germany's young rowers, at the outset of their careers, were beaten into bronze-medal position by the reigning European champions New Zealand and by a surprise American crew in a photo finish. East Germany's tally was three golds, one silver, and three bronzes. The next-best nation on the medal table, the Soviet Union, had two golds in the sculling events but nothing else. West Germany, New Zealand and Czechoslovakia had two medals each, and six nations had one apiece. GBR ranked 14th on the results table. Manfred Ewald and SED secretary Walter Ulbricht should have rejoiced at the result of their directives.

The team and its coaches were rewarded with a cruise to Cuba, the only resort that combined an exotic location with the minimum risk of escape. Even for champion swimmers, Florida was a long way off.

Jürgen Grobler had fulfilled his state-sanctioned quota when Güldenpfennig took a medal at the first international experience for either of them. Both had been outsiders for selection in the winter before, but were now recognised members of the team and would not be dislodged easily. Grobler told Michael Calvin, writing for The *Independent* in 2012, that 'I know I cannot run away from my past… some things that were going on at that time might not have been correct, but I can look everybody in the eye and not feel guilty. I am not a doping coach. I am not a chemist.' That comment might be true superficially but, once deconstructed, it looks disingenuous.

In the winter of 1971–2 Grobler and Güldenpfennig had pushed themselves into the front line of a demonstration of state power focused on winning Olympic medals. In their climb through the ranks they had pushed weaker men aside. The East German team for the 1971 European rowing championships in Copenhagen had seventeen names later selected for Munich.

There was no obligation on Grobler or Güldenpfennig to force their way into the national reckoning. They chose to put their names into the record book. They achieved it by doing the training better than their contemporaries and by embracing the system wilfully and willingly. They knew about the Oral Turinabol and knew its benefits. At no point in his denials has Grobler said, 'We tried it and found that it did not work.'

When the doping issue became a subject for debate in the 1990s after the collapse of East Germany, Grobler at first said he did not know about it. When that became untenable he said that 'some things that were going on at that time might not have been correct, but I can look everybody in the eye and not feel guilty.' It is perfectly conceivable that he does not feel guilty and does not think of himself as 'a doping coach' or a 'chemist'. In the morality of that place and time he did no wrong. The list of drugs that were banned was short and badly defined. There were wide pharmacological roads around most of the bans. When Oral Turinabol was given to athletes it was proven to be extremely stable and in a therapeutic setting it had high safety ratings. It was effective in building lean muscle and bone mass. It was perfect for their purposes and it had two other qualities essential for the East German Olympic programme: it could be matched with epitestosterone to mask the evidence that the extra testosterone was synthetic, and it would be flushed out of the athlete's body in a short time after the dose was stopped.

However, doping played only a small part in Grobler's application of the best science flowing from the German College of Physical Culture in Leipzig and elsewhere. The East German team used boats built beside the River Spree in Berlin using a hull profile that was unique at that time. It was designed to have the lowest wetted area — that is, the amount of skin in contact with the water — to reduce the friction or drag. It was designed to pitch and yaw less as the oarsmen moved their weight back and forth on the runners of their sliding seats. It had enough stiffness not to wallow as the weight within it shifted, but was flexible enough to absorb much of the counterforce of rough water to minimise slow-down.

Up to this point, individual boat yards had modified existing designs to seek incremental improvements. They had been subject to fashion but not much hydrological research. The East Germans went about it with legendary thoroughness and seemingly unlimited financial resources. The naval architect who bossed the programme from the start, Klaus Filter, had started rowing at sixteen in Berlin when he began an apprenticeship with the racing-boat builder, Friedrich Pirsch. As his rowing and sculling improved he was steered in the direction of the newly empowered College of Physical Culture in

Leipzig 'to fill his time while in training'. After graduation he went back to work at Pirsch. By the mid-Sixties he was obliged to look for new materials to build the fine shells because East Germany was finding it difficult to import the South American cedars which were then deemed the only material combining strength and flexibility in appropriate measures. The East German state aircraft manufacturer, EFW, had been put out of business in 1961 – probably as a result of Russian interference – and its facilities were made available to the burgeoning sports-equipment research programme.

Filter was able to start experiments with light and strong plastic 'sandwich' materials and in his thirties he decided to enhance his boat-building skills by taking a two-year naval architecture course at the university in Rostock. From that he began developing boat designs from first principles. Theoretically they were the fastest built, but they were impossible to row. The means to a solution for the 'perfect design' versus 'practical for humans to row' was ready-made because rowing as a national sport was already functioning in all its aspects through a committee of the leading coaches, training scientists, experts in biomechanics, medical men, with Filter heading up the technology side with boat designs and materials. Filter says Grobler was, from the beginning, an authoritative voice who understood that collaboration with the other key elements would bring the results the state required.

Biomechanical work with athletes, combined with Filter's hull dynamics, was crucial in developing the style of rowing which obtained the best out of boats and men. East German crews rowed a long arc by curving the back forwards to enable the arms to reach a long way forward without unduly compressing the legs onto the foot-stretcher that is fixed to the hull. The boat is then levered past the point where the blades are locked into the water. The large flat area of the blade prevents it being torn through the water while the boat is drawn past the lock point by the strength and skill of the oarsman. This rowing style places more strain on the lower back muscles than could be borne by many western oarsmen who trained under a shorter but more intense regime. The East German coaches had full-time professional athletes and so could indulge themselves with long sessions at less intense pressure. They could develop the lower-back strength slowly and carefully over time. The bodies, the style and the boats were each designed for maximum compatibility. Filter, assisted by Grobler, was working to perfect the knowledge of the amount of flex and best hull shape for the boat to match the reaction time of the athletes. If the boat rolls, the rowers must adjust their weight and application of power to match. If the reaction is too slow the roll becomes worse and the boat speed is impaired. The task at which they excelled was to match training to boat shape so as to produce the style of propulsion desired to cover the endurance distance of 2000 metres. It was not a sprint: Grobler and Filter succeeded in developing a type of training that matched athletes and their boats to the distance.

In 1972 Güldenpfennig was given a boat with a plastic laminate hull, finished in soon-to-be-ubiquitous Wehrmacht grey, fitted with a wooden seat and washboards. It was the latest development. Götz Draeger, the man he replaced, had won silver in the European championships in Copenhagen in 1971 in a wooden shell, along with all his teammates. Film of the final in Munich shows Güldenpfennig sculling in the same style as the sweep oarsmen, using his curved back and outstretched arms at the start of the stroke to place the blades in the water as far forward as possible.

The ironies of East Germany's dominance of Olympic rowing in Munich were many. The original award of the Games to the Bavarian capital by the International Olympic Committee had given immense satisfaction to its president, Avery Brundage. Brundage had risen from poverty on Chicago's east side to own the largest construction group in the city and to forge a dominant role in US athletics. He had one obsession, which was a hatred of communism and communists, and one closeted dislike, which was for Jews. To hold the Games in a state that shared a long, walled-off border with a communist one must have pleased him.

Munich's organising committee rose so high to meet the expectations of the Olympic family that hubris was almost certainly heading for a fall. From the start, the Soviet Union and East Germany were winning half as many golds again, with fewer athletes between them, than the United States and West Germany combined. Then on 5 September, early in the second week, came the devastating hostage-taking and murder of thirteen members of the Israeli team by Black September terrorists. The East German rowers were not there to see the shaming of the West German security services in their botched response to the crisis. They had been sent home immediately after their medal ceremonies to avoid western temptations in general and defection in particular.

Brundage, aged 85, who was due to retire as president of the IOC at the end of the Games, spoke at the hugely moving memorial service in the main stadium on the following day. He said that the 'Games must go on' and was applauded warmly. But some later revised their opinion after noting Brundage's deemed hostility to Judaism had been particularly evident in his support for US participation in the Berlin Games of 1936.

The circumstances of Munich's embarrassment left the East German leadership enjoying a moment of *schadenfreude*. Although beaten by two scullers, both of whom could be described as idiosyncratic and brilliant, Grobler's protégé, Güldenpfennig, was a great example of a socialist team ethic. He had only himself to rely on in his races, but he was shaped in the classic East German mould, an interchangeable cog in a bigger machine. He would race the single again in 1973, with the same bronze-medal result, but thereafter he moved into the quadruple-sculls event, introduced to the programme at the 1974 world rowing championships and won by East Germans every year without interruption until 1993.

Jürgen Grobler was hitched to this star and accompanied him, as coach of the quadruple scull, to his first Olympic gold in Montreal in 1976.

2

1976
The Montreal Olympiad

'He began informing quietly eighteen months after the first approach. He was given the lightest disguise possible with the codename, "Jürgen".'
— HUGH MATHESON

The Olympics crossed the Atlantic after Munich but, before the flame reached Montreal in 1976, international rowing had changed profoundly. The last European championships of the era were held in 1973 on the Krylatskoe course on the western edge of Moscow where winning medals had been turned into a lottery by a ferocious wind which allowed the crews on or close to lane one an advantage of up to ten seconds over lane six. Güldenpfennig finished third behind the new West German sensation, 20-year-old Peter-Michael Kolbe, who had drawn 'lucky' lane one.

The IOC added six women's events to the Olympic rowing programme for 1976. FISA, the international federation, set the distance for women's events at 1000 metres – half that for men – in the mistaken impression that women lacked endurance strength in the same way they lacked explosive strength compared to men. But the shorter course gave the advantage to athletes with more explosive strength and greater muscle bulk while taking it away from the longer-limbed, leaner and more lithe athletes. In its preliminary selection of women likely to enjoy and prosper in competitive rowing, East Germany sought out the same body type favoured for field events such as shot put and discus. Coincidentally this short, three-minute race gave added scope for the use of synthetic testosterone. It was another twelve years before FISA corrected this mistake by extending the women's distance to 2000 metres in time for the XXIV Olympiad in Seoul in 1988.

Meanwhile, Jürgen Grobler's next fortunate break after bringing Güldenpfennig from his provincial club to an Olympic medal was the introduction of the men's quadruple sculls to the world and Olympic regatta schedule from 1974. The IOC agreed to the addition in 1971, but FISA only ratified the boat in its programme in October 1973, ten months before the world championship regatta in Lucerne the following August. It was hardly surprising that the 1974 East German team came closest to a total shut-out, when the men's team won six golds and one silver medal, with the eight in fourth place. The GDR women were similarly dominant with four golds, a silver and a bronze medal.

The quadruple sculls, with the added weight of a coxswain, had been introduced to the women's international programme in 1957, when East Germany won its first medal, a bronze for the crew from the Sports Institute of Leipzig. By the mid-seventies the East German system was producing a squad of scullers – both men and women – big and strong enough to win the single, double and quadruple categories. Athletes rotated between boats according to the finest calculations of coaches as to which event had the weakest foreign competition and could thus be won without necessarily absorbing all the talent. There was a bias in favour of the sculling events, which arose from the national policy – set out in full in *Das Rudern* – that the novice should begin with, and master, sculling and the technique of handling an oar in each hand. Most of their time was spent in the single-scull boat before they took up 'sweep' rowing, in which a single oar is held in both hands.

Das Rudern asserted: 'It may be pointed out that youths can learn sweep rowing quite early on without hesitation, but on orthopaedic grounds, they should not be allowed to take part in sweep boat competitions until boys are fourteen and girls are sixteen. Learning periods for sweep rowing should not exceed one hour.' The outcome of this early concentration on sculling up to the years of competition and selection is that the best and most able athletes were trained and tested as scullers first, and promoted to the elite programmes as scullers, leaving lower achievers to crew the bigger sweep boats.

Throughout the 1960s and 1970s East German teams had an extraordinary record in the smaller sweep classes of coxless pairs and fours, but more patchy outcomes in the larger eights. The results in the two sculling events were also not so glittering because the single and double scullers were more likely to be pitched up against a lone outstanding athlete, representing a minor rowing nation that was not sufficiently organised to manage a coaching and training programme like East Germany's.

The GDR single-sculling representative always had the hardest task of the team. Gossip was fed to western rowers by Ulli Schmied, two-time Olympic medallist in the double sculls, that the East German sculling squad would endeavour to race hard enough to stay in the top seven but not to be top dog because that would put them in the 'hard to win' singles event. They preferred to rank from fourth to seventh to ensure a place in the quadruple sculls. Good evidence backs Schmied's claim. From 1962 to 1989 the winner of the GDR national team trials and most years, when the timetable allowed, the national championships was selected as the single sculler for the world or European championships (with the exception of 1981 when Rüdiger Reiche raced and won the single at the world championships in Lucerne after Uwe Mund had won the national title). The same principle applied to the double and quadruple sculls: the national champions, drawn from state sports clubs but trained as a composite group, were selected to travel abroad to represent their country.

Because of its unified nationwide programme, all top athletes were matched in style and technique. There were no eccentric coaches in outlying clubs with bees in their bonnets about laying back at the finish until their spines touched the breakwater or other stylistic flourishes. *Das Rudern*'s chapter on the technique of sculling is inflexible: 'Since the ends of the inboard levers cut across one another in the pull and in the slide forward, one hand leads slightly and goes slightly under the other at these two points. The rule in the DRSV is: Left hand in front of and under the right hand.' The passage concludes: 'This general rule is important and must be binding to avoid losing time when national crews or racing teams are being assembled.'

In the Seventies and Eighties none of the major rowing nations followed such a simple policy, and consequently their top coaches found themselves teaching fully developed scullers to change the leading and higher hand to match new partners. The exceptional results for the GDR came at least as much from ruthless application of very simple rules as from any real difference in style.

The GDR coaches could take the next-best finishers after the single and double scullers had been selected and fit them into a quad boat with little or no adaptation required save to set the rigging to accommodate physical differences in height and reach. Jürgen Grobler was able to place Rüdiger Reiche (1m 98cm) and Güldenpfennig (1m 82cm) together in the 1974 quadruple scull, which won the world championship event. Filter assisted him in this by measuring the most efficient arc of each athlete – some taller, some shorter, some with a short torso and long arms, some blessed with longer legs. Filter then adjusted the length of each scull overall, and the amount of lever from the sculler's hand to the fulcrum or 'pin' and the amount outboard of the pin. What Grobler and Filter devised – in collaboration with the biomechanical expert Schwanitz and all the other branches of their rowing committee – was a particular set-up from the boat's keel to the tip of his blade for each athlete which would maximise his output while leading to greater uniformity of the whole crew. Thus, to the spectator, the crew looked perfectly uniform in its movements on the water but once they had lifted the boat out of the water and put it on the rack you could see that Reiche and Güldenpfennig were entirely different body types.

Decades later in 1991, when Grobler first started coaching Steve Redgrave and Matthew Pinsent, he invited Klaus Filter to advise on the best boat and rig for them to employ. At that time Pinsent was 15 kg heavier and rowing in the bow seat which pushed the boat down into the water at high speed, creating unnecessary drag. Also Pinsent was trying to pull the boat round to demonstrate his strength on every stroke. It was mechanically easier for him because he was closer to the bows. Filter came to live with the boat-builders, the Ayling family, while he redesigned the hull and the material of its construction to suit the two athletes. While Grobler worked on their strength, fitness and race plan, Filter calculated and built the perfect platform for their exceptional strength. The crew improved from bronze medal in 1990 to gold in the 1991 world championships.

None of the small two- or three-athlete nations could compete in the quads. It was a boat type not much used or known in the West until the world received a masterclass from a crew coached by Grobler. By the early Seventies East Germany had 300 professionals involved in coaching and supporting its international rowing community. They were attached to one or other of the fifteen sports centres, and were drawn up from there to train composite international crews selected from several competing centres. Grobler's star may have been hitched to Güldenpfennig, but he had other Magdeburg athletes like Martin Winter, Peter Kersten and Stefan Weisse up his sleeve. The quadruple scull was the perfect vehicle for his thorough and scientifically tested ambitions, offering the greatest speed per athlete of any boat type. (An eight will go faster, but it has twice the number of bodies to pull it along. All other things being equal, an international eight will cover the 2000-metre course about twenty seconds faster than a quadruple scull.) Jürgen Grobler saw the quad as providing his next step up the coaching hierarchy in East Germany, and it was important that he used the prominence his success with Güldenpfennig had given him wisely. From his first appearance in the national coaching hierarchy, he was known to be ferociously ambitious and he soon acquired the nickname 'Schweinsdick' or 'Piggydick', which should be translated in an almost admiring way rather like the British would say 'Goldenballs'. Sometimes the nickname was adapted to 'Schweine Schlau' or 'canny like a pig' – again generally used affectionately. He was recognised as a man who was 'always clever' and who would 'spot the opportunity and make the right decisions' to achieve his ambition.

The East German training plan was to row up to 13,000 km a year, which breaks down to about 40 km per day taken in two sessions, with a third session of weights in the gymnasium or cross-country skiing in winter. At this huge quantity, Grobler once said: 'sometimes we made the work too hard and we got no improvement, [so] it was necessary to do most of the training at less than full pressure.' The crucial skill in a coach who is pushing athletes to the limit of their natural endurance is to know when they are overtrained. If, at a set time in the cycle, a piece of work is usually done at 80 per cent of gold-medal time and the crew is only able to manage 75 per cent, he must look hard for the reason. In the absence of a better explanation, overtraining is suspected, and either the load is reduced or the capacity of the athlete is increased.

If the speed required to win an Olympic gold medal is 100 per cent, then all training over a measured distance can be expressed as a percentage of gold-medal time. Grobler is well known for his accuracy in predicting the expected improvement in times for each event in the four years leading to the next Olympics. In the autumn of an Olympic year he will make his calculation taking all factors into account, and then correct the time for flat water conditions with no wind assistance or hindrance. The world best-time, usually set in a tight race by one of the best crews in the most favourable following wind, is inevitably much faster than the Olympic gold target. Grobler imported this systematic method to the British team when he arrived at Leander in 1991, having used it with his quadruple scull ten years before. Once the gold-medal standard is set, the coach has a baseline to measure all training, and once he has followed one or two super-compensation cycles he knows how his athletes can be expected to perform.

East Germany's first generation of athletes trained in its pioneering use of sport as an instrument of foreign policy raced in Mexico in 1968 and retired after Munich in 1972. Four years later the men's team for the Montreal Olympics looked different, with more opportunities for athletes to push up into the team. Grobler wanted the best of the Magdeburg boys to be among them. In addition to Güldenpfennig and Winter, he had Weisse. He took these three to national trials and formed the quadruple for the world championships in Nottingham in 1975. The final crew, which won the national trials easily, had Güldenpfennig at stroke and Weisse in the number-two seat. His new protégé Winter was selected in the singles and won the bronze medal behind the brilliant but inconsistent Peter-Michael Kolbe of West Germany and the 'lone wolf' Irishman, Seán Drea. Joachim Driefke and Jürgen Bertow who had been in the inaugural world-championship quads took the silver medal behind Norway in the double sculls. These results made Ulli Schmied's point that a gold in the quads was the more certain and easier option.

In a nation where success in international sport was the most praiseworthy achievement a citizen could manage, this shuffling to stay out of the top three, but to finish in the top seven, was almost comic. The presiding genius who somehow ensured that he had most of his club members in the crew and was thus selected to coach them at the world championships and Olympics was 'Schweinsdick' Grobler.

There were fifteen trainers in SC Magdeburg when he arrived straight after graduation in 1970, but Grobler soon asserted himself and began to dominate the coaching set-up. When the authors visited the club in June 2017 — on the day before some of the buildings put up at the time of maximum investment by the regime were to be pulled down — they found a group of men in their seventies who had been elite rowers at the time Jürgen arrived. They were reminiscing around a table in the upstairs office, with a half-empty case of beers at their feet. They remembered him as just one of the coaching team — "he was nothing special at first" — but, with frequent breaks to argue about how hard they did or did not have to work and who was in the crew when they won the championships, they gradually recalled the socially adept, seemingly artless man who always spotted the coming talent and then trained it to perform at the highest level. They also remembered how Hörst Häckel, one of the first-team coaches, had taken two of the club's boys, Friedrich-Wilhelm Ulrich and Manfred Kässner, in the coxless pair to win the world junior championships in 1971 to make SC Magdeburg's first success on the international stage. Jürgen found another club member to take the first Olympic honours in 1972, and a year after that he had nailed his personal flag to Ulrich and Kässner. Perhaps Häckel had meant it to work out like that, perhaps not. The former rowers had a shrewd idea that Grobler would abide by whatever imperatives the world he lived in required: if success, and the space required to achieve it, was reached by being a member of the party or by paying attention in the daily political education classes, Grobler would conform unobtrusively.

The system needed both the coaches who would tune the engines for its success and it needed plenty of engines ready and willing to be trained. Jan Frehse, later a national and a junior world champion, describes how he was recruited by SC Magdeburg at the age of 14. After a class at his school's gymnasium a representative from the club asked the assembled pupils: 'Who here is 1m 80cm tall?' Frehse was measured as 1m 86cm and asked if he wanted to become an elite sportsman by joining the rowing programme. He says in that winter of 1976–7 there were too few large youngsters in the rowing clubs of the district, so all the schools were searched for suitable candidates. Frehse spent his spring holidays at the club with nineteen other boys. They were measured by strength tests, running competitions and their first attempts at rowing a boat. When Frehse finished top of the group he was subjected to more tests, including a prediction of his fully grown height that turned out to be accurate at 1m 94cm. He was told that rowers from SCM 'always fulfil their performance orientated mission.'

Throughout the history of the GDR and up to the present day, the Magdeburg club was best known for its handball teams which have been out of the top spot in Germany only rarely since it was founded in 1959. But on his arrival in the club's rowing arm, standing on the Großer Werder island in the Elbe in the heart of Magdeburg, Grobler found 'a boat house and a river and nothing else.' By his intervention a hostel and a state-of-the-art fitness centre were added. It would be wrong to attribute all of this success to Jürgen. He was part of a team of thirty people at the club: fifteen trainers, two administrators, two boat-builders, two drivers, three physiotherapists, a nurse, two doctors and two cooks. The reputation of the club's education section, which looked after the children who had been taken out of normal school to be trained as athletes, was high too.

The structure of elite sport in East Germany originated in the Politbüro, was encouraged by the SED's secretary Walter Ulbricht, and driven by the Ministry of State Security, known universally as the Stasi. The Stasi guided every enterprise whether industrial or social. It commanded the scarce resources and directed them where the Politbüro demanded. Every successful person in any walk of life was a member of the party, and every place of work and sports club had at least one informer. According to his personal Stasi file, Jürgen was first approached by the party in 1973 and is recorded as having been recruited in 1975. That means that he was not embarrassed into informing by being caught out in a misdemeanour. Such an occur-rence would have made recruitment immediate, a sentence of guilt by blackmail. Instead, he and his Stasi handlers took their time, and he began informing quietly eighteen months after the first approach. He was given the lightest disguise possible with the codename 'Jürgen'.

Grobler's party membership, status as an informer and coaching ability were all crucial to obtaining investment and ensuring appropri-ate support for athletes at the spearhead of the national reputation. From the 1972 Munich Olympics to Moscow in 1980, the coach's loyalty to Magdeburg athletes was his prime motivation, while his national responsibilities increased.

**

If the men's quadruple scull was what would now be called a 'gimme', the men's coxed pair was the hardest and slowest boat in the regatta. The world champions in 1975 at Nottingham were Jörg Lucke and Wolfgang Gunkel and it was assumed that they would proceed seamlessly to the Montreal Games. But they were beaten in the East German trials by two Magdeburg men trained by Jürgen – at least after he had taken them from Häckel. Friedrich-Wilhelm Ulrich was a world-champion junior and Harald Jährling had won the Spartakiade – an exclusively East German youth championships – in the coxless pairs in 1972. Lucke was 34 at the time of the trials and Gunkel was 28, while the pretenders were both 22 that summer. It was an enormous coup and piece of cheek that put SC Magdeburg and Grobler even more firmly on the map.

Once selected, the team flew to a training camp at Sudbury on Lake Ontario, Canada, and spent weeks in acclimatisation and intense training leading up to the taper, during which the last super-compensation cycle was completed and the athletes recovered in time to arrive at the Olympic final in the highest possible state of fitness. There is one comic footnote in the GDR rowing story in the Stasi report on the 1976 team which lists the competitors, the entourage and – more important than the event they have trained for over a lifetime – their membership, or otherwise, of the party. Also listed is the duration and destination of telephone calls outside East Germany and other trivia that obsessed the Stasi. Buried in the notes on conversations with girls in Copenhagen is an urgent message to the managers of the rowing team to destroy their stocks of Oral Turinabol, Clomiphen and other anabolic steroids before leaving Sudbury for Montreal and the Games. The GDR boxing team had arrived in Montreal with the pills in their baggage, and to avoid detection they had been obliged to tear off the Jenapharm labels and throw everything into the St Lawrence river. The rowers were instructed not to make the same mistake.

Once they reached the Montreal finals, both Jürgen's crews exhibited his even-paced tactic demonstrated in Munich four years earlier. The quadruple scull, stroked by Güldenpfennig, tussled with the Russian quad for the first three 500-metre segments of the course with just fractions of a second separating them. Then in the last quarter the East Germans maintained their pace as the Russians faded, and the GDR quad took two seconds off the Soviet Union to win by half a length. In the coxed pair, Jährling and Ulrich came off the start slowly into the headwind and were seemingly stuck in third place until the 1500-metre mark, before sustaining then raising their race pace at the close to finish two seconds clear of the field. Grobler had seen his crews take the first two of his extraordinary collection of gold medals.

**

Of little concern to Grobler in Montreal were the shoots of a revolution growing in Britain. Bob Janoušek, the two-time Olympic bronze medallist, had trained at Charles University in Prague to a similar curriculum to the one in Leipzig but with less Marxist-Leninism or biochemistry of testosterone. Czechoslovakia had its big crisis with communism in 1968, and in 1969 Janoušek was allowed to take up the offer of a job from the Amateur Rowing Association (now British Rowing). His family came with him on the understanding that they would not be allowed to return to Czechoslovakia. When he arrived in England, he wrote a training programme for international athletes which adapted tried-and-tested East European methods. After a year, however, he found that nobody was following it and that the British national team's results were as bad as ever. Where, in odd cases, a crew and a coach could be found who did manage the long endurance training, there was an increase in lower-back injuries since the change of style required building up muscles and joints to take the stress, which meant a different regime from that of the traditional style of rowing in England.

After the debacle of the gale-torn 1973 world championships in Moscow, Janoušek decided that he would coach a national squad crew himself. He redesigned the system around training once a day after work, starting at 6 p.m. and attempting to be back in the boathouse in two hours. In an hour and a half of useful training he squashed as much as he could from the four- to five-hours system he had learned while reading sports science at Karlovy University and as a rower in Prague. The programme meant masses of intense work to build up lactic acid in the joints and pushing his men to exhaustion on every piece of work. Because they had not developed strong enough back muscles to lift their body and boat up from a long lean forward, Janoušek trained his crew to sit upright and use the sliding seat to compress their legs, so that the buttocks touched the ankles at full compression over the foot stretcher. From there they started the pull of the stroke with an explosive lift of the legs and the back together. Janoušek's trademark call was 'Smash it in'. His technique was the epitome of the *Kernschlag* (solid stroke with a hard beginning) style as opposed to the *Schubschlag* (thrust stroke) style around which all the East German boats, training, diet and medicine were designed.

After one winter of this method Janoušek took his squad to Mannheim to race in the docks over a slightly short course of 1800 metres for the first international regatta of the 1974 season. His coxed and coxless fours beat both East and West Germans at a canter on the first day. Combined as an eight on the second day, Janoušek's crew was beaten by the West Germans when they tried to row in the same style at thirty-six strokes to the minute, using fewer, stronger strokes to cover the distance. Janoušek drew the squad together on the following Monday and told them they would never win against endurance-trained athletes unless they learned to race at forty strokes to the minute for the whole distance. They did so. Janoušek's eight developed very high speeds and generally won races by sprinting to the front and holding on in fast conditions, but in long slow races against a headwind, they tended to lose against endurance-trained crews. Janoušek knew that his methods devised to meet the need of those in full-time employment might fail in a race that favoured endurance over speed. But he also knew that, in the unsupported world of British sport, there was no other way.

In Montreal, Janoušek's eight led the final until the East German crew pipped them at the post. Mike Hart and Chris Baillieu also won a silver medal in the double sculls, in their case ahead of East Germans but behind Norwegians.

3

1980

The Moscow Olympiad

'In New Zealand it was a unique occasion for any Westerner to witness the East German rowing team actually skiving. Despite this, the regatta yielded the usual crop of medals for the GDR.'

Jürgen Grobler's niche in the East German hierarchy was irreversible after his double gold-medal success in Montreal and his ever-strengthening programme at SC Magdeburg that pushed new, competitive athletes to the verge of national selection. By now it was engrained in East Germany's strategy that after each Olympic Games the tactics for the next cycle were subjected to the full Marxist dialectic of thesis, antithesis and synthesis in the following January. The predicted gold-medal times were set and the training of the elite squad switched to the new standard at a new intensity. By luck or judgement the Magdeburg scullers finished trials in the right spots to earn places in the quadruple scull for the 1977 world championships to be held in Amsterdam, while the single and double scullers hailed from Rostock, Halle and Berlin.

Thanks to the universal style and Klaus Filter's rigging adjustments, the new quad was remarkably uniform, with Martin Winter and Wolfgang Güldenpfennig as bookends. The post-Olympic year is often the season when athletes retire or take a year out. In the West they needed to pass exams or earn money, while in the East they were pushed underwater by young bullies coming up behind them. For example, only two members of the British eight that had beaten East Germany into fourth place in 1974 and had finished second in Montreal continued to row in 1977. One of them, Jim Clark, took a silver medal in a pair with newcomer John Roberts. The other, Tim Crooks, finished fourth in the single sculls. His switch from eights to singles, sweep to sculling, was regarded as remarkable and a move that the East Germans would never have allowed.

The East Germans cleaned up in Amsterdam, taking five out of eight gold medals in the men's events. Curiously, Grobler's Magdeburg coxed pair of Jährling and Ulrich, Montreal Olympic champions, were beaten into second place by a couple of even bigger Bulgarians. The major upset in 1977 was the win by the British double scullers Mike Hart and Chris Baillieu who had followed their own idiosyncratic path since winning the Boat Race for Cambridge a decade before. They took two seconds off the East Germans Rüdiger Reiche and Ulli Schmeid. This world medal was Britain's first gold since the London Olympics of 1948.

* *

East Germany had no need to search out British crews when Jürgen Grobler began coaching at international level in 1972. The first time the East Germans had taken notice of Brits was at Mannheim regatta in 1974 when Bob Janoušek entered two British fours which beat the components of the GDR eight. Janoušek had been one of the first East Europeans to take a senior job in the West. He brought success to British crews by using the super-compensation cycle combined with a precise and cleverly worked-out style that combined the skills of men moulded in a variety of club traditions to train in his squad.

An exit from communist society as achieved by Janoušek was denied to that generation of East Germans. The carrot that brought them home from trips abroad was the high standard of daily life that they enjoyed over the ordinary citizen. As the years passed and the East German economy performed less well in relation to the West, this became more marked. Few athletes saw a better life for themselves outside their ever-generous and grateful state. Retribution for flight was swift and tortuous on families and even on scant associates of defectors. People caught trying to cross the fence were shot. Border guards were brutal, starving and beating their dogs to increase the viciousness with which they chased and ravaged anyone found in the vicinity of the fence. The state authorities did not get the irony that anyone who chose not to share in their 'socialist happiness' would be shot for being unhappy. The only rower to defect and quit the good life was Matthias Schumann, who won gold in the eights at the 1978 world championships. He absconded in 1981 when racing in Amsterdam, and settled in Dortmund, West Germany, and worked as a sports reporter and photographer. He does not discuss the cost to his relations left behind in East Germany.

**

The prospect of the 1978 world championships at Lake Karapiro on the North Island of New Zealand was enticing for anyone held behind the Iron Curtain. It meant at least six weeks abroad and would be the most prolonged taste of life on the other side that they would experience. Grobler took the quadruple scull – this time with Martin Winter in the number-three seat behind Frank Dundr at stroke – and duly won.

Karapiro Lake is formed behind a hydroelectric dam in the Waikato River. Coaches were unable to use motor launches because of restrictions to conserve the wonderful, wild nature of the site. There was no waterside path for cyclists either, so the best that coaches could do was to set up a deck chair camp on a prominent hill and observe training through binoculars. In the fortnight before competition, East German crews covered their normal massive number of kilometres per day at low intensity, and were instructed to follow the river upstream and out of sight of the coaching team and its Stasi informers.

The British spare man at Karapiro had been a member of Janoušek's 1976 eight and had recently followed Tim Crooks in converting from rowing to sculling. He wanted mileage to develop the new skill and was following a similar training programme to the East Germans. About a week before the start of racing, when he was far upstream of the course, he rounded a sharp bend into a steep-sided, sheltered cove to find the entire GDR team sitting in their boats and quietly enjoying a long rest – while their coaches imagined they were grinding out the obligatory daily paddling ration of 35 km. It was a unique occasion for any Westerner to witness the East German rowing team actually skiving. Despite this, the regatta yielded the usual crop of medals with the men taking five golds and two silvers in eight events and the women three golds and one silver in six events.

**

The international federation had awarded the championships in the year before the Moscow Olympics to Bled in Slovenia. Slovenia was the richest province in the state of Yugoslavia and resembled its western neighbour, Austria, more than the rough side of the Iron Curtain. The East German contingent performed as before, with nine golds between the men and the women. Grobler's quadruple scull won, with his Magdeburg oarsman Peter Kersten at bow, while the double scull with Martin Winter at stroke finished third. Because

Frank and Alf Hansen of Norway competed in the double sculls at almost every championships from 1972 to 1979 and usually finished first or second, it was an event that was hard for East Germany to be sure of a medal, and so the preference for a place in the quadruple sculls became even more marked. Grobler had to innovate little in these years to keep his golden record.

If the Politbüro generated an imperative of success over the hated capitalist Federal Republic of Germany in the 1972 Olympics, the target for the 1980 Games in Moscow was the Soviet Union. The USSR treated East Germany as a vassal, a tiny buffer state on the edge of the Russian empire. The East Germans set out to capture Soviet gold on Russian flat water. For the Moscow Games the stakes were high: to finish third in the table, and closer to the masters than before.

Grobler was still attached to his club athletes at Magdeburg. His coxed pair of Harald Jährling and Friedrich-Wilhelm Ulrich, steered by Georg Spohr, was a club crew that even when missing selection as a pair usually found seats in an eight or a four. In 1980 they hit form and reached Moscow under Grobler's charge. Peter Kersten – who had been in the quadruple scull and in and around the top group of scullers and who was, like Wolfgang Güldenpfennig, on the small side – won the trials and took the single-sculling spot. Martin Winter was allotted the stroke seat in the quad.

Preparation for Moscow was disrupted on 20 January 1980 when the US president, Jimmy Carter, decided to use the Olympics as a bargaining counter to persuade the Soviet Union that its December 1979 invasion of Afghanistan should stop and an immediate withdrawal follow. Carter said that the United States would boycott the Games unless the Soviet Union withdrew its army. An American boycott posed no threat to any of Grobler's athletes, but much depended on whether West Germany and Norway aligned themselves with the Americans.

While argument raged, the rowing nations continued to train through the spring and summer, culminating at the traditional last try-out before the championships at Lucerne regatta. Peter-Michael Kolbe of West Germany and the Hansen brothers of Norway were on stunning form, and their eventual withdrawal from Moscow led to speculation as to whether the Olympic results would have been the same without Carter's action. The US president declared that any US citizens who travelled to compete would find their passports revoked on return. In Britain, prime minister Margaret Thatcher made similar noises but parliament allowed individual governing bodies to make their own decisions. The Amateur Rowing Association – amid much opprobrium and in the teeth of its president Christopher Davidge's conviction that it should drop out – went to Moscow anyway, but on a shoestring after its sponsors withdrew. There was almost no government money in British Olympic sport then. Ironically, in spite of her criticism of those who defied her wish and competed, Mrs Thatcher appointed the cox of the eight, Colin Moynihan, as her minister for sport in 1987.

The one beneficiary of the boycott was Henley regatta, which obtained a stunning last-minute entry for its Grand Challenge Cup. Four teams which boycotted Moscow – the United States, Norway, West Germany and New Zealand – fielded eights in Henley's premier event. The US defeated New Zealand in a thumping final.

The Hansens and Kolbe competed in the Grand at Henley, but were spitting with anger at the wreckage of their careers. The politicians who did the wrecking were too short-sighted to understand that a decade of war in Afghanistan would drain the Russian treasury, much as Vietnam had drained the United States a decade earlier. It was the reforming president, Mikhail Gorbachev, who pulled his country back from Kabul in 1989 after ten years of engagement. Within a year his Soviet empire had collapsed.

Although Moscow was the least glamorous Olympics of his career, Grobler was satisfied that his crews had peaked at the right time. He might have been surprised that his single sculler, Kersten, was beaten by Vasily Yakusha, a Belorussian competing for the Soviet Union. Yakusha had finished last in the Bled final a year earlier. He came from fourth place at the 1500-metre point in a close field, and swept through in the last 500 metres to take the silver behind the Finn Pertti Karppinen who had led from gun to tape.

When Grobler came home to Magdeburg and reviewed his career and its numerous gold medal successes, he was in a strong position to decide for himself where 'Schweinsdick' should go next.

4

THURSDAY 9 NOVEMBER 1989

East Berlin

'Grobler was the most curious one who reads, listens and tries everything.'

— KLAUS FILTER

Jürgen Grobler's status among the East German team coaches had risen because the crews he was responsible for performed well and his application of the methods and science of rowing and sculling was as good as anyone's.

In the months after each Olympics the GDR trainers, medical researchers, boat-builders, biomechanics, dieticians – all the members of the Committee – wrote reviews of the training and results of the past four years and made their proposals for the next cycle to be presented and discussed in a grand wash-up meeting, usually held in the following January. It was at this meeting that the next batch of gold-medal times were predicted and the baseline set for the trainers to work from. In 1981 it was the route map from Moscow to Los Angeles, with three world championships as marker posts along the way.

The men's and women's teams were run separately, although they shared most of the facilities. Hans Eckstein took charge of the men's team and Grobler became director of the women's squad. Eckstein was six years older than Grobler and, like him, a graduate of the German College of Physical Culture in Leipzig. Unlike him, Eckstein was a two-time national champion in eights and fours. Grobler rowed competitively from the age of 16 up to the student championships, but his rowing had been subordinate to his teenage dream of becoming a cameraman, which was quelled when he realised that fewer than four film graduates were required each year in East Germany. But the GDR was offering hundreds of openings for graduates in sports science. Strategically wise even in his teens, Grobler responded to the laws of supply and demand in what was, nominally, a purely command economy when, aged 19, he enrolled at Leipzig.

Ten years after his graduation Grobler was one of the top two operating coaches under Dr Theo Koerner, the chief executive, whom he regarded as one of his greatest influences. The other was Eckstein who had been his instructor during teaching practice at SC Enheit Dresden. That Jürgen took the director role for the women's squad is attributed by some to the canny 'Schweine Schlau' character that realised the probability of more international medals equalled the reward from a grateful state of a higher standard of living. He was expected to produce consistent success in the six Olympic events available. At the 1979 championships East German women had won three golds and three silvers, and at the 1980 Olympics one better with four golds, a silver and a bronze, so this was a daunting target and in his first season as director the team flopped, if only by its own dominant standards.

The 1981 world championships returned to the Oberschleißheim Olympic course near Munich, and the conditions were benign. The women's medal yield dropped sharply to one gold by the coxless pair and three silvers. Two boats missed medals. With the huge number of athletes being given the best possible training to compete for seats, it was particularly galling that the eight finished fifth, just ahead of Great Britain who enjoyed no investment of any kind.

Jürgen applied the standard selection rule for sculling boats, allocating the winner of the trials to the single boat. Sylvia Schwabe won the 1981 trials and inherited the single-scull slot that had been graced for six seasons by Christine Scheiblich, who had won the first women's Olympic sculling medal in 1976 and was unbeaten abroad until her triumph in Moscow. Meanwhile, expectations for Schwabe were high and disappointment deep when she was beaten into fourth by, among others, the British sculler Beryl Mitchell who – to add insult to injury – was a lightweight and would have been too short and slight to qualify as a top-tier athlete in the rigid East German system.

As director of women's rowing, Grobler had no responsibility for any particular crew. He was, therefore, slightly distanced from the failure. A high proportion of the 1980 Moscow women's team, having held off the selection challenge from below despite the large number of candidates, had then performed badly. Grobler's disappointment will have lingered only a few hours before he subjected his programme to severe analysis. In such circumstances his conviction that quality of training matters more than quantity was developed. Crews from the West, who had perhaps learned to fear the East Germans and regard them as well-nigh unbeatable, would be amazed to watch them paddling light on the way back to the rafts after a warm-down. The boat would bang from side to side and the crew slide back and forth with no care for the movement of others. It was the opposite of teamwork. It was ragged, like an army that has thrown away its weapons. Most pressure work at less than race pace was sloppy and contradictory to the excellence of competitive performance. In the men's squad some of the distance rowed served to keep the oarsmen tired and out of trouble rather than to go faster in races. They behaved as military conscripts behave: did what they were told without engagement or enthusiasm and let standards fall the moment authority is out of sight.

In contrast, western athletes were volunteers who had given up most of their free time and sacrificed earnings, comforts and a social life in order to compete. Their energy was spent to the point that they could not climb the stairs at night without concentrated effort. They could afford little more than a couple of hours' training a day six days a week, and so coaches made their lives as easy as possible by looking for constant rhythm and unified movement. Western athletes thus felt almost insulted that the crews who had all the apparent advantages, handed to them by a political machine that yearned for success, could treat the enterprise with such disdain.

The East German women were never as bad in this respect as the men, but they still treated their boats and their kit as if it was someone else's property in which they had no interest. Grobler wanted a shift of attitude and character, and gradually he obtained it. Rather than increase pressure on the West, and the Federal Republic in particular, Grobler looked east. After all, it was the Russians who had pushed his crews down the table. The Soviet Union had suffered insult in their 1980 'home Games' in Moscow, where the gold medal score was four to one in East Germany's favour, and so they had doubled their efforts, engaged in systematic doping of athletes, and used every advantage in a most cynical manner. At the 1981 championships, the Soviet Union took four of the six women's golds to East Germany's one, and in 1982 it was five to one. The Soviet Union was drawing on a population sixteen times greater and investing the equivalent of the GDR national programme in each of its satellite states.

The science was also, in effect, the property of the Soviet Union. When the German Democratic Republic was created out of the Soviet zone in 1949 the occupying force removed machinery and productive resources from German factories as war reparations and continued to regard the Warsaw Pact satellites as colonies to be plundered at will. All of the science developed at the Sports Institute of Leipzig had to be transferred free of charge to Moscow. Whatever the Germans had learned of the benefit of synthetic testosterone to those enduring heavy training, the Russians had to be told. The Soviet Union had a more cynical view of synthetic assistance: 'anything that helped was a good thing, a good thing was better if you doubled the dose', regardless of whether or not the rest of the world had banned it.

Grobler's task was to get back ahead of the nation that had significantly less regard for the welfare of its athletes or international law. He could not simply raise the dose of training and testosterone to match, and hope that he could find enough athletes from a population of sixteen million to beat the best selected from 260 million.

Grobler has said recently that he thought the GDR was overtraining at that time. His experience told him that he should monitor performance daily to be aware of the dangers of pushing athletes too hard. The sloppy, 'couldn't care less' style of the men when they were not racing was the outcome of thousands of kilometres on the water each year. Increasing the load would lower the quality of the work still further. He also knew that the synthetic testosterone given to the women was at the upper limit of what would be helpful. Women were showing the effects of permanently deepened voices, burgeoning body hair and – according to Brigitte Berendonk, a West German shot-put champion, and her husband, the microbiologist Werner Franke – markedly increased libido. In rare cases, mental instability was an added risk. The strongest, top-tier women may have had more useful bulk and endurance strength, but they themselves were beginning to question the balance of doping and training.

Grobler, staying in character, analysed every aspect of the training and racing programme and then improved the quality of work by making each part count for more. It is still his mantra today. When he growls 'more power' through the megaphone at his crews he is not simply calling for more kilowatts of energy but for better application of whatever strength the athlete has left. He wants the contraction of a muscle to translate directly, with minimum slippage, to lever the boat past the point at which the blade locks into the water. His exemplar was Christine Scheiblich who had been the women's single-scull champion in Montreal. Klaus Filter tells how one of the difficulties that humans have with boat propulsion is that as the rower reaches the end of the recovery phase of the stroke and is preparing to put his blade into the water, he concentrates his weight onto the balls of his feet while pushing against the foot stretcher. For a moment this negative force is pushing the stern down and stopping the hull before the blade is locked on and the oarsman is pulling the boat forward again. Stopping the boat at the catch is universal except in rare cases like Scheiblich's. Her timing at the catch was proved to be perfect in every type of test that Filter could devise. Scheiblich was one of the weakest athletes in the team and yet she won all her world championships races by large margins. The first Olympic final for women scullers in Montreal was one of the closest and untypical when the American Joan Lind chased her to within half a length. Scheiblich was followed by Thomas Lange and a few others on whom Grobler has modelled the ideal stroke. He has since asked athletes to treat the foot stretcher, which fixes all the thrust of the rower as the oar is levered past the pin, as if it was as fragile as an eggshell. He wants the power to build off the stretcher, not be applied with a macho bang. More power is to be used to make the boat go fast, not just to build big shoulders.

Grobler was known, then as now, as a man in constant search for the different angle, the unexpected factor which would make a difference to boat speed. Although he had worked closely with Peter Schwanitz and Filter throughout his career and knew the biomechanic's and boat-builder's reasoning and science as well as his own, he was aware that parallel work was being carried on in the West. After his eight had finished third in 1982 in Lucerne, he bought a new eights shell from the manufacturer Empacher in West Germany. Although he asked his sweep oarswomen to train in it for months, they were unable to make any sense of it. Percentage gold-medal times were well off the mark. As Filter told him before and after the extremely expensive experiment, the way the East German boats were designed and built and the way the East German athletes were taught to row was compatible. The Empacher was designed for a different, more universal style, with more compression of the legs and less reach of the body and arms. In the language of *Das Rudern*, it was made for a *Kernschlag* not *Schubschlag* style.

Characteristically Jürgen learns from mistakes like that and absorbs the new information into his formidable bank of rowing experience which, after nearly fifty years as a professional coach, cannot be matched. The following year, in the 1983 world championships, his team earned the result he wanted: four golds and two silvers put the East German women back on top of the table. The Russian flare was waterlogged.

**

Grobler entered the final year of preparation for the 1984 Los Angeles Olympics with every expectation of being able to repeat the success of Moscow. The preparation went well, with altitude camps in Mexico and Silvretta on the Austrian–Swiss border, and a European season of regattas that would culminate in Lucerne on 7–9 July. Then without warning, on 8 May 1984, the Soviet Union declared that it was so concerned about the commercialisation of the Los Angeles Games and was so worried about team security that it would withdraw its competitors. Two days later East Germany and Vietnam announced that they, too, would withdraw.

Whatever your position in East German society, whether one of the chosen *nomenklatura* or a factory worker, you could not protest or gainsay an edict from the Politbüro, which ran the state from the top to the very bottom. For the Politbüro to be denied the chance to exhibit German superiority in competitive sport was as bitter for its members as being cut out of a chance of Olympic glory was for 20-year-olds who had spent four years and 50,000 km at the oar. The instruction came from Moscow, intended as a Cold War strike against the US president, Ronald Reagan. It was a plain tit-for-tat response to the American boycott of Moscow four years earlier.

As a consequence, rowers who did win gold on Lake Casitas, outside Los Angeles, speak of their results at Lucerne regatta beforehand as the real marker of their quality. Martin Cross – who rowed at bow in the four stroked by Steve Redgrave and that won the first British Olympic rowing gold since 1948 – always takes a second breath to speak of beating the East German coxed four in Lucerne. The GDR, whether it won or lost, was the benchmark for all international rowing events in those years.

From the announcement of the GDR's withdrawal on 10 May 1984, Grobler knew that there was no chance of a change of mind. He set about measuring how much improvement in standard times was likely at Seoul in 1988, and then refined his programme to ensure that his cohort would be in the lead once more.

Through all these years he had been drafting new faces into the senior group, most of whom had won gold at world junior championships. There were not enough places in the senior squad to accommodate everyone with world junior championship golds who might have expected to rise to senior success, and Grobler was obliged to cut those who would not make the step up. All who experienced it said that

Grobler was clear and kind in the way he told people that they were about to be dropped from a programme in which they had striven ridiculously hard and from which they, their families and schools, had benefited. He had no need to blend youth and experience because those in the lower women's ranks had been exposed to international racing from the beginning and fought their way into the top group by winning hard races. They knew about survival from experience.

One of his juniors, Jana Sorgers, was picked up during her eighth year at school as a naturally athletic girl who stood at 1m 82cm. She was offered a place at SC Dynamo in Potsdam, near Berlin. This involved living at the clubhouse, with trips home every fourth weekend. At first she was homesick and asked to return to her family. Her mother argued that hers was an opportunity not to be missed. She knew what her 14-year-old daughter could not know: that the life of an elite athlete would open a whole new world for her. There were also benefits for the family, including a better flat and access to higher-paid employment. A compromise was reached: Jana was allowed to spend every weekend at home, and her projection into the sports training elite provided a lift for the Sorgers family.

Jana's schoolwork continued at SC Dynamo through teachers seconded to the club, but the emphasis was on training, perfecting and cementing the movements of her new sport. For two years her training load was increased steadily. Racing and testing was continuous, and culminated in her winning trials for the junior national team to race in the championships in Jönköping, Sweden, in 1984. The East German juniors were even more dominant than the seniors, partly because few other nations were organised to select composite crews drawn from across the country. When composites were formed, the training period was short. But in the GDR the team was being built from the earliest stage possible. Sorgers won again in the 1985 junior championships in Brandenburg, and consequently transferred to the senior squad, directed by a coach she had not come across before: Jürgen Grobler.

When asked if Grobler had favourites among the women's squad, she admits that she was perhaps one of them, but the relationship did not extend to him doing any favours for her or anyone else. He was supportive when any athlete was struggling or under-performing. He would modify the programme and give the athlete every chance to recover their form, but if improvement didn't come, he dropped them. He had a gauge, which became more sophisticated with experience, based on his understanding of psychology and physiology on whether there was another good championships performance to be had from an athlete. If he concluded they could not raise their game for another great effort he would end their careers gently but firmly. He knew the cost in physical training and emotion of a gold medal and he hated a futile enterprise.

All juniors started out in sculling boats. After the basic skills were mastered and their bodies had matured, they switched to sweep rowing. The very best remained in sculling boats because the coaches assumed that international sculling events would be filled with the best athletes from other countries. Sorgers had won twice at world junior championships: in the quadruple scull at the age of 17 and in the double scull a week after her eighteenth birthday. She took the stroke seat in the senior quad in her first year after moving up. This was unusual but not unheard of. Her recollection of the training is that the quantity was massive despite Grobler's mantra of quality being more important than quantity. She remembers how, when he came to watch a session managed by her crew coach, Jutta Lau, everyone perked up, pulled harder and polished their style. He was a hugely respected and slightly frightening figure.

The winter work Grobler insisted on was exhausting, particularly the cross-country skiing. At altitude the combination of thin air and side-by-side track racing left even the most athletic gasping. The importance of this exhaustion was to root out the weak in body or will. For the survivors there was the 'assistance' available by means of Oral Turinabol. Sorgers opined that the blue pills were given to and taken by the whole squad. If they wished to survive in the privileged world that they had come to expect, they took the pill. It was so much a part of the system and morality that the question of side effects that obsessed critics never occurred to the athletes. The long hours of Marxist-Leninist discussion had a purpose and effect. They believed in their coaches as agents of a state that, to them at least, was benign and extremely generous.

Sorgers says that the synthetic testosterone was used only during periods of very heavy training and was accompanied with the explanation that it was to assist a more rapid recovery. As this was perceptible and could be measured by the coaches, it was easy to believe. Nevertheless, athletes were aware that the drug was regarded as illegal. All East German rowers gave regular urine and blood samples which were tested at Kreischa near the Czech border to determine that no trace of the synthetic testosterone remained after the little blue pills had been changed from Oral Turinabol or Clomiphen to a harmless placebo. The accuracy of the tests resulted in no East German rower testing positive, ever. It is a nice irony that today the laboratory at Dresdner Straße 12 in Kreischa is one of the few approved by the World Anti-Doping Agency (WADA) for tests to catch twenty-first-century cheats.

Sorgers sculled on in the quad to Atlanta in 1996, where she and her coach Lau represented a united Germany. Lau's programme was the same as her old East German one although, Sorgers said, 'it felt much harder.' Because it did not include any synthetic testosterone.

**

While Jana Sorgers was going for her second world junior champion-ship in 1985, the seniors gathered at Hazewinkel in Belgium. The boycotters of the Los Angeles Olympics were all back in the boat and the East German women resumed their position at the head of the medal table, with four wins, a second and a third, while the Soviets took one gold and one silver. Jutta Lau retired from competition after several illustrious years as a prominent sculler and was fast-tracked into Grobler's coaching team. She knew his methods well and was a reliable disciple.

For the 1986 season the 18-year-old Sorgers, with two junior world golds in her kit bag, was transferred to the senior squad in Grünau on the outskirts of East Berlin. She made the top seven in the sculling trials and moved into the quad. She was with a future Olympic champion single sculler, Birgit Peter, and two older women. By now the international federation had extended the women's racing distance to 2000 metres, and at the world championships in Nottingham the quad racked up a seven-second margin over second-placed Romania. This was a sweet revenge because Romania had evaded the Soviet Union's Los Angeles boycott by Warsaw Pact nations, and had taken five of the six rowing golds in women's events there. For Grobler to assert so convincingly that the Romanian success would be countered was part of the realpo-litik of his role. Despite this success, Romania's heavy investment in its women's programme was to become a force equal to his own.

Immediately after his team missed the libido and booze-fuelled post-championships party to catch its charter flight from East Midlands airport, Grobler set the targets for the 1987 season that would climax in Copenhagen. The programme performed with its customary authority in the early regattas, when Grobler's super-compensation cycle required his athletes to race without full recovery early in the season. They would compete with measured tiredness at continental regattas, so they had to work harder to win than when they were in the pink. They would then reach the final of the championships with 100 per cent of their available energy, and were able to race more easily and improve their position relative to the best crews.

In 1987 the conditions were awful on finals day. Martina Schröter, the single sculler at Copenhagen, raced in such a headwind that she took nine and a quarter minutes to cover 2000 metres and finished fifteen seconds behind the Bulgarian whose lane afforded shelter from the cross-headwind. The women's double scull of Beate Schramm and Sylvia Schwabe went to the 1500-metre mark in the fastest two places, as expected, and then lost ten seconds after a crab (catching the top edge of the oar under water resulting in a sudden – often dramatic – brake on the boat), fading to fifth. Only the quadruple scull with Sorgers in the bows came good and won.

In all, Grobler's team took one gold and three silvers, with the eight and the coxed four out of the medals. It was a poor result by East German standards, but he will have calculated the lane differences and known where his preparation or selection was deficient and where it was appropriate to blame the conditions. By this time in his career he was more likely to blame his training programme – now tailored to each athlete – than to assume that the weather or any outside factor was the cause.

The next stop was the Olympics in Seoul. For Korea in 1988 Grobler stuck to his usual approach, calling for quality and applying his objective method of selection. Lau was now personally responsible for the quadruple scull and, although obliged to take the women who finished fourth to seventh in trials, was allowed to allot seats. Sorgers moved from bow to stroke and was made responsible for changes of pace in a crew that – assisted as ever by Filter's subtle adjustments to the rig – enjoyed nigh-perfect uniformity of movement. Sorgers' strength off the start and her ability to hold the length of the arc of the stroke while dropping the rate to race pace were two reasons for her crew being able to complete the first 500 metres in 89 seconds, and then pass through the next quarters in 98.5 and 98.3 seconds. This was as close a call as Lau or Grobler could ask for, and when the Russians came from the back to push towards the line, Sorgers raised the pace again to cover the last 500 metres in 95 seconds, a well-nigh perfect race profile. In addition, the East German coxed four and eight won their events. Grobler had delivered again, although his crew coaches took the honours. East Germany's women had five of Seoul's six gold medals.

Seoul would be the last Olympic games in which East Germany would compete as a separate nation. For the third time it finished second to the Soviet Union and ahead of the United States. The political point of the country's sporting prowess had been well made, and now the economic cost of the socialist path was draining the patience of the people, just as it was doing in the other Warsaw Pact countries languishing behind the Iron Curtain. By the time the Olympic family would meet again in Barcelona, the GDR would no longer exist and many of its rowers would be competing for a unified Germany. But as the Olympic flame was extinguished in Seoul, no one knew that. On the long flight home from the Far East, Grobler would have asked himself what his next GDR Olympiad would bring, and what his next trajectory of crew improvement would look like in each of his boat classes – beginning with a world championships in Bled, less than a year away – just as he had done after the previous four Olympiads.

The post-Seoul conference of the East German rowing federation in January 1989 set out the next expected gold-medal times and the training structure required to achieve them, led by the technical director, Dr Theo Koerner. Grobler stayed in his post as director of women's rowing and prepared his team for Bled in September. He had few new faces, and the experienced team took four gold and two silver medals, including a gold for the coxless four that replaced the coxed four in the world championship programme. He had little to report on his return to Germany because it had all gone eerily to plan. He gave his squad three weeks off and planned the trip to Lake Barrington in Tasmania for the next world championships, scheduled for November 1990.

* *

On the evening of 9 November 1989 Wilfried Hofmann, the president of the East German rowing federation, was seated in front of a big television set at the Columbia Club in Indianapolis. In company with others attending FISA's international coaches conference hosted by US Rowing, he was paralysed with incredulity at what he saw. Men and women atop the Berlin Wall were attacking it with hammers and pickaxes. Dr Theo Koerner was in a similar quandary as he lay in bed at the Calvary Hospital in Canberra, Australia, having suffered deep vein thrombosis while lecturing to the Oceania Olympic Solidarity rowing seminar on talent identification. In East Berlin, Jürgen and Angela Grobler watched the same scene during a party for a fellow coach, and then drove toward the Brandenburg Gate to see what was going on for themselves. In one extraordinary evening, the GDR vanished before their eyes, and their livelihood hung in limbo.

East Germany's collapse came about when Günter Schabowski, the government spokesman, botched his announcement of travel visas being made available in the days that followed. When asked on camera when the free visa system would begin, he answered 'this evening', thus triggering the opening of the borders to the West. The border police were ordered to lay down their arms. By dawn on 10 November there was still a wall, but no longer a border with the Federal Republic.

Jürgen Grobler, like every East German citizen, would have been reminded from a young age at school and by the state newspaper *Neues Deutschland* that socialism was right and everlasting, while capitalism was corrupt and destined to end cataclysmically. Whatever he felt deep down, the high-ranking coach was obliged to rub along with the Marxist-Leninist philosophy that underpinned every action of the state. But by 1989 the state was resorting to increasingly desperate measures to stay afloat, and people were apprehensively aware of what was afoot. Soviet newspapers were suppressed because they reported President Gorbachev's *perestroika* in too much detail. West Germany was invited to pay for exit visas to allow East Germans to leave. The leavers were branded as troublemakers for seeking a better life on a different path. For the GDR these visas had two benefits: they transferred wealth from West to East and they got rid of the riff-raff.

When the East German bubble burst, the rowers' training continued toward an uncertain future. The economic system that had supported elite athletes so well persisted for a while as the country moved swiftly to reunification with the Federal Republic. Many rowers and coaches stayed on as they looked about them for what was next, while many suffered from depression. Jana Sorgers was a case in point. After stroking the quad to her fifth successive gold medal at the 1990 world championships in Tasmania, she 'fell into a hole' and dropped out of rowing for two years before making a successful comeback wearing a German shirt in Atlanta in 1996. Half of Grobler's squad went to Tasmania, where they won three golds and three bronzes. 'Not brilliant, but acceptable', he would say in another year, but this time the surprise was that his pair and coxless four were beaten by West German crews. The Wall had truly disintegrated.

A year before the Wall fell Ian Wilson, Europe Agent for the oar makers Concept2 (and the enormously successful Nottinghamshire County Rowing Association), was negotiating the sale of hundreds of the company's new carbon-fibre blades to Klaus Filter, the East's equipment guru. As Filter checked every single blade with meticulous attention to detail, Wilson casually asked if there was an East German coach who might be suitable for a post at Leander Club in Henley. Filter suggested Grobler as the experimenter among the East German coaches and as the most curious one who reads, listens and tries everything. Wilson remembers Filter and Grobler measuring oars with one-metre rulers and giving them five-metre retractable tape to aid their labours.

After the deal was struck and after the Wall was breached, several senior GDR officials and their wives, including Jürgen and Angela, were invited to the world indoor championships in Boston, Massachusetts. Klaus turned up with a bagful of chunks of the Berlin Wall that he distributed as souvenirs. Wilson brought a bagful of five-metre measuring tapes to the party.

One of the competitors in Boston was Britain's outstanding talent, Steve Redgrave, and Wilson the matchmaker ensured that Grobler at the very least set eyes on him. What followed was an invitation to visit Henley-on-Thames that summer, where Redgrave was based at Leander Club.

5

Henley-on-Thames

'I am a club man. I like the physical existence of a clubhouse where you can gather and talk to the old guys.'
— JÜRGEN GROBLER

Henley Royal Regatta was a quintessential blend of Britishness in 1990. After a heady year in 1989, when it celebrated 150 years of rowing and garden-partying with a record entry for its fourteen events, it relaxed into its normal self. Normal, that is, for the home crowd, but surely bewildering to a quizzical family from, say, Magdeburg.

In the generally glorious summer of 1990, rain fell intermittently and heavily on the first two days, before sunshine and warmth prevailed for the weekend's semi-finals and finals. The two-by-two racing was enlivened on all five days by blustery crosswinds that fanned wobbly steering and controversy over umpires' decisions.

Meanwhile, there was some serious rowing going on in the competition for Henley's coveted trophies, witnessed by a visitor in transition from one indulgent elite to another, and who would give British rowing a charge of East European science and ruthlessness. The visitors came from a state that had lost all its gloss for the majority of the people but where the elite had the same sense of entitlement as the high command of British rowing. The fashions in clothes, hairstyles and spectacles may have been different, but there was little distinction between the hangers-on of the GDR *nomenklatura* who turned out for luxury state occasions and those towed through the Stewards' Enclosure by retired rowers in their finery.

The main British hope in the regatta lay in the Silver Goblets for coxless pairs. The star oarsman of the day, Steve Redgrave, had two Olympic gold medals and was hoping for a third in two years' time in Barcelona. Andy Holmes, the man who had shared both of Redgrave's Olympic medals, had retired and Redgrave was at Henley with Simon Berrisford, a congenial fellow nicknamed Bungalow. On Saturday morning, however, mishap struck when Berrisford had damaged his back in a collision with a sculler and the British boat was forced to withdraw from the Goblets.

Later that day, the *Guardian* correspondent, strolled past the boat tents to Leander Club, known colloquially as the Pink Palace, and hesitated by its riverside gate. The garden and dining marquee were crowded with blazers of blue and many stripes, peppered by distinctive cerise ties and pink socks. Women in summer dresses and Ascot hats sipped Pimm's. What stopped him at the gate, however, was catching sight of a small group by the doors of the boat shed. Steve Redgrave and Ivor Lloyd, the club's captain, were talking to a man in a blazer and silk tie accompanied by an attractive woman and a small boy. Although they were dressed for the occasion, he sensed that the Stewards' Enclosure was beyond their comfort zone. He knew he had seen the guy in a different context — but where? It soon dawned on him that the blazer's owner was a coach from East Germany, a familiar tracksuited figure at international regattas. His presence here — chatting to the top British oarsman in the pink-tinged enclave of Britain's rowing establishment barely eight months after the demolition of the Berlin Wall heralded the end of East Germany's promise of lifetime careers – could mean only one thing. The reporter made his way across the yard and joined the little group. 'Meet Leander's new coach, Jürgen Grobler,' Lloyd said. 'He starts in January.' For 'Leander' read 'Britain and Redgrave', the reporter said to himself. The *Guardian* had an old-fashioned scoop.

Informal discussions took place before the formal interview in the committee room at Leander. On hand was a native German speaker, Roswitha Zarach, to aid translation. She remembers two discussions – one to negotiate Jürgen's terms and a second addressing Angela's concerns about schooling for her son and employment opportunities for herself. Later, Grobler told the journalist Neil Allen that: 'I spoke so very little English that my wife acted as interpreter for me. I was wearing a blazer, she had on a smart dress and my then 10-year-old son Christian was furious because we made him wear a tie and blazer, too, which turned out to be two sizes too big for him.' The interviewers put him at ease by giving him a sense that they understood his nervousness.

After the interview came the grand tour. 'It was a club of great contrasts,' Grobler said. 'Upstairs with the beautifully furnished rooms, the bar, the committee room, comfortable chairs, like an English country house. But downstairs it was very different. The changing rooms and a gym that was hardly worthy of the name, it was more like a dungeon. There were spiders everywhere, maybe some rats as well. It was very basic, just a corner where you did weights.' It was crucial to Jürgen's self-esteem that he transferred his skills seamlessly from preparing a large squad of the best athletes in the world's top rowing nation to the two best athletes in the sport. These facilities were certainly a contrast to those he was used to, but he was less worried about the dungeon appearance than about the limited number of athletes who could train at any one time and the absolute absence of testing equipment. There was no point in writing a programme for training if you could not measure whether it was working.

Steve Redgrave, twice an Olympic champion, was the bait dangled in front of Grobler by Ian Wilson when he sounded him out about moving to England at the Boston indoor rowing championships. Redgrave recalls Wilson saying to him: 'We know of this really good guy in East Germany who's keen to come to the UK. Did I think Leander would be interested? I was sceptical because I thought it was the East German machine that got the results and not really an individual. Taking an individual out of their system, could he cope in a western world with how we do things? I didn't think that would be possible so I took a back seat. But Leander was interested.'

For Grobler, the novel aspect of visiting Henley — more than its regatta bearing no resemblance to the multi-lane courses familiar to him in the international rowing arena — was that his wife Angela and son Chris were with him. East Germany's regime had never allowed its coaches to travel with family members. Leander sent John Peters to collect the Grobler family from Heathrow in a rather flash Jaguar.

'It was like a dream really from the moment John picked me up,' Grobler said. He remembered seeing pictures of the Beatles on tour in Germany being driven around in Jags. 'It all seemed very rock'n'roll. Henley looked magnificent and right at the centre was Leander, which of course I knew all about. I had never been lucky enough to make the trip to Henley, although I did prepare some crews for the regatta. I had been disappointed with not being allowed to accompany them.'

Those from East Germany who did go to Henley had given an hour's presentation on their return. As he arrived at the regatta in 1990 Grobler felt an emotional attachment right away. 'I had already seen the footage. I am a club man. I like the physical existence of a clubhouse where you can gather before and after your sport and talk to the old guys and see the history of what went before you on the walls. I liked many sports in the GDR – water polo, swimming, track and field, canoeing – but one of the things that made me choose rowing was the clubhouse element. We didn't have great buildings like Leander, but we did have our own bases at Leipzig University and my hometown club SC Magdeburg, where I had learned to row on the Elbe.'

The Grobler family were chaperoned in the Stewards' Enclosure by John Pilgrim-Morris, a coach at Leander, and his wife Jenny. 'They looked totally out of place because of what they were wearing,' Pilgrim-Morris says. 'The boy had a flick-knife which he was throwing into the lawn, stressed. I'm ashamed to comment on it in a way, but it was relevant at the time because of the oppressive background they had come from.'

They watched the prizes given away by Mary Glen Haig, a member of the International Olympic Committee. Outside the boat tents, Soviet oarsmen were, as every year, selling their shirts as the only currency they could exchange for a beer. Klaus Filter says that the East Germans avoided this problem by taking their own beer with them to all training camps and championships abroad, evading customs difficulties by loading it underneath the oars, seats and riggers on the trailer.

**

The Groblers' visit to Henley was the penultimate stage in a series of contacts between Jürgen and Ivor Lloyd, the captain at Leander. Lloyd was in his fifth year of captaincy and tasked with continuing to make the club more accessible by changing the membership requirement from whom you know to what you can do. He began in 1986 by enticing Steve Redgrave's coach Mike Spracklen from Marlow Rowing Club. Lloyd perceived that Leander needed a Pied Piper, and Spracklen played the pipe. Redgrave came with him. At the same time the Amateur Rowing Association's international programme was in disarray, and international oarsmen began to follow each other to Leander.

Lloyd realised that coaching was the key to Leander's success, and when Spracklen accepted a post with Rowing Canada at the end of 1988, he set out to find a worthy successor for the deep hole in his club's resources. John Peters and John Pilgrim-Morris kept Leander's coaching on the river for a year until Wilson, advised by Filter, identified Grobler as the coach most likely to adapt from East Germany's sports factory. Lloyd was aware that several other countries were bidding for his target. Jürgen was quite elusive, while Lloyd's aim was to create a nurturing environment to convince the Groblers that Leander would look after them. This was no short-term plan. The offer came with a house, with schooling for young Chris, and with career introductions for structural engineer Angela – not to mention a salary, good equipment, the biggest man on rowing's campus, and some of the British men's squad based at the club. Leander set out to embed Jürgen and make his family comfortable in a place they felt they would like to settle.

The formal part of the interview at Henley took place in the clubhouse. Only Lloyd and Grobler were in the room, Leander's committee having declared that they were 100 per cent behind the scheme but leaving it to the captain to negotiate. As Lloyd says, the meeting was not so much an interview: 'The facts stood for themselves. It was creating a cradle-to-grave scenario. The whole package was the attraction, and what the club stood for in international terms. All the powers of persuasion to elicit the signature.'

Lloyd says the question of doping did not arise. 'We didn't ask because at that time no one really understood. There was always this thing of all the Eastern Bloc countries are all a bit shady. When I was in the British team, if you started to talk to any of the athletes a minder would whip across and words would be said and you were broken up, and so you couldn't get to know the athletes or the coaches. I don't think they were free to mix. So there was a vacuum into which people put a whole load of circuitous information. Some of it ended up to be true, as we now know. At the time there was no tangible evidence, so you pushed it to one side.'

Thus another Henley drew to a close in its unique combination of rowing prowess and tradition. One incident was that Peter Coni, the chairman of the management committee, was infuriated by a BBC programme broadcast on the second day, alleging that his regatta had a vault full of cash but contributed nothing to Britain's rowing. Neither allegation was remotely true, and the Stewards forced the national broadcaster to withdraw the programme, correct its 'misleading impressions', and donate £1,000 to British international rowing – to augment the regatta's £127,000 contribution towards coaching, training camps and equipment between 1988 and 1991.

This was the impecunious world that Jürgen Grobler was about to enter. In East Germany they had proper gyms, training equipment, nutrition, medical support and good facilities. They were an elite under pressure to perform, but also pampered. 'Britain in 1990 was very different to this,' he recalled for Leander's two-hundredth anniversary book. 'But that was the challenge, and despite having a very good offer at one of the top clubs in Germany I did not hesitate. This was an important moment in my life. I needed to know more about myself. I had worked with great Olympic champions in the GDR but was it really me making any difference at all? Was it the system, from start to finish, which was producing this conveyor belt of champions? Was I just a cog who could easily be replaced, or was I a coach with ability and talent? One way or another I was going to know soon enough.'

In November on the last day of the world championships at Lake Barrington – deep in the rainforest of Tasmania where Redgrave and his new partner, Matt Pinsent, had just won a bronze medal behind the 'East Germans' Thomas Jung and Uwe Kellner and the Soviet twins, Nikolai and Yuri Pimenov – Grobler and Pilgrim-Morris sat on a grassy bank and went through the German's six-year contract written out in Klaus Filter's English translation from German on flimsy fax paper. The German version banned pets in the premises that Leander was providing. Jürgen announced that his son had a fish, and would it be allowed? John replied that the English did not recognise fish as pets. When the deed was done, Jürgen turned to John and said: 'Why does Redgrave stroke the pair? He is not a stroke. I will switch the order.'

When the East German and his family moved to Henley a few weeks later, John Peters drove Jürgen back to Berlin to collect his things. Peters was surprised to find that the Grobler apartment was equipped with all imaginable western appliances, testament to the hold that East Germany placed on its high-profile operatives. Peters's van was directed to a hut by a railway siding where the two men loaded it with a lot of rowing equipment, including Concept2 oars and some pretty rudimentary telemetry in army-style boxes labelled DDR. Peters drove the van nervously out past the security guard and through customs without incident.

In the event, it was to take Jürgen and Angela very little time to adapt to the British system — in fact, Grobler even Anglicised his name by tossing away Jürgen's umlaut. Leander was incredibly hospitable. The Grobler family was put up in the club for a couple of months while they waited for their house to become available. Christian was allowed to keep a rabbit on the premises, 'which I feel certain was against some club regulation which they chose to overlook,' said Jurgen. A place had been arranged for Christian at Badgemore Primary School. 'Everything Leander promised me was provided – and much more – so now it was time for me to start delivering.'

From the start of his work in 1991, Grobler ran the training for everyone at Leander even though his contract was to coach Redgrave and Pinsent. He introduced an unsophisticated, brutal gym regime on day one. It was not what the rowers expected.

On Grobler's second day in the post he found Wade Hall-Craggs with his feet hooked on the edge of a bench while his torso projected rigidly parallel to the floor. The oarsman stared fixedly at a stopwatch on the carpet. The *Guardian* reported that Leander Club, with its partiality for cerise socks and schoolboy caps, had carpet and curtains in its weights room. These seemed to be the only comforts in the tense silence, however, as Hall-Craggs made the first circuit of the 1530-movement programme presented to the club's oarsmen by their coach of two days. Several tortures later, Grobler revealed with a smile that the programme written on a scrap of paper was his most recent East German one. The guinea-pig was by then bouncing through fifty bunny-hops and looking as if his Hall was about to part company with his Craggs. Outside, the Thames was grey and inhospitable. 'It's better to do less rowing and more of other things at this time of the year,' Grobler said. 'Weights, running, cycling. It makes training more interesting.'

Impatient to start making improvements, Grobler went to work with a passion. The first thing he did was to ask Peters to hammer white posts into the bank at 250-metre intervals so that every moment, every effort, on the river could be timed and recorded accurately. He set about learning the quirks of wind and water on Henley Reach so that he could set benchmark times for pieces of work in a variety of conditions.

Next he altered the basic training loop used by Leander crews by extending it by 250 metres, amounting to 500 metres there and back. The loop henceforth extended to the bridge by the clubhouse instead of ending at the regatta finish line. An extra section of quality work was added to the day at a stroke.

* *

While Leander Club was busy breaking with tradition by recruiting its first full-time professional coach, the Amateur Rowing Association was in turmoil. In the autumn of 1989 the Leander coach who had guided Redgrave to two Olympic golds, Mike Spracklen, had moved to Canada after his written offer to take charge of Britain's open men's squad was ignored by the governing body – an unforgiven slight. The post of director of international rowing held by Penny Chuter was abolished. Bruce Grainger – the chief coach for juniors, and a man who had sat at the feet of the great West German coach Karl Adam for six months on a Churchill fellowship – was appointed to the new post of international performance director. Brian Armstrong was made international rowing manager and David Tanner was reappointed men's chief coach, a part-time post shared with his day job as a headteacher. Chuter was relegated to being the ARA's principal national coach.

During the following February, nineteen club captains held a meeting to express dissatisfaction with the governing body and its financial management, and tension was rife between the clubs, including Leander, and the ARA. The governing body had been advertising for a full-time professional coach without success, and so when Leander hired Grobler, the ARA began to explore possibilities of cooperation. This resulted in Tanner's resignation on the premise that his job should be a full-time one, and subsequently in Grobler's appointment as 'technical advisor' to the ARA in the spring of 1991. In April performance director Grainger then resigned, citing two reasons: that Armstrong was named above him in the ARA's line management, and that Grobler's ARA appointment in tandem with being a club coach placed the German in an invidious position. Grainger told the *Guardian*: 'I feel inevitably that he will favour people he is coaching. That is why you are supposed to have an independent person in such a job. You need safeguards. I think it is unfair on someone who has not had time to get his feet on the ground in Britain. It is playing into the hands of politicians in rowing.'

Grainger also had philosophical issues with the ARA: 'I don't believe in the division between the domestic and international sides. There should be a continuum from novice to international oarsman. That's crucial. I don't believe in elitist groups.' He also thought that Britain's rowing should be more scientific, a theme he reiterated at a conference of physiologists and coaches he ran in February that year. He cited both the message emanating from Eastern Europe and Adam's academy at Ratzeburg, where he had studied.

Grainger had kept such a low profile since his appointment as international performance director that he was dubbed the 'Lone Grainger' and became subject to criticism by athletes (who had also run a 'dump Tanner' campaign). Meanwhile, letters to the *Times* bemoaned the ARA's governance by amateurs and its squandering of funds on administration.

The lightweight-squad coach Mark Lees replaced Grainger, but the die had been cast. Inevitably, Grobler was set to make the leap from Leander to the national team after the Barcelona Olympics.

6

1992
The Barcelona Olympiad

'A typical debrief would be, "Steve, the catch... not so bad. Matt, the finish... not so bad. Now another lap."'
— STEVE REDGRAVE

Broadly speaking, Britain's international rowing became stuck in the doldrums after two gold medals at the London Olympics in 1948. Apart from a silver medal at the Tokyo Games in 1960, British crews trod water while the rest of the world, in particular Eastern Europe, moved on. The return to the podium came in 1976 when GB's eight won silver in Montreal after being pipped for gold by the East Germans in the last 200 metres.

When Great Britain topped the medal table of twenty-seven nations at the 1948 Olympic regatta, its coaches and administrators decided that all was well in a discipline that had been transformed from a necessity into a sport throughout the nineteenth century. The greatest concern was how many of the medallists came from Oxford and how many from Cambridge. Having got through the war, they wanted to put England back together again — just as it had been. Honest and tough men in the clubs and universities trained for the Boat Race and Henley, and sometimes went on trips to European championships and

Olympic Games, but in hope rather than expectation. In the clubs there was no international vision.

There was, however, more ambition among national servicemen in the RAF who were steered to Benson airfield and trained on the river in nearby Wallingford. They worked hard and did quite well. Once military service was over they moved to London and formed Barn Cottage Rowing Club, remaining detached from the internal strife of the leading clubs. Later they developed links with Molesey Boat Club and then re-formed under Lou Barry, a former squadron leader, at Tideway Scullers. They knew what they wanted, and four of them achieved a silver medal in Tokyo in 1964.

For the Munich Games in 1972 Barry negotiated to put three from his own club, Tideway Scullers, in a coxed four with one traded from Leander. Because his number 2 man was working a full day as hod carrier the four did very little training by the standards of its competition, and finished a slow tenth in the Munich Games that year where the best Brit result was fifth in the double scull.

By now even the more backward administrators knew that something was wrong, and so they changed their attitude to Bob Janoušek, the coach they had hired in 1969. They gave him the power to organise a squad drawn from all the clubs. They resisted complaints from club captains who saw their talent on the move, and allowed Janoušek to get on with organising and training his group in a fit-for-competition manner.

British crews have stood on the Olympic medal podium (and the world championship podium with the exception of one year) ever since Janoušek's success. In his six years at the top of British rowing, he adapted his knowledge of Eastern European methods to resources and practices unfamiliar to him. One of his successes was to break the hold of powerful clubs by handpicking and personally coaching a national squad, a system that would haltingly gather strength after he resigned at the end of the 1976 Montreal Games to become a boat-builder. In 1980 in Moscow, Britain's coxless four and pair won bronze in addition to a silver for the eight. Then, at the 1984 Los Angeles Games, on Lake Casitas, a British crew burst onto the Olympic gold standard for the first time since 1948.

Lake Casitas is a magical place in wooded hills to the east of the Pacific Coast Highway near Ventura, California. For the Games, the lakeside was decked out in the signature pastel shades of the 'Tinseltown Olympics' in downtown LA, several hours' drive to the south. But on finals day, when the coxed fours began, all the spectators could see was mist.

A *Guardian* correspondent was high on the scaffold of the press stand in sunshine, seated next to *The Sunday Times's* Richard Burnell, who was shaking with nerves because – as the most recent Brit to win a gold medal, back in 1948 – he was desperate to lose his nine-Olympiad stewardship. The course was about 200 metres from the shore, but invisible. The top of the TV catamaran was just visible above the mist, and the deep-throated intonations of Dick Erickson, the commentator on board, were barely audible. As the race progressed, Erickson announced that the Americans were leading and the Brits were giving chase.

The mist lifted a few feet at the moment when Martin Cross, Richard Budgett, Andy Holmes and Steve Redgrave broke through, and cox Adrian Ellison, lying on his back in the bows of the boat, could see nothing but clear water ahead. Burnell hit the stratosphere as the four stormed through his record. This medal was sensational, long awaited and performed by a crew whose individual tensions – in some cases, a refusal to row together – had been smoothed away by a man each wanted to be coached by: Mike Spracklen. It was a perfect day for the Brits.

The achievement on Casitas also marked the start of Steve

Redgrave's remarkable Olympic career. He was the first of a small contingent of super-athletes who would come under the influence of Grobler's move to Britain seven years down the road – a chain of multi-medallists who would keep Jurgen and British rowing on the gold standard. But nothing of this was in the German coach's imagination, for in 1984 he was seething back at home, a victim of East Germany's boycott of the LA Games.

Redgrave won his second Olympic gold in Seoul in 1988, accompanied by Holmes and coached by Spracklen. Seoul was a completely different affair. The course had been created by moving a few hundred villagers (who had no say in the matter) to enable the Han River to be dammed. It had a shimmering mountain backdrop but no spectators, save for bussed-in school children and contingents of East German athletes and officials on organised time out from other sports.

A rib injury to Holmes – arguably the finest oarsman of his generation – disrupted the pair's regatta season. But Seoul was memorable for the British pair's comfortable victory. It was also memorable for their failure to achieve the double when they started in the final of the coxed pairs the next day, steered by Pat Sweeney. The Italian brothers Carmine and Giuseppe Abbagnale took the race in hand, while the Brits were slow to start before managing to haul themselves into second place. They held this until the East Germans sprinted past them to take the silver medal.

'We ran out of legs,' was Sweeney's straightforward explanation to the *Guardian*. The moral is that doubling up is a big ask, even for athletes at the top of their game, and especially when there are crews around of the calibre of the Abbagnales. The Italians dominated the coxed boat with Giuseppe di Capua in the cox's seat until they approached the Olympic finish line in 1992.

Holmes walked out on rowing soon after winning his second gold. Redgrave refused to row with him again because Holmes would only commit to a further year whereas Redgrave had set his sights on the Barcelona Olympics. At the 1989 trials a young four containing new boy Matthew Pinsent slugged it out with Holmes's boat, and afterwards Holmes tried to contact Pinsent with a view to trying a pair. His approach failed, and he retired wondering what would have happened if Pinsent had crewed with him instead. Holmes closed the door on his rowing life, put his medals in a sock and broke contact with Redgrave. The *Guardian*'s Frank Keating caught up with Holmes just before the Barcelona regatta, which he said he had no intention of watching. He did, however, confess to one potent rowing memory:

'I can remember one thing about that previous life of mine, starkly and vividly. Our first training session at the camp when we got to Korea. It had been a wretched build-up for the Olympics. We hadn't won a race all year, there had been rows and mopes, and then I'd sprung a rib. We got to Seoul and on our very first race-simulation outing we realised we'd got it all back together. Just like that. It was uncanny, almost surreal. Suddenly we came as near to perfection as I'm sure it's possible to get. I still think in that outing we achieved a perfection that no pair of oarsmen could ever have experienced in the whole ancient history of the sport. It was utter resplendence, just totally sublime. I wonder if Steve has experienced such a feeling since. Perhaps it's that mystic passage that drives him on and on still...'

**

In January 1990 a significant sidebar on East German sport was revealed by the *Guardian* correspondent who went to Leipzig to knock on Professor Hermann Buhl's door. Buhl, a former middle- and long-distance record-holding steeplechaser, was director of research in the department of medicine and biochemistry at the German School of Sport Science. He had confirmed to a news agency that a doping programme existed in East German sport, the first professional, at that time, still in post to do so.

A willing interviewee, Buhl was keen that readers should understand the structure of the East German system. In 1975 the head of state, Erich Honecker, said: 'the GDR must be the first in the world... I get my orders, then is the problem.' As a physician, Buhl said, he might have said 'no' to what he was being ordered to do, but as an employee 'I must make the research and make the knowledge known.' For ten years his institute worked on basic theoretical knowledge of hormonal regulation. It employed seventy scientists of whom half a dozen worked on hormones and the rest on the central nervous system, respiratory system and muscle tiredness.

Professor Buhl's department had direct connections with coaches, government and sports associations, including about fifteen Olympic disciplines. But rowing was not among them. It had its own medical centre in Grünau. The consequence of Leipzig's work was that physicians and coaches had information about 'regulation' of an athlete's system. 'We reported on how the body of your athlete works.' After that it was up to coaches and physicians as to whether doping products were used, without knowledge of the laboratory.

'It is a difficult situation for scientists in the GDR,' Buhl said. 'Other countries ask how it is possible that a little country like the GDR has such a good performance in medals and records. Some think this is all due to doping. Not correct. The system is very good. Rich countries cannot beat it.'

Buhl summarised the society under which the likes of Grobler and himself worked: 'The aim for all coaches, officials, sportsmen and scientists is to get medals, and a medal is money. If I don't do this work I can go into the hospital or clinic, and my job is at an end.'

In the decade before the Iron Curtain was breached, the international federation FISA engaged in pioneering control of doping and in forward-thinking about the development of its sport. Thomi Keller, FISA's president until his death in 1989, and his treasurer, Peter Coni, had devised the first dope-testing programme to operate 'out of season' when athletes were attending altitude or warm-weather training camps. The FISA medical commission sent two representatives to carry out tests, one from the East and one from the West, to allay fears of geopolitical bias in 'taking the piss'. Licensed laboratories in Cologne, London, Lausanne, Los Angeles and Sydney analysed the samples, and the programme was supported enthusiastically by East Germany.

Throughout his period at FISA's helm, Keller – a born diplomat – sprinkled his council and commissions with people from the Eastern Bloc. Among them were several from East Germany including Wilfried Hofmann (president of GDR rowing) as chairman of the youth commission, Helmut Pohlenz (chief doctor for GDR rowing) as a member of the medical commission, and Klaus Filter (GDR boat-builder) as a member of the materials commission. Pohlenz – along with the performance director Theo Koerner and Lothar Trawiel, coach to the double Olympic single-sculling champion Thomas Lange – were adamant in repeated testimony that they were hostile to sports doping and wanted to see cheating athletes prosecuted. They volunteered to lead the fight against them.

Curiously, Grobler was not questioned about his involvement in doping when he was appointed technical advisor to the ARA in 1991. Colin Moynihan, then an MP – who was minister for sport from 1987 to 1990 and had coxed the British eight to a silver medal in the Moscow Olympics – says that other MPs and journalists frequently asked him whether Grobler was implicated in the GDR's doping programme. Moynihan was obliged to ask his civil servants to enquire on an answer which would stand parliamentary scrutiny. In turn the civil servants would consult Grobler's employer – both Leander and the ARA – which would reply that neither had reason to believe the coach was in any way involved. Moynihan, who believed along with many of his crew that doped athletes from East Germany might have cheated them out of gold, was obliged to tell parliament that Grobler's employer was sure he was clean. Moynihan believes he was telling the truth because neither employer – Leander nor, later, the ARA – had asked the question or, if they had, they had taken any denial on trust.

Denis Oswald, the Swiss lawyer who succeeded Keller in late 1989, shared Thomi's view that international rowing should be run for the rowers and not for the oldies in blazers. He hoped, therefore, that rowing across the world would benefit from the theoretical and practical expertise of the East German coaches newly on the market. The signs were that events would become less skewed towards the state-supported Eastern Bloc nations, and that medals would be spread more evenly.

Oswald's main message was 'universality', and the collapse of the Soviet Union and Yugoslavia gave him, almost overnight, a hike in the number of countries affiliated to FISA – important for a sport anxious to maintain its inclusion in the Olympic Games. He was also cautious about preventing anyone who had not been convicted of a crime from working in the sport. Although most western athletes knew that they had been beaten by oarsmen who had advantages in resources, including anabolic steroids, they had no legally confirmed evidence. It was all hearsay and suspicion. In the absence of evidence, anger was generalised and diffused. Although some individuals sought redress, there was no coordinated effort to assemble evidence for a conviction. Oswald the lawyer overruled Oswald the bronze medallist who might have had silver in Mexico 1968 in a coxed four which finished just behind East Germany.

In 1991 Grobler arrived in a Britain that – far from the dry rowing creek his East European predecessor, Bob Janoušek, had found twenty years before — was on the verge of thriving. As well as Redgrave and Holmes winning bronze and gold in the coxed and coxless pairs in Seoul, sixteen men comprising the eight and the two fours had finished fourth. Various combinations of those sixteen men had reached the podium, mostly in bronze place, and the squad competing for places in the team for the 1991 world championships in Vienna was stuffed with ambitious, big, strong men.

Behind them came a generation of boys who had begun to win gold medals at world junior championships while moving on to university clubs — notably Tim Foster from Bedford Modern, and the two pairs of brothers, Jonny and Gregory Searle and Rupert and Anton Obholzer from Hampton Grammar School. Although it was achieved by quite different methods from East Germany's, a capitalist western state had put together a decent squad, so it might have seemed to Jurgen that all he had to do when he arrived at Leander was organise the training and selection along his well-proven lines in order for results to follow.

At that time Leander regarded itself as the epicentre of British rowing and was the national squad's base on the upper Thames, while remaining a distinctly amateur club with a nice stretch of river to row on. Crews who trained there were given all the support that was available, which is why Redgrave and his former coach, Mike Spracklen, had moved to Henley from their home base at Marlow Rowing Club. But Leander had none of the back-up facilities that Grobler was used to at Grünau or SC Magdeburg with its full-time coaches, doctors, nurses, physiotherapists, cooks and bottle-washers. At Leander he could ensure that his athletes were fed properly, but only he could tell the club kitchen how to meet the nutritional requirements of his charges. He had to manage the boat racks and decide what type of boats his men would use. There was no input from the groundbreaking VEB boat factory in Berlin, although Filter was busy exploring opportunities in the new Germany.

More significant than the shortage of support staff was the number of full-time athletes. There were only two: Steve Redgrave had been winning consistently since 1984 and was available to train all day, while Matthew Pinsent was reading geography at Oxford, less than an hour away from Henley. Others nominally attached to Leander had commitments of work or study and could not manage four to five hours of training a day – training that was, and is, Jurgen's only style.

The squad training regime Grobler found in 1991 was close to that laid down by Bob Janoušek when he started work in 1970. Redgrave, who had been coached by Spracklen up to 1988, had always been treated as special, to the fury and sometimes disdain of his partners. But he had followed an endurance programme and, while far from easy, found that he could follow Grobler's regime without too much adaptation. Pinsent did most of his training under Oxford University Boat Club coaches and could manage his intensity as he grew into full adulthood by rowing in two places with little overlap or oversight.

It was Grobler's luck that the two men he took responsibility for immediately after his ten years as director of rowing for the GDR's women were the two outstanding physical specimens with the wherewithal to do as he asked. They had the desire and habit of winning at the highest level. He could apply his method, see that it worked and provide them with the scientific reasoning that justified his decisions. His principal task on arriving at Leander Club was to coach them to the 1992 Olympic podium via the 1991 world championships in Vienna. Redgrave saw Grobler's arrival as a big punt on his own part and Leander's:

'Were we getting an incredible coach, a maker of champions, or were we getting a small part of an incredible system... which many also had their doubts about concerning the use of drugs. Back in the summer of 1990 we were just operating on our gut instincts. But at the start he was very much on trial as well. I told him bluntly that first day that I would do anything and everything he asked me to do in 1991 regardless of results, but if at the end of the year I felt I wasn't beginning to turn the corner and get back into Olympic gold medal shape I would go back to my old routines for '84 and '88. Jurgen seemed to have no problem with that. At one stage I announced that I intended to compete in the next two Olympics and he immediately stepped in, waving his hands a good deal, saying, "No, no, no, no, Steve, let's just talk about a third Olympics, Barcelona. Nothing else matters at this stage." He was right of course.'

Before going to Vienna, Grobler delivered a significant and valuable lesson to the innocents of British rowing. He took the squad to a summer altitude camp in the Silvretta Alps, where he used to take his East German athletes. As chief coach of the East German women he had become convinced that such training was an essential final step to achieving Olympic or world success. Aware that the West Germans had their eye on Silvretta, one of the first things he did after landing his Leander job was to book the facility for the use of Redgrave, Pinsent and other members of the British team.

John Pilgrim-Morris was one of the coaches who accompanied him on the camp, and the experience was a real eye-opener. The lake at Silvretta is owned by a hydroelectric company and was frequented by the East Germans because, once filled by melt waters in June, the highest lake in Europe afforded 2000 metres of rowable water at an altitude of 2000 metres. The approach to the site was a steep ascent from Schruns with thirty-four hairpin bends in foul wet weather. The accommodation was in huts below the dam, adjacent to an Austrian army camp.

It was clear as soon as they arrived that Jurgen was in charge. The first thing he did was to send the athletes to the bottom of the ascent and make them walk up again. Meanwhile, he and Pilgrim-Morris visited the cellar of one of the Austrian huts that turned out to be full of East German kit, including a rubber boat, life jackets, and wire and buoys to mark out a full 2000-metre course. The temperature of Silvretta water is four degrees, and as an extra safety factor, all scullers were required to wear life jackets and other boats to carry them on board.

The second morning was given over to laying the course. The 2000-metre wire was paid out from 500-metre drums with buoys attached at 12.5-metre intervals and towed into place. Jurgen led the whole procedure with military precision. Redgrave and Pinsent were put in charge of laying the wire, a task they performed for the next ten years.

For water training sessions Jurgen sat on a promontory halfway along the course offering a commanding view of the lake. With binoculars and a stopwatch he measured the time taken for every boat over 2000 metres. He also required the men to walk round the lake because the theory was that you must exercise continuously at altitude to maximise adaption. There were no indoor rowing machines; all the work was on foot or on water. Initially, water training was at a low rate of twenty strokes a minute and low pressure. This was in part to allow the oarsmen's blood acid to change to altitude values. Once boat speed and pulse rates had settled to sea-level numbers, the intensity increased.

Everything was logged, and coaches would provide statistics at a meeting after every session. Feedback was quite limited, however, says Pilgrim-Morris. At that time physiological support in Britain was very basic. For example, day-to-day measurement of lactate levels was not available as it had been in East Germany. 'Jurgen showed me a graph of how much race speed was reduced due to altitude, and another on reduction of boat speed due to water temperature. The point is that he came with a huge background of knowledge about how to go about training, particularly altitude training. For the altitude camps to be so effective, his knowledge and expertise provided that vital path to gold.'

When asked if altitude training provides a significant advantage, Grobler replied: 'Do you think we are stupid? Even if it doesn't, would you not prefer to train up here in the sunshine where the air temperature is about 15–20 degrees rather than down at Varese in 34 degrees?'

Pilgrim-Morris says the point Grobler was making was 'that mileage is possible at altitude to enhance training regardless of the altitude aspect.' But Grobler also admitted that he got it wrong once with his East German women: 'Three hundred-plus kilometres in three weeks was too much.' Grobler was firm and demanding of his athletes, but he was also always prepared to listen.

Pilgrim-Morris says that watching someone who knew his stuff at work was a great experience. 'I realised that he really knew what he was doing, and my thought was that the East German system for the oarsmen was so far ahead of what we were doing because it was based on decent research. They didn't need drugs. In a way that's been proved because the consistency with which Jurgen's crews that have been to altitude perform at the top demonstrates that if you have a properly thought-through, balanced training system, you'll get results if you have the right athletes.'

Earlier that year, the first thing that Grobler said to Pilgrim-Morris on the riverbank at Henley when coaching the Pinsent–Redgrave pair was to reiterate his remark in Tasmania: 'Redgrave is not a stroke. I switch it.' Grobler showed that he was an astute technician. He recognised that switching Redgrave from the stroke seat was no small matter because the oarsman had already won two Olympic gold medals at stroke. It was the dynamic that counted, he said: 'I could see that Steve could not lead Matthew as well as Matthew could lead Steve. Or to put it the other way round, Matthew could not follow Steve as well as Steve could follow Matthew.'

When he made the switch he told Redgrave it was temporary. 'At first I think perhaps Steve was not too happy about it, but he was good to his word of doing everything I asked for that first year.' Grobler said later: 'For him it was always "my pair" and Matt was young and starting out. I felt Matt was seeing Steve as his hero. When we changed, Steve became a better leader from the bow seat. I think he agrees now that it was the best thing to do.' Redgrave confirms that he was sceptical about the three-week experiment. But he never went back.

At the Vienna world championships Redgrave and Pinsent claimed their first title, accomplished in the fastest time in history for the coxless pairs of 6:21.35. Once the Germans Thomas Jung and Uwe Kellner had fallen into the psychological hole left by the fall of the Berlin Wall, the most experienced crew was the Pimenov twins of the USSR, and they, the French and the Yugoslavs went off like bats out of hell. After 1500 metres Redgrave and Pinsent were fourth and Pinsent, in the stroke seat, kept looking round at the other crews until Redgrave told him to desist. The crucial move came 750 metres from the line when Redgrave started to talk about the Pimenovs. With 500 metres to go he said to Pinsent: 'Come on, this is the last 500!' Then he said: 'You're a world champion.' They went clean past three boats to cross the finish, marked for the first time by an airstream of bubbles across the course. Grobler had switched his men, and proved his point.

Redgrave eventually appreciated the change, saying: 'It's got more out of Matthew with him at stroke. Jurgen had to do something to make the crew his own, and it works so well. I can read the racing quite well from the bow seat while Matt has the confidence of being stroke of a successful pair.' The fascinating thing according to the oarsman Martin Cross was that the pair 'never went with Redgrave at stroke. Matthew pulled Steve round. Matt is very strong psychologically in what he wants to do. The other way round it didn't work.'

In Vienna the British lightweight four won gold in the last three strokes of a sensational race, setting a world fastest time. The Abbagnales earned their seventh world title in coxed pairs, while the newly united Germany finished top of the table with twenty finalists from twenty-two starters.

During the championships there was an attempted coup in Moscow against President Mikhail Gorbachev. FISA vice-present Leonid Drachevski was hauled into the Soviet embassy for a briefing, and the Estonian sculler Jüri Jaanson and a couple of Latvians learned that their federations would no longer make them available for the Soviet team. Yugoslavia was on the brink, too. Iztok Čop and Denis Žvegelj pulled Slovenian t-shirts over their Yugoslav uniform for the pairs medal ceremony. On a lighter note, the stretch of water beside the Danube was notable for the nudists' sunbathing area near the warm-up water and kamikaze mosquitos that came out in the evening.

* *

Vienna had revealed that the new British pair possessed stardust. It was Redgrave's third world title and Pinsent's first. They had filled the gap in their mentoring opened by Spracklen's departure. Redgrave and Grobler had kept their bargain, and their trust would continue.

The training regime imposed by the coach was different to Spracklen's. 'People always comment on the huge mileage Jurgen asked his rowers to do when he arrived at Leander, and we certainly put the hard yards in, but in my case at least I was probably doing less,' Redgrave says. A typical training block with Spracklen might be 150 miles one week, 200 the next, then a week of 150 and then 100. Then repeat. 'To hit 150 or 200 miles a week you need to be on the water three times a day. That didn't leave time or energy for anything else, so I did virtually no weights at all. With Jurgen, cross-training became a big part of what we did.'

They spent increasing time in the gym and on rowing machines. Keeping athletes on the move was a big part of his philosophy. 'When you completed a circuit the norm was to pull over for a decent breather and a technical debrief,' Redgrave says, 'but he always kept them short. He didn't want us going into recovery mode. A typical debrief would be: "Steve, the catch... not so bad. Matt, the finish... not so bad. Now another lap."'

The biggest challenge was to maintain the intensity required for long-distance training. 'Jurgen liked most of the mileage done at a low rating – say eighteen strokes to the minute – which gives you time to recover, but because he always wanted your heart-rate to stay high he wanted you to really work hard through the stroke.'

Sometimes Jurgen cracked his men up from the towpath when he became lost in language, shouting 'Apple strudel, apple strudel!' repeatedly.

That Spring, Grobler tuned into the Boat Race on TV, which for a century has been an important feeder for the men's national team. Oxford's coaches Steve Royle and Pat Sweeney sought his help to set a training programme. When Oxford won by a length and a quarter after holding a powerful Cambridge crew round the outside of the long Surrey bend and being effectively down to seven men for the last three minutes, oarsman Pete Bridge told *The Times* that 'we really felt the strength that we had built up over six months under Jurgen's methods.' Their stamina, Bridge said, came from Grobler and his next important tip to British rowing – his one-race philosophy. 'We had to peak for the Boat Race [in March] so for six months we worked step by step to do the right thing at the right time.'

The following year – Olympic year – Grobler's crew had a tense ride. At trials before Easter they were beaten by Greg and Jonny Searle of Molesey Boat Club, setting up a head-to-head for the spring regattas. The contest between the Molesey and Leander pairs was indicative of the division of the men's squad into two parts. Athletes who trained at Leander followed Grobler's regime and grew to have faith in it. Athletes based in London and trained by the University of London's coach, Marty Aitken, followed a different beat.

Aitken, a native of Melbourne, had been recruited when he brought the Australian development eight to Henley in 1988, taking the post on the understanding that he would be invited to coach international crews through the summer. His British eights won bronze at the world championships in 1989, slipped to fourth in 1990, and took bronze again in Vienna in 1991. There were crew changes over the three years, but the coach had a strong squad that followed his more intense programme to reach the world podium. His men felt no reason to be more like the Leander crowd. At the same time there was a strong national group of lightweight men who never made it onto Jurgen's programme. The lightweight and women's squads had their own programmes. In effect Grobler, one of the best coaches available, had only two people who were listening intently.

Mark Lees, the ARA's performance director for the Barcelona Olympics, set out a conventional selection plan that had the squad clustered in various centres and training in coxless pairs. Anyone who wished to make the team was required to enter long-distance trials in November 1991 and 2000-metre trials at Holme Pierrepont, Nottingham, in April of Olympic year. As expected, the open men's November trial was won by the reigning world champions, Redgrave and Pinsent. Second were the Searle brothers from Aitken's squad. The margin between the two pairs was five seconds. Jonny, three years the elder Searle, says that as he and his brother had both been junior gold medallists coached by Martin Cross from the Redgrave 1984 golden four, they had no doubt that winning the Olympics was feasible. And the best way to start was to beat Redgrave.

The brothers and their coach Steve Gunn – who, like Cross, was a teacher at Hampton Grammar – planned their approach to the April trials on a principle of improving potential by one second each month. This was linked to a breakdown of the cycle of each stroke so that the perfect movement was grooved into their style and would not break under extreme pressure in the last quarter of a tight race. They planned, too, that their start would be fast because they knew that neither Redgrave nor Pinsent was at his best when trailing in a race.

At Holme Pierrepont a lorry with scaffolding seating mounted on it followed each trial, affording a perfect view from three metres above the water level. For the final of the men's pairs, the moving stand was filled with press, coaches and athletes. Everyone knew who would win, so there was little excitement while waiting for the start. The speculation was all about who would fill places two to six, and whether Lees would opt for a coxless four or an eight as his second boat after the Redgrave–Pinsent pair.

Jonny Searle now says that the race that followed was the best the two brothers rowed together. They took a lead, they built on it in response to Pinsent's push to get back on terms, and they rowed out as five-second winners. Even that achievement of reversing the November result by ten seconds was not as shattering as it would seem. It was assumed on the lorry that one, or both, of Redgrave and Pinsent was ill. They couldn't have been beaten like that if they were on equal terms. The only person who would have none of this speculation and treated the result as absolutely right was Steve Redgrave. He told Mark Lees, who now had a real puzzle to solve, that it had been a fair race with a fair result.

As it happened, Redgrave was being generous with the truth. In training camp at altitude in South Africa that January he had come down with food poisoning. In spite of treatment he took a long time to recover, attributed to the fact that he stayed with the full Grobler training programme. Terminal exhaustion was expected. In May he

94

was diagnosed as suffering from inflammatory bowel disease, or IBD, but this was not made public until some time in June. The fatigue and distress that this condition can cause defeats most people, and the fact that Redgrave went on for another eight years of Olympic competition with that and diabetes is just another aspect of his heroic career. It also brings Grobler's skills and quality into focus. In the GDR, notwithstanding Redgrave's brilliant success in 1984 and 1988, he would have been discouraged from trying to carry on rowing. If he had been diagnosed with IBD, let alone diabetes, he would have been dropped without a backward glance. He would have lost his place in the squad without recourse, although he might have been encouraged to take a coaching qualification or other sports-related work.

Grobler's response, however, was to do what he was trained to do and what he had a reputation for: ensure that his crew had a second chance. Both pairs were entered in the coxless event in Cologne regatta a month later. Problems occurred on the first day when the Searles were not ready as the final started, and Redgrave and Pinsent duly won. The next day the Searles entered the coxed pairs instead, finishing third, while Redgrave and Pinsent won the coxless event again.

The duel was reset at Essen two weeks later. The Searles again fluffed their start on Saturday and withdrew on Sunday because Greg had a sore throat. Čop and Žvegelj beat Redgrave and Pinsent on both days. Pinsent was alarmed: 'I thought, God, this is so heavy, we're not working together. Steve thought the same. It looked like the wheels were coming off.' As for the Slovenes, they were also puzzled by their unexpected victory, with Redgrave's condition not yet having been made public.

With the 1992 Games approaching, nobody yet knew if the Searles were the fastest pair, although many suspected them to be so. The two leading boats were crocked, and the press was busy suggesting that the laid-back brothers required a cox to get them out of bed on time. What was clear was that Britain had two exciting pairs to fill two Olympic team spots. The question was, if both were able to win the coxless, who was the best bet to beat the Abbagnales with a cox? At the same time, there was pressure on Lees to push all the best people into a big eight that might go one, or even two, better and win gold in Barcelona. But Lees knew that two medal-quality pairs carried less risk than what might be a horribly incompatible eight of all the talents. Besides, even if the eight won, there would be only one medal.

Meanwhile, Jurgen was certain that his best chance was to nurture Redgrave to Barcelona to race with the young, keen and healthy Pinsent. If there is a characteristic of Grobler's time in Britain, it is that he will always recognise the most likely talent in the squad to win Olympic gold, and he will work out which event will give that talent the higher probability of a win. Then he will coach that crew as his own, without deflection. In 1992 he was telling Lees, throughout the season, that his men would be ready and would win the pairs event on the lake at Banyoles on 2 August.

Lees kept faith with Grobler by selecting Redgrave and Pinsent for the coxless boat immediately after Essen regatta, despite their poor showing. It was too risky to allow the selection dilemma to stumble on until the last regatta before the Olympics in Lucerne. As it turned out, Lucerne regatta was a British disaster. Redgrave and Pinsent were absent while Redgrave continued his recovery. There was no sign of the Searle brothers (and the Italians, still the crew to beat in the coxed pairs, were taking it easy in sixth place because Giuseppe had gastric trouble). The fancied coxless four saw their own race pass them while they paddled, late, up to the start, and the understudy British four were under instructions not to challenge the first boat.

So nothing was gained in Lucerne, while much was lost. Far from being in twos and fours, the British team was at sixes and sevens as it entered its final preparation weeks before the Barcelona Olympics. But the Searle brothers were selected in the coxed pair among a team that Lees promoted as 'the strongest Britain has ever sent to the Olympic Games'.

While Jurgen Grobler and Steve Gunn each strove to bring his respective crew to the Barcelona start line in full health and fitness, another spat at the ARA did not improve circumstances. In June, a week after the crew announcement, the *Guardian* reported under the headline 'ARA bumps Lees from Olympics' that the international performance director 'has been told there is no place for him at the Games or the altitude and acclimatisation camps, and that the men were refusing to fly if he was not going to be present.' Lees told the paper that he had not been asked to resign. 'As far as I am concerned,' he said, 'I am the performance director and I am attending the Olympic regatta. But I am not in charge of tickets.' The newspaper commented that the ARA 'has a long, unfortunate tradition of pursuing excellence by sitting on the bank and facing backwards.'

Lees was a canny fighter and had the full, if discreet, support of Jurgen Grobler, who also knew a thing or two about public explanations for events being no reflection of the truth. Eventually, the ARA issued a press release on 26 June that said: 'The ARA is pleased to confirm that Mark Lees is continuing in his appointment as International Performance Director (Seniors) and enjoys the full confidence of the Association's Officers. In this role, Mark will attend the remaining stages of the training of the British Olympic team. Britain has the strongest ever Olympic rowing team and all the efforts of the athletes, coaches and administrators must be devoted to achieving excellent results at the Games.' Neatly the two roles had been officially combined in the one man and fortunately the two pairs had managed to avoid most of the politicking and were training like fury.

**

When Redgrave and Pinsent arrived at the pretty lake of Banyoles for the 1992 Barcelona Olympic regatta, Jurgen Grobler could tick four boxes on the progress chart for his star pair. He knew that their endurance was greater. He knew that their speed on the water was faster. He knew that they were capable of a faster time than they achieved when winning the world title in Vienna a year previously. He knew that the colitis that had attacked Redgrave seventeen weeks before the Olympics was cured. But the box he couldn't tick confidently was the one marked 'motivation'.

During the year between Vienna and Barcelona, Redgrave and Pinsent had faced a strong selection challenge from Greg and Jonny Searle and strong competition from the Slovenians Iztok Čop and Denis Žvegelj and the Germans Peter Hoeltzenbein and Colin von Ettingshausen. But, despite a rocky season of question marks over their results and potential, Redgrave and Pinsent were a different pair when Steve returned to the boat. They arrived at the Barcelona start as the pundits' favourites to take the pairs title. The Britons were at very different stages of career development. Redgrave came to the line with two Olympic golds already round his neck. For him Barcelona meant gold or nothing. Pinsent, however, was arriving at his first Olympic starting line. Gold may be the ultimate aim, but other metals would also spell achievement.

As it turned out, the pundits were right and Grobler could now tick another box. The British pair won their heat ahead of Slovenia, Switzerland, USA and Hungary for a place in a semi-final without having to work up a sweat. They won their semi-final against Germany, Slovenia, Norway, Austria and Switzerland by two seconds and in a faster time than the French victors of the other semi. They had met and defeated all their main rivals.

In the final, Čop and Žvegelj went in front from the start but the Brits were first to the 500-metre mark where they turned on a punishing show of strength. They opened a length lead very quickly and mastered the race for the remaining 1500 metres, crossing the finish line five seconds ahead of Hoeltzenbein and von Ettingshausen, with the Slovenes in bronze position. One German and one Slovenian required medical attention after the chase. Their partners stepped into the same boat to paddle to the medal ceremony, and the exhausted men recovered just in time to do likewise.

It was a commanding, regal performance if not high on the excitement scale for the grandstanders peering across the reed beds of the Banyoles lake. Any doubt about the result for British spectators was drowned by the boom of a normally gentle-mannered English vicar, the Reverend Ewen Macpherson Pinsent, yelling: 'That's my boy… that's my boy!' from the back row of the grandstand. The reporters heaped purple prose on Redgrave's third gold and his rank as Britain's greatest Olympic athlete in living memory, on Grobler's fifth gold for a crew under his personal care, on the engagement of the German as a brilliant move, and on rowing planting at least one foot firmly in Britain's upper sporting echelons.

Then, unexpectedly, British rowing planted another. The coxed pairs was supposed to be a grand finale for Italy's Abbagnale brothers after their ten years of domination and two Olympic titles. But there was a tingling feeling among aficionados that the Searle brothers could give them a fright.

As the finalists moved into the last 500 metres, though, the British supporters on the bleachers realised they would not be rising to their feet. The Searles were a long way back in third position, and the crowd's roar was voiced in operatic Italian, increasingly sure they would be hearing Italy's national anthem played after the Abbagnales crossed the line first. However, cox Garry Herbert was challenging

Greg and Jonny: 'Do you want to make a little magic for ourselves? Do you want to make a little bit of history? If not you, who? If not now, when?' Suddenly it *did* look possible, and suddenly hundreds of Brits were on their feet, hollering as they witnessed an explosive burn by the Searles to anoint themselves with gold in a flash of lightning. The last stroke of the race saw the destruction of a legend and perhaps the finest, most sensational victory in Olympic rowing history. Herbert wept unashamedly as the Union flag fluttered for a second gold-medal ceremony.

The Searles' achievement hailed the end of an era. They were the last Britons to triumph as unpaid amateurs, coached by their school-teacher. Their compatriots were engulfed in a system designed for full-time professionals training four or five hours a day for 320 days a year. Grobler's endurance training enabled his athletes to achieve the near-constant 500-metre split times over 2000 metres. In contrast, the Searle brothers trained for less time at much higher intensity to beat the kings of endurance. It was an heroic win, an achievement of outstanding character rather than carefully managed victory. They only sped faster over the last quarter.

In the sunshine at Banyoles, Redgrave had his third consecutive gold and Pinsent his first. They were a proven unit with a coach to guide them. If they were to continue – and it was a big 'if' – their motivation was now united: gold or nothing. The Searle brothers, meanwhile, would be looking for a new boat when the international federation's plans came to fruition, for the coxed pair was about to be ejected from the Olympic programme to make way for events for lightweights.

And this was not the only change afoot. When the ARA advertised for a chief coach for men, Grobler asked Ivor Lloyd, his boss at Leander, what he should do. Lloyd replied that there was only one candidate. Jurgen Grobler was appointed Britain's chief coach for men three months after the Olympics. He continued to work out of Leander but was henceforth paid by the governing body instead of the club. And now he had four exciting Olympic champions on which to build his team for Atlanta in 1996.

7

1996

The Atlanta Olympiad

'I feel the stress. Steve says: "OK, you're the coach, I trust you, tell me what to do," and I feel that is bloody hard. Everybody in the world likes to beat that monument.'
— JURGEN GROBLER

Those ambitious rowers who had cheered Pinsent, Redgrave, the Searle brothers and Garry Herbert to their gold medals at Banyoles in August 1992 found the international waterscape little changed a month later when they reported for training up to Atlanta, four years hence.

As the ARA's chief coach for heavyweight men Grobler found there was no viable national training centre in which to base a national squad. In 1970 Bob Janoušek had started to work from the new National Water Sports Centre at Holme Pierrepont, but few of the international-calibre oarsmen who lived and worked in the south-east followed him. Janoušek moved to London three years later and trained his crews from the small boathouse underneath the ARA offices in Hammersmith. He had some boat racks and a rudimentary gym in the changing room, but the bigger handicap was the turbulent tidal Thames on the other side of the esplanade. Janoušek described the situation as being like 'training a sprinter on Piccadilly'. The national squad thrived because he was a charismatic leader and because, for the ambitious, there was no alternative.

In late 1992 Grobler might also have chosen Hammersmith, but Henley was where most of GB's training took place and Leander offered better facilities than elsewhere. Besides, he had an office there, and his family celebrated the new job by buying a house in Henley where Angela entertained team members to a traditional German bread-and-cakes tea.

The characteristic most repeated by the athletes for whom Grobler has unlocked the richest of experience is that he is honest – ruthlessly so. In Britain it began with Redgrave and Pinsent. Matthew Pinsent has a mantra for his leadership lectures: 'You expect honesty from the people around you. There is not a lot of room in a really high-performance team for a hidden agenda.' Jurgen creates such genuine emotion in people willing to test it, to an extremity that few can imagine, by managing the personal relationship between himself and each athlete as if it was the only one. He practises group psychology, but more usually he builds a separate relationship with each person in his squads and uses that leverage to push the athlete to his or her limit. The consequence is that all the components of a crew know and trust each other to keep going when 'the man with the hammer' starts bashing away at arms and legs. That is why his crews win gold again and again.

At Leander 'everything was interlinked,' Grobler says. 'Sometimes it was even just a matter of a little bit of living money for a rower I wanted involved with the squad, a student perhaps with no income who was giving me his all. The committee and club spent a lot of time and money trying to make things happen.' The club housed and fed all the rowers in the squad.

For his part, Grobler demanded more from Leander men. 'I was very aware of possible accusations of bias against me regarding

Leander rowers so I made it quite clear to them that they had to be demonstrably better – 10 per cent better – than rivals from other clubs before I would pick them. There would be absolutely no decisions weighted in their favour. Quite the contrary.'

The Thames at Henley was liable to flood, but it was more manageable than the Tideway in London or, for that matter, the Elbe in Magdeburg. Whenever he needed verification of his recorded times and performance measures, or to set up trials within the squad, Grobler could find still water at Holme Pierrepont or at Hazewinkel in Belgium. Above all, while the ARA was much derided as incapable of nurturing a national team, Leander was keen to support success and hoped that some of his glitter coupled with Pinsent and Redgrave sweating in its gym and winning races would inspire the club's cadets and ordinary members to higher standards.

Not everyone was convinced. There were plenty of berths for dissenters. There was a cluster of Hampton School old boys at Molesey Boat Club opposite Hampton Court. The Nottinghamshire County Rowing Association was brimming with world-champion lightweights who were captivated by the inclusion of lightweight fours and double sculls in the Olympic programme. More lightweights were ensconced at London Rowing Club in Putney, and the women were close by at Thames Rowing Club and in Marlow. Each of these units had a champion to fight for boats and training facilities and argue the politics of selection. Jurgen may have come from a more hierarchical system but he was adept at ensuring that, even when things went wrong, his crews received enough chances to prove themselves.

One opportunity Grobler gave his squad was to compete at Grünau regatta in Berlin. The bonus of the trip was to show his men the facilities at the former headquarters of East German rowing, a place set up by professionals for professionals. This wide stretch of the River Spree was where the 1936 Olympic regatta had taken place in front of extensive lawns and large boathouses, as Adolf Hitler witnessed German crews winning five out of seven events – the exceptions being Britain's Jack Beresford and Dick Southwood's gold in the double sculls and the University of Washington's *'Boys in the Boat'* in the eights. In 1993 the multilane course had floating pontoons every 250 metres with monitoring cameras mounted on them. There were buildings for doctors and psychologists and a bio-feedback boat equipped with strain gauges and computer connections to simulate the rowing stroke. After harbouring an image of East Germany as downtrodden, Tim Foster – a junior gold medallist with Pinsent in 1988 – was amazed how rosy life had been for an athlete.

The 1993 world championships were at Račice beside a bend in the Elbe, 40 km north of Prague. For Grobler the Czech Republic was not so unlike home. The Iron Curtain had been pulled aside simultaneously in East Germany and Czechoslovakia, and both countries had been following the path to capitalism at similar pace. Consequently, the world order of rowing was turning on its head. The French team which had not won a championship gold in living memory, won three. Britain's team, lifted by wins for a lightweight single sculler from Loch Lomond, Peter Haining, and for the women's lightweight four, took four golds and second place on the medal table behind Canada. Unified Germany's strength in depth put them third with fourteen medals of all colours, but only three golds and France ranked overall fourth.

Grobler's pair beat fellow former East Germans Detlef Kirchhoff and Hans Sennewald into second place by a length, and the Slovenes Iztok Čop and Denis Žvegelj finished third. It was not a standard Redgrave–Pinsent race. Their start was sluggish, allowing Belgium and Slovenia to hold them off to the halfway point. As the Belgians faded, the Germans advanced to keep the pressure on the leaders. Pinsent had to raise the rate and sprint to take the Slovenes in the last quarter, and although they pushed Britain over the line first, the Germans were fastest over the last 500 metres. The silver and bronze medals had gone to athletes who had spent their youth and early adulthood in supportive, closed federations, and now they were learning how to compete without that systematic support.

Jonny and Greg Searle remained in the coxed pair and pushed through another season of mixed results to reach the Račice course with no guide to the odds of a repeat win. At the start of the final their supporters groaned as Jonny raised a hand to indicate 'not straight' at the moment that the flag fell and the other five crews took off. The British pair were stuck in last place for the first half, although they were only three seconds adrift at 1000 metres. There they moved – probably as they had planned to do off the start – and took the Abbagnale brothers out without a real shift in pace. They reached the finish line 1.5 seconds in front.

The results of Grobler's two pairs left the question of whether Britain would win more medals if everyone followed his plan. The spread of medals across the nations showed that there were now few athletes anywhere with rowing as a full-time occupation, and that success came to the federations that could organise their squads to make best use of limited time.

**

The 1994 season was framed around a mid-September world-championship race on Eagle Creek in Indianapolis. Grobler stuck with his familiar pair and was obliged to bite his nails as Redgrave and Pinsent trailed a new German partnership of Thorsten Streppelhoff and Peter Hoeltzenbein until the last sixteen strokes. While the Grobler training method was clearly working, it was not clear whether a fast last quarter was the result of a tendency in the ever-confident Pinsent for showmanship rather than settling the race from the start.

Meanwhile, with the coxed-pair event having been cut from the Olympic programme, the Searle brothers had put together a coxless four with Rupert Obholzer, a contemporary of Jonny at Hampton and Oxford, and Tim Foster. In true Searle fashion the four started slowly and reached the 500-metre mark in last place before grinding their way through the field, only to run out of water as they closed on the French who snatched silver behind Italy.

The athletes in the coxless four were all in work or study, and so trained at higher intensity known as Utilisation One or UT1. This involved a higher level of lactate in the blood. Grobler was used to measuring the optimum lactate in the blood for each athlete at each level of intensity, and then designing a programme that would deliver each oarsman to the start line of the last race of the season in the condition most likely to win. His was the aerobic method of rarely, if ever, allowing the lactate in the blood to increase above 1.5 millibols. It involved sessions of 25 km at seventeen strokes to the minute. A consequence of this very boring routine was that rowers could become careless of the stylistic niceties of the stroke. The method worked physiologically but did not always produce the most efficient boat-moving technique. As Janoušek had discovered twenty years earlier, training at a higher intensity for a much shorter time produced comparable results.

By this time, Pinsent and Redgrave were attracting celebrity earnings. The column inches devoted to them resulted in enough fame to appear on the odd sports gameshow and obtain sponsorship deals. But there the gameshow stopped. None of the others, even the Searle brothers with their Barcelona gold, could afford to give up the day job.

The Leander Club management filled some of the athletes' financial shortfall and enabled a small group of them to train alongside Redgrave and Pinsent, but nobody was able to match the pair's results. The British open-weight men's team had reached a zenith with the regular wins of the two strongest rowers in the world operating from their Jurgen-inspired platform, and others winning medals from the Molesey crowd. The rest of the British men's crews were finishing regularly between fifth and ninth at world championships, rarely able to show the pace or endurance to race for medals.

**

Henley regatta turned into a testimonial for Steve Redgrave in 1995 when the press realised — mistakenly, as it would turn out — that this would be the great man's last appearance at the regatta. The following year the team would be away at Olympic training camp, so now was the final opportunity to see the man who was determined to win a fourth consecutive gold medal in Atlanta. It was time to reflect on the giant who went rowing at Great Marlow comprehensive school at the age of 14 and grew up to win three Olympic and five world titles, three Commonwealth golds and thirteen Henley medals.

In the beginning there was Adam and Steve, who begat Andy and Steve, who begat Simon and Steve, who begat Steve and Matt. Adam Clift was Steve's partner when they won a junior silver medal in double sculls. From that early partnership, for Steve, it was a story of single-mindedness and the ability to persuade others to join him. Francis Smith, his school coach, told the *Guardian*: 'One of Steven's great achievements was that people would go through a wall with him. In whatever he did he was going to be a winner.'

This was borne out by his crewmates in the Los Angeles four coached to gold by Mike Spracklen. Martin Cross said: 'It was awe-inspiring for me to sit in the bow seat and try to keep up with power I hadn't felt in a boat before. There was a brutality because it wasn't smooth rowing. The crew maker at that speed was Redgrave.' Richard Budgett, later to become doctor to the British Olympic Association and from 2014 IOC representative on WADA, said rowing with Redgrave was ecstatic: 'He lifted us from a medal crew to a definite gold-medal crew. Steve outperforms everyone, and has overcome a serious illness.'

His Atlanta partner Pinsent described their relationship: 'In so many ways we are alike, such as tactically in racing and the way we organise our rowing life. We want to win all the time.' And Grobler described him as a 'benchmark in rowing', declaring: 'I feel the stress. Steve says: "OK, you're the coach, I trust you, tell me what to do," and I feel that is bloody hard. Everybody in the world likes to catch and beat that monument Steve Redgrave.'

Nobody caught the monument at Henley in 1995. Redgrave and Pinsent won the Silver Goblets and Nickalls' Challenge Cup – in Redgrave's case for the seventh time, surpassing the record of Guy Nickalls who gave his name to the trophy. The pair also won the Prince Philip Challenge Cup for coxed fours when they teamed up with Laird Reed, Joe Michels and steersman Neil Chugani.

For the 1995 championships the rowing world tripped off to Tampere in Finland where the British pair did the usual with a 1.5-second margin over the Australians Richard Wearne and Robert Walker, and the four improved to finish second, half a second behind the Italians. Meanwhile, the lightweight men were regulars on the podium – as, less frequently, were the lightweight and open-weight women. It was not really a contest between two training systems, but rather between part-timers and full-timers, and it was not going to get any better until all British Olympic sport was ripped up and restarted from scratch.

**

Atlanta 1996 produced one of the most iconic moments in rowing history, caught by Peter Spurrier's camera, as Redgrave and Pinsent reduced their own Olympic record by seven seconds on Lake Lanier. They had burst into a lead of more than a length halfway along the coxless pairs final and then held off a sprint finish by David Weightman and Robert Scott – Aussies coached by Grobler's Magdeburg protégé, Harald Jährling – to scamper over the line in first place by less than a second in 6:20.09.

From the stands the last hundred metres were heart-stopping, so close did the Aussies come to victory – quite different from Redgrave and Pinsent's assured and comfortable win in Barcelona four years beforehand. For a full five minutes the British pair remained motionless, heads down, gasping for oxygen. By Redgrave's reckoning, this was the cusp of their power, the moment of perfect equality of the two best oarsmen in the world. In Barcelona, Pinsent had been the apprentice to Redgrave's mastery. In Atlanta they were of equal stature and status. Whatever the future held, Pinsent would be on the ascendant while Redgrave slid downhill. Spurrier focused his lens on them long after the other boats had turned and paddled away. Eventually, Pinsent extended an arm behind his back and Redgrave took his hand. Spurrier's shutter clicketyclacked. It was both men's seal on what we all thought was the finale of a remarkable partnership.

When they were able to move the boat again, the pair came alongside the television dock where reporters from the BBC and Olympic News Service waited for flash quotes. Redgrave's exhausted utterance went round the world: 'Anyone sees me go anywhere near a boat, you've got my permission to shoot me,' he said.

At the end of the medal ceremony, Pinsent walked up to an IOC official and asked if he could have the Union flag. It was handed over, without the need of climbing the flagpole to pinch it. It now resides at Leander.

Despite this victory, Atlanta was not the happiest Olympic Games. The regatta opened to harsh words from Mike Sweeney, FISA's technical delegate, at the first team managers' meeting: 'This is the Olympics. This should be a showcase not only for the sportsmen and women of the world but also for the venue organisation.' Sweeney was expressing the federation's 'anger and disappointment' at the chaotic transport situation on the 55-mile route between the Olympic Village and Lake Lanier. The first day of competition was characterised by gridlock and breakdowns. Transport difficulties such as late buses, no-show buses, buses that caught fire, drivers who didn't know the route, drivers who fell asleep at the wheel, drivers who were frightened to take the freeway, all threatened to undermine the Games and regatta. Rowers of several nationalities demonstrated at the Olympic transportation hub more than once. Buses destined for other venues were hijacked and redirected to Lake Lanier. Redgrave was among those who spoke out: 'We've given up on the transportation system on race days; you just don't know when the buses will run. It's obvious that nobody's in charge.'

The service improved gradually, but the damage was done. Peter Haining, Britain's single sculler, summed it up when he said: 'I've spent twenty-eight hours in buses to race for twenty-seven minutes. It's not really on.'

Many rowers moved out of the village to hotels or houses near Lake Lanier. Among them were Redgrave and Pinsent who were pursued relentlessly by the world's media once word spread that they were about to make history. Paranoia struck the British team management, and the pair moved clandestinely to a discreet student residence in Gainesville, near the rowing lake. Next morning Peter Spurrier and *The Herald*'s correspondent Mike Haggerty could not believe their luck to see the British oarsmen consuming a giant's breakfast. Sportingly, they muttered: 'You're secret's safe with us' as they walked past Redgrave and Pinsent's table.

A more tragic blemish on Atlanta was the terrorist bomb attack on the Centennial Olympic Park on 27 July. The blast claimed a life and injured 111 people, while another person died of a heart attack. Security guard Richard Jewell discovered the bomb before detonation and cleared most of the spectators out of the park. The FBI falsely implicated Jewell as a suspect, and the news media focused aggressively on him as the presumed culprit. But in October he was cleared. In 2003 Eric Robert Rudolph, a carpenter, was convicted and sentenced to life imprisonment for the bombing. He claimed to be motivated by the US government's sanctioning of 'abortion on demand' and wanted to force the cancellation of the Olympics.

A little levity was one casualty of the tragedy in Olympic Park. That evening the Olympic News Service published an edited version of the epic novel set in Atlanta, *Gone With The Wind*. The new edition substituted international rowing stars for the story's original characters and reduced the book from 600 pages to a modest 400 words. It was posted at close of play but removed from the Olympic wire during the night as the news of the bomb unfolded. The Olympic 'thought police' decided there was no place for humour on a morning of sombre tragedy.

From a British rowing point of view, the most remarkable thing about the Atlanta Olympics was not that Redgrave and Pinsent won their fourth and second gold medals respectively. It was that their medals were the *only* golds won by the British Olympic team. The only other crew to medal was the four of Rupert Obholzer, Jonny and Greg Searle and Tim Foster – all from Molesey Boat Club and coached by Steve Gunn. Weakened by sickness, they were forced to settle for a bronze. The gold went to Australia's 'Oarsome Foursome' of Drew Ginn, Mike McKay, James Tomkins and Nick Green. Foster managed a broad smile on the medal rostrum, but the others were heads-down glum. The result was less a comment on their preference for UT1 training than on a combination of other circumstances – circumstances that would not be changed until all in the team were professionals.

During the closing ceremony the nation was jolted to the realisation that British sport had been flushed down the five-ring pan, while the heroes of the fortnight were Redgrave, Pinsent and Grobler. It became apparent that rowing was the one and only sport in Britain capable of delivering in the Olympic arena. The sports pages were filled with 'something must be done' pieces, while surveys showed that the British public was keen on medal-table ranking and would not be put off by athletes being paid to achieve it.

With that in mind, shortly after the team returned home, the state National Lottery set up by John Major's government in 1993 was extended to fund Olympic sport. It was designed to support Olympic success, not wider participation. Its clearest precedent for allocation of funds was Manfred Ewald's arrangements for East Germany in 1965. Win gold medals and the money will follow.

Not only had rowing won Britain's sole Olympic gold in Atlanta but the sport had substantial grassroots in clubs, schools and universities. It had the semblance of a national training system, and it enjoyed three or four coaches led by Grobler who showed proven experience at the highest level. Furthermore, the ARA was ready with a well-prepared application for Lottery funding, led by David Tanner, the newly appointed international manager and performance director.

The ARA scooped the pool, and for the second time in his life Jurgen found himself at the top of the tree in the best-funded international rowing programme in the world. That was not mere luck. He had helped to create the conditions that persuaded the UK Sports Lottery to place its bet on rowing's square.

8

2000

The Sydney Olympiad

'The four is not a gift shop. Many of the squad learned to win with Steve. I am very confident in having him in on performance.'
— JURGEN GROBLER

When Britain awoke on the morning after the Atlanta Olympics closed, the country faced an empty medal bucket – with the notable exception of Redgrave and Pinsent's gold. At the same time, British rowing awoke to contemplate a world without Steve. His 'shoot me' retirement comment had sounded final at the time. But the reverse of the coin was that the sport was in the ascendant and – as the only sport on the gold standard – when it came to funding for the Sydney Olympiad, British international rowing was assured of a lion's share.

No open-topped buses waited to parade the Atlanta Olympic team around the capital on their return. The country turned its attention to electing a new government in 1997 after seventeen years of rule under the Tory party. Change was in the air, and along came the National Lottery to fund things, such as elite sport, that were desired but not on offer from the Treasury.

Thus began the professional era. Shortly after his fiftieth birthday, Grobler took the reins of a fully funded rowing programme which promised to avoid the wider disappointments of Lake Lanier. On his return from Atlanta he set aside the memory of the Olympic organizers' incompetence and began to work on the next Games, just as he had after each of the previous six Olympiads. One of his first actions, once he had taken a well-earned cruise with Angela, was to discuss with each of his athletes how they felt about carrying on for another Olympiad. His role was to estimate whether they had another four years of training and competing in them and if they would meet his physical endurance assessment, and to gauge if they had the desire and the will to go on winning every day. He has never urged an athlete to train who does not really want it, although he has often persuaded an athlete to retire if he felt they no longer had the motivation to raise standards and targets every day.

A lifetime of such assessments means that Grobler has a very acute understanding of each athlete's sense of himself. Whether he really believed that Redgrave's fourth gold was his last or that the lure of a fifth – unprecedented in an endurance sport – might bring him back is unknown. However, he did know Redgrave was a driven competitor, well supported at home, and would now enjoy financial security. There was good reason to hope and to talk, but only when Steve himself was ready. In the meantime, Grobler the smart psychologist worked out his expected gold-medal times for Sydney, modified the training programme to accommodate the expected increase in full-time athletes' performance, and sat on his hands until Redgrave called him for a chat.

Redgrave's retirement comment while gasping for breath after the Atlanta final meant no one was surprised that he was nowhere to be seen when training began in October. Towards year's end, however, he knocked on his coach's door and said he wanted to carry on for Sydney. Grobler advised him to make sure this was what he really wanted, while knowing full well that Steve had no problem with motivation. Once he was certain that Redgrave's decision was for real, Jurgen told him that, whatever was to happen, his life in a pair was at an end. Instead, assuming he made the cut, Redgrave would be in a larger boat in Sydney. Grobler pulled Pinsent aside at Leander and told him that Steve was coming back. Pinsent was furious and wouldn't believe it at first, metaphorically stamping his foot at the realisation that his short-lived position as top dog was on hold.

Grobler told *Regatta* magazine that a four was in his mind. 'Steve has never stopped training for four months before. It will take time to get him back. We never train in the pair, but we need to re-form the pair as soon as possible as a measurement boat.' The magazine's December cover picture showed Redgrave and Pinsent afloat in a four under the headline 'Seats available for Sydney'. The two of them landed a £1m sponsorship from Lombard to see them through the Olympiad, and in April 1997 their club, Leander, secured a £1.8m grant from the Sports Lottery Fund for development by voting to admit women as members and offering community facilities.

Meanwhile, the ARA's David Tanner secured an admirable coaching team despite the uncertainty of his funding situation. Harry Mahon, a former Swiss and New Zealand national coach, was hired to take charge of scullers, replacing Steve Gunn who had taken Mahon's old job in New Zealand. Sean Bowden, Nottinghamshire County's coach who was on the move to Oxford, was in charge of lightweights, and Mike Spracklen came back from the USA to take charge of women. The ARA landed £1.8 million from the Lottery Sports Fund, the first tranche of a sum that would build to £8 million, affording them six full-time coaches and grants for athletes.

In the spring of 1997, Grobler found he had a much enhanced group of men from which to draw, and was personally coaching twice as many oarsmen as when his career in Britain began six years earlier. But his crew makers had not changed: Redgrave and Pinsent were set to lead for another four years. That May's *Regatta* cover pictured James Cracknell and Tim Foster bookended by Redgrave and Pinsent in a boat under the headline '...and then there were four'. Inside, Grobler told the magazine: 'Once we were three and now we are five.'

With the aid of assessment trials that had begun in January, Grobler composed his lead boat. Redgrave was still harbouring thoughts of sculling but was hammered by Greg Searle who emerged, under Mahon's guidance, as a strong contender for the single boat. Foster stroked Oxford to Boat Race victory a week before finishing third in the Nottingham pairs trials with another Oxford Blue, Rupert Obholzer. Cracknell and Bobbie Thatcher, who had been together in the Atlanta Olympic double scull, came second behind Redgrave and Pinsent.

Grobler's new four went on show in the Stewards' Challenge Cup at Henley. The entries were thin, and a Nottinghamshire County Rowing Association four was moved up a category from the Visitors' to the Stewards'. The regatta justified the upgrade on the grounds that the NCRA crew were all world champions in lightweight boats, although that hardly addressed the point that they were 25 kg per man lighter and trained part time in contrast to the fully funded Leander group.

Knowing they had no chance of a win, the NCRA crew rowed a time-trial race pattern in preparation for a selection race to be held a week later in Lucerne. As they came alongside the enclosures, the NCRA crew raised their rate for a finishing sprint and closed the gap on Britain's lead international boat. Mystifying the crowd, Pinsent dropped his rate to a paddle, allowing NCRA to close to his stern, before bouncing his crew into a superb fifty-strokes-to-the-minute power burst and racing away to win by two and a half lengths. The losers were disgusted to be treated as the saps in a bully's parlour game and said so during the customary 'three cheers' exchanges. No mention of this appears in Henley's official record. It merely says that Leander's finishing burst 'was extraordinary'.

Grobler has not commented on this incident, but the big men's behaviour towards honourable and defeated opponents fell well below the standards set in *Das Rudern* and the other training manuals the East Germans produced for the vanguard of the revolution. The NCRA managers were obliged to quote the 1997 race many times in the future, however, when the Stewards promoted their lightweight crews above their proper station as cannon fodder for the British open-weight team.

The world championships that September were on France's Lac d'Aiguebelette, known as 'Egg Omelette' to the athletes. Just before the event opened, Britain went into mourning when Princess Diana was killed in an accident in Paris. The president of the ARA, Martin Brandon-Bravo, contemplated withdrawing the British team when it became clear that finals would coincide with Diana's funeral, but after calls to London and consultations with officials, sanity prevailed. Martin and his wife Sally set about making bows of black ribbon for the athletes to pin to their strip.

Bluntly, to succeed in competitive sport, you have to become more than averagely selfish. You must adopt a singular concentration of emotion and effort and push aside consideration of others. Politicians who withdrew teams from the Olympics in 1980 and 1984 were cursed by athletes. If a competitor thought the political gain justified a wasted four years, the sentiment has never been voiced. The death of Diana, which unleashed unprecedented public grieving, was perceived in the same way by the British team. There was more concern that the Dutch were reported to have done a blistering 500 in a heat or that the lake water was circulating to the disadvantage of lane one.

In the event, the four took an early lead in their heat, semi-final and final, and hardly raised a head of steam to reach the podium on

Saturday 6 September. However, when the winning had been done and 'God Save the Queen' was played in their honour, the Union flag was raised only to half-mast. Triumph was shared with lament for Diana.

The Aiguebelette regatta had set the new 'dream team' on the path to Sydney but it had also produced an excellent overall result for Britain. There was gold for the women's four, silvers for the women's double scullers and the lightweight men's eight, and the sculler Greg Searle was among four bronze-medal winners. Thirteen out of nineteen crews reached top six finals.

** **

Just when the shadow of East Germany's doping programme seemed to be receding into the myths of time, the issues of spying, social engineering and pill-popping erupted in the media early in 1998 when witness statements and recovered Stasi files that had been in the public domain for years suddenly caught the imagination of newspaper and television editors. The East German secret police had taken meticulous care in filing millions of personal records reported by thousands of informers.

To wake up to news that the Berlin public prosecutor's office was investigating 113 sports coaches and officials. Fortunatley for Grobler the list had no East German rowing staff on the list. To hear accounts by swimmers and track athletes of health problems that they laid at the door of their former doctors and coaches – was the last thing that high-ranking professionals such as Grobler wished to hear. The press at last began to do its job and directed awkward questions to bodies like the UK Sports Council and the ARA, now the former East German coach's employer: how was the coach vetted before his appointment in 1990? Does Grobler have a Stasi file and, if so, what lies within it?

The editor of *Regatta* magazine, who was independent of the ARA, when accusations began to appear, offered Grobler the opportunity to tell his story in his own words. The coach declined, but during the next few weeks was forced to break his silence, particularly in answer to a sustained series of insinuations made by the *Mail on Sunday*. In its May 1998 edition, *Regatta* published a spread summarising the *Mail*'s campaign and the denials issued by the ARA and FISA (reproduced on pages 237-245).

Eventually, the *Mail on Sunday* sent Michael Calvin to the British training camp in Hazewinkel, Belgium. His story put an entirely different twist on the trail of misinformation published previously. On 19 April Calvin had written:

'The faceless men haunted Jurgen Grobler for 15 years. They preyed on his fears, held his family hostage and forced him to compromise his principles... As ever, perception is more powerful than reality. His personal Stasi file might summon the stereotypes of John Le Carré, but in essence, his 15 years reporting to the Ministry of State Security, from July 1974, was an exercise in bureaucratic mundanity that would have done Sir Humphrey proud.'

Calvin quoted Grobler as saying: 'Some things that were going on at that time might not have been correct, but I can look everybody in the eye and not feel guilty. I am not a doping coach. I am not a chemist... It was my job to bring in gold medals, but to do that I had to be a diplomat in a GDR tracksuit. You must understand that hundreds of thousands of people were contacted... The most insidious informers within rowing were the coxes, who tended to be specially trained secret policemen.

'I wanted to leave Germany because I wanted to prove I could succeed in a different system... I love it here. People in Britain have been really great. I've had letters, faxes, phone calls from people I don't know. They tell me: "Stay here, be strong. We are with you."'

Regatta magazine also printed quotations from Redgrave: 'He is held in amazing respect by his past athletes. That must tell you something.' And Pinsent: 'If Jurgen had done badly by them, they would have been the first to stick the knife between his ribs.'

When the doping issue hit the fan, Martin Cross reflected on it in April's *Regatta* in the light of his own experience in 1980, when two Russian oarsmen failed dope tests at Mannheim regatta and received a two-year ban. Long after the Mannheim regatta, members of Cross's coxless four who had finished behind the Soviet crew received medals in the post. 'There is no doubt that the equation of drugs = you win, no drugs = you lose is false,' he wrote, pointing out that in 1983 British crews won no medals but in the Olympic season of 1984 his undoubtedly clean crew had beaten East Germans and Soviets whatever they were or were not swallowing.

'I did not want to see the tawdry spectacle of people I respected because they were great athletes having to renounce their titles… there are serious issues involved, particularly relating to the influence that coaches may have had in threatening athletes, or inducing youths in their care to take drugs unknowingly, and these must be dealt with through the law courts as appropriate. But it is easy for us in the West to moralise about the choices athletes or coaches "should" have made when we did not live in the grip of a communist regime.'

Time heals, he went on, but so is truth a painful healing agent. 'I do not want "my" medals back but I do want my children and the young rowers whom I teach in school to know the truth about what drugs were taken and why. For this reason I am calling for the IOC to institute a "truth commission".' Cross argued that this would enable the story of athletes who took drugs to be told without recrimination.

In July's *Regatta* magazine, the *Independent*'s correspondent, revealed what the Stasi files said about Grobler in a piece entitled 'Wall Game'. He described the coach's role as an informer under the codenames of 'Jurgen' and 'Berg' reporting to Stasi case officers Ratzel and Schoen. He concluded that: 'it is very hard to see that anything harmful was passed on or that any damaging consequences followed... He was, as he has claimed, a minor player in a system that enveloped the entire society and from which no one escaped as both informer and victim. Throughout the period the record in Grobler's day job as a rowing coach was outstanding.'

Jurgen was pulled through hell and high water when the Stasi papers and doping hit the headlines. He was particularly incensed by the publication of a photograph of him in his Leander coaching jacket, resplendent with the club's insignia. He was extremely proud of his Leander connection, describing it as his only club. Ivor Lloyd, the club's captain, said: 'He was absolutely fuming and furious. The jacket ended up in the rubbish bin because he said he wouldn't wear it again because Leander was implicated in the question of whether he was involved with the doping that took place in the GDR. I think his professionalism was being questioned about something outside his control. Even if he knew about it, it was part of somebody else's decision.'

By 1999 the Berlin prosecutor's office was conducting seventeen preliminary inquiries involving those 113 former East German sports coaches and officials as part of its investigation into the use of drugs in sport. No charges were brought against Jurgen Grobler.

That same year, on 4 February, the comprehensive Lausanne Declaration on Doping in Sport was adopted by the world conference on doping in sport. It set up WADA to promote, monitor and coordinate the fight against drugs in sport. FISA was a signatory.

* *

Coming into the spring regatta season in 1998, the wheels came off Grobler's four. One Saturday evening, Foster made a sweeping gesture during a party at Oxford's boathouse and put his right arm through a window, damaging several tendons in his hand. He was out of the boat for ten weeks, forcing Grobler to find a substitute for the first round of the world cup in Munich at the end of May.

Redgrave and Pinsent's record of winning together since 1990 and the four's unbeaten run of eleven wins came to an end on 31 May when, with Luka Grubor replacing Foster, they finished fourth. 'Today was the difference between being very good and average,' Redgrave said, and the regular members were quick to dispel the notion that Grubor was to blame. 'The quality of crews we are up against compared with last year is a different kettle of fish,' Pinsent said. 'We would have needed a very good row to finish second and an excellent one to win.'

Redgrave noted that Grobler had taken them by surprise again when he switched Redgrave to the number-three seat and Grubor to the number-two between the heat and the final. It was a rare example of an ineffectual move by the coach.

Foster had lost two pints of blood in his accident and was incapable of opening a can or slicing bread, but he was sent to the national rehabilitation centre at Lilleshall and was back in training before the Munich regatta. He cycled the daily round trip from Oxford to Leander, where he pulled on a rowing machine and lifted weights with the aid of an inner tube to serve as a pulley.

Meanwhile, the four's entry in the second round of the world cup was withdrawn to concentrate on Henley regatta and the final of the cup in Lucerne. Foster's absence taught coach and crew how vulnerable they were, and the frustration of being out of the boat taught Foster how important it was to be in the group. For him, there was a whole new meaning of 'in' and 'out'. They all knew a little more about themselves, and the incident set them on guard against becoming complacent.

The restored crew made their second start of the season at Henley in a semi-final against the Australian 'Oarsome Foursome'. The victory was exuberant, so much so that stroke-man Pinsent raised a triumphant arm in front of the enclosures before the race was over. The race umpire, Mike Sweeney, said: 'I didn't realise that Pinsent was such a juvenile. If he'd caught a crab he'd have lost the race.' The final was against the Danish Olympic and world-champion lightweight four, honourably fought and well rowed. Afterwards in the boat tent the Danish stroke, Victor Feddersen, told the Duke of Edinburgh (who was awarding the regatta prizes that year) that they were happy to get so close, and 'happy that they are not our real opponents'.

A week later the British crew took the field apart on the Rotsee in Lucerne. The first stroke of the final put their bow ball a fraction ahead, and they recorded the quickest time over all quarters, consistently inching their boat ahead until the Aussies were left for dead and clear water appeared between the Brits and the tenacious Romanians. The rest – Germany, Poland and Norway – were out of sight. After the line was crossed and before the customary quick turnaround, one arm soared skywards. This time it was Foster's outside arm, the right one, with all muscles and tendons save the thumb functioning normally. Winning on the Rotsee, that's what your right arm's for.

September brought the final of the 1998 world championships in Cologne – the crew's hardest race since their formation in 1997. The Brits were ahead at all the splits, but Italy probably had the lead at some points in the howling following wind. Redgrave called for lifts three times, and Cracknell had the puff taken out of him. The winning time of 5:48.06 was just outside the world's best, and three other crews finished in under 5:50.

Redgrave said: 'Everyone knows we can win when it's all going well, and we train to go pretty quick on bad days. Today was one of those days. After I came close to chucking it in for health reasons, I've proved to myself that I'm still there. I think I am stronger that I was this time last year. Basically, becoming world champion is the statement of the year.' It was his eighth world title.

After that result, David Tanner told *The Times* that the four was no longer a selection issue for Sydney 2000. But an issue it soon became. During an outing at Henley in October Foster's back went *ping!* and seized up. Just like it did while sitting in a bus in 1992, an incident that resulted in removal of a bulging disc and a six-month recovery period.

This time the diagnosis was a bulge in one disc and a tear that had prolapsed in another, causing a crooked walk. Foster traced his trouble to a spectacular diving catch performed while playing cricket at altitude camp in Austria. An epidural at Lilleshall rehabilitation centre gave him temporary relief, but in December the ex-rower surgeon Matt Stallard offered him three options: Foster could bugger about, which had been tried, or he could bugger off, or they could take the disc out that Friday. On 18 December Foster awoke at Harpenden Hospital minus another piece of his spine, and returned to his parental home in Bedford for gentle rehabilitation.

As he suffered agonising pain while trying to do ordinary things such as turn over in bed, Foster hungered after Olympic gold that now seemed a long way away. His crewmates kept in touch by phone and were enjoying a camp at Hinze Dam on the Gold Coast in Queensland, plus an acclimatisation visit to Penrith Lakes in Sydney, site of the Olympic regatta. They sent him a postcard of a topless Australian beauty.

Foster also missed Jurgen's altitude camp in the Sierra Nevada, instead returning to Lilleshall to resume training. Grobler's programme for his top men included two visits to altitude each year to increase the amount of oxygen-carrying molecules of haemoglobin in the blood. This camp near Granada in Spain was the first of 1999.

Cracknell described life at 2350 metres in his column in *Regatta*, saying the aluminium building on top of the mountain 'looks like a Bond villain's hideout' and had an indoor track, pole-vault pit, pool, gym, basketball, football and volleyball courts 'and, unfortunately, rowing machines'. He continued:

'Doing an ergo [ergometer session] at altitude with less oxygen, and watching people ski below, makes you think you might be in the wrong sport. Apart from ergos, our training includes weights, circuits and football. The tactic of mindless enthusiasm does not seem to work at altitude. After five minutes of the first game there were a lot of volunteers for goal.

'Being without Tim Foster here and throughout the winter, due to his back injury, has been difficult both for our training and for me personally. I share with Tim when we go away and it has been strange not to have him around. His approach to training and to life on a camp certainly helps me through them. During the time Tim has missed it has been frustrating being unable to help him. I wish I could do his training for him (so does he, probably). But only he can do that.'

The athlete's selfishness is a trained response. As it becomes more important for your results that you sleep properly, get a hypoallergenic pillow, more pasta and the last of the hot water, you learn the limits of the socially acceptable arts of pushing others out of the way. Of course you have sympathy for other people's suffering, but sympathy comes more easily if that suffering is going to affect the speed of your boat. Grobler's crew wanted Foster to get well soon because they desired the boat to flow. Only secondly did they want their mate not to be in pain.

Cracknell also noted that: 'None of us have a divine right to remain a part of the programme, and we should be continually driving ourselves to retain our place and reward those who have the confidence to invest in us.' Ed Coode, a charming old Etonian and marine biologist from Newcastle University, had given impressive performances as substitute through the winter that 'identified him as the one to move forward with'.

Meanwhile, Foster was driving himself towards recovery at Lilleshall. He started on his bike. Two hours in incessant rain on his first ride froze him, but he was happy – the one thing he couldn't feel was his back. He found himself explaining rowing to injured footballers, cricketers and rugby players, likening Pinsent to the reliable leader on the field Alan Shearer, himself to the creative midfielder David Beckham, Redgrave to Tony Adams, the motivator who leads at the back and sticks it in, and Cracknell the bowman to David Seaman, the last line of defence. Beckham-Foster's challenge now was to turf out the substitute Ed Coode.

As he progressed, Foster imposed a curfew on his social life, went to bed before closing time, and dedicated himself to being nothing but a rower. On 17 March, three months to the day since his operation, he tiptoed out of Leander with his sculling boat and went out on the water for the first time in nearly four months. He sculled 5 km on Henley Reach and imposed a regime on himself as a reaction to the coolness of his crewmates who had clubbed together for a postcard but had not cared to send flowers or grapes. Each day he arrived at the club before anybody else – itself a challenge to Grobler who prided himself on being the earliest bird.

Having spent two months 'making tea', Foster was now up and running again. He summarised it as going from world champion to asking his mum for help to put on his socks. By the time of his sculling venture he could dress himself, stretch, touch his toes – which he admitted he couldn't do before the operation – and view rowing machines through rose-tinted spectacles. He had even looked forward to training on the 'devil's machine', but as he improved every day in his sculling boat, so he passed the most telling of mental tests: he hated ergometers again.

In April Foster was game for inclusion in selection trials at Holme
Pierrepont, but he was left on the bank. In atrocious conditions – and
in the absence of Pinsent – Cracknell and Coode won the time trial.

Grobler's four entered the world cup season with Coode in the
hot seat. At Hazewinkel they won without being challenged beyond
the halfway mark. A second British boat consisting of Jonny Searle,
Richard Dunn, Jim Walker and Jonny Singfield finished third behind
Poland. Grobler was noncommittal about Foster, who was 95 per cent
fit and unlucky not to qualify for the final in a single-sculls repechage.
The four's performance secured a seat for Coode in the next round
of the cup in Vienna. Grobler would have noted that the British eight
came second to Romania. He was also harbouring the possibility that
Greg Searle, omitted from Hazewinkel because of a minor injury, was
a possibility for a pair with Foster.

The regatta season took place in a period of three months training
at Henley that had begun on 10 March after the altitude camp in
Seville. This was the longest period that the squad would spend at
home before the Sydney Olympics. It was, according to Cracknell, an
annual battle with fishermen and cruiser drivers on Henley Reach. It
also included 'everyone's favourite' exercise, a 2000-metre ergometer
test, and trials in pairs that were the only occasion when the men raced
each other. These were fun as well as important because, Cracknell
said: 'your result affects which crew you end up in for the season.
Splitting down into pairs provides some excellent training for the
four. Side-by-side, steady-state training becomes a competition of
who can go fastest without looking tired while giving calls about
how easy your pair is moving.' He was paired with Coode to try and
beat Pinsent and Redgrave. The unwritten rule was that the winners
would get the best room at the summer altitude camp in Austria. 'The
best room contains single beds… As nice as Tim is…'

At the showcase of Henley regatta, Coode's four won the Stewards'

The 'scion of Magdeburg'
Wolfgang Güldenpfennig with
the Holland Cup.

Grobler's career critical moment in Grünau when Harald Jährling and
Friedrich-Willem Ulrich of SC Magdeburg overtake the reigning Olympic
Champions in the coxed pair to win GDR selection for Montreal in 1976,
where they took the first Olympic gold for a Grobler crew.

Klaus Filter, GDR rowing
championships, Grünau, 1955.

Manfred Ewald, President of the DTSB the GDR Sports Federation,
member of the central committee of the Socialist Party and architect
of the GDR sports revolution, addresses Margot Honecker, wife of the
future GDR Leader, 1968.

Grobler amongst members of the mid-80s GDR women's squad.
A. Fercho, K. Peters, Grobler, S. Heinicke, B. Schroer, J. Geracik.

Day 1 for Leander man, January 1991.

Atlanta 1996: Gold for Steve Redgrave (bow) and Matt Pinsent in 2-.

Sydney 2000: Gold in 4-. Redgrave and Pinsent hug in relief,
with Tim Foster (l) and James Cracknell (r).

Athens 2004: Pinsent crunched up after winning his fourth Gold, with Steve Williams (bow), James Cracknell and Ed Coode.

London 2012: Racing for Gold – Alex Gregory (bow), Pete Reed, Tom James and Andy Hodge (stroke).

Rio 2016: Gold for Alex Gregory (bow), Moe Sbihi, George Nash and Stan Louloudis (stroke).

Grobler tending to Steve Redgrave after a rowing machine duel with Matt Pinsent.

Rio 2016: Grobler gives a crew a talk before GBR eight goes afloat to win.

Henley: Jurgen flanked by Mrs Grobler and Lady Anne Redgrave
in the umpire's launch.

Sydney 2000: Jurgen congratulates Steve Redgrave
on his fifth consecutive Olympic Gold.

Challenge Cup by a length over the Danish lightweights who were unbeaten in lightweight events since winning the 1996 Olympics three years earlier. Thomas Ebert, Thomas Poulsen, Eskild Ebbesen and Victor Feddersen thought that the verdict was generous because Poulsen reckoned he was alongside the British stroke, Pinsent, when he heard the finish buzzer. Grobler's comment was: 'You know the boys; they only do what they have to do. But you can't win against the Danes on one leg.' This was Redgrave's eighteenth Henley medal.

Foster was rowing in the number-seven seat of the British eight that lost a storming final of the Grand Challenge Cup to a new German crew by a half-length. He was losing his battle to deselect Coode from the four but had been persuaded against initial reluctance to bring some gravitas to the feisty eight coached by the Imperial College wizard Martin McElroy.

A week after Henley came the final round of the world cup in Lucerne. The four came through a fast Norwegian boat in the last 100 metres to win by canvas. The Norwegians had set a world record of 5:46.12 in their heat. The Brits started at fifty strokes to the minute, dropped to race pace, and rose to forty-five at the finish. They never led by more than a second, and were challenged by Australia and Italy. The eight, again with Foster at seven, rose from sixth to second place in the latter 1000 metres of the final to finish less than a second behind the Russian winners.

The question now awaiting an answer was: would Foster be sent to the four's pre-world championships altitude camp or the eight's Fenland camp at Ely? 'I feel I could make the four go faster,' Foster said diplomatically. 'I want to row in it, but the eight's a nice alternative. It's been great for me to be in it. I've set myself high goals and achieved them.' Three days later, Grobler named Coode in the four for the world championships at St Catharines, Canada, but he also announced that Foster 'is not out of the four'. Foster stated publicly that he had changed his mind about wishing to row in the four or nothing.

Regatta commented that Grobler was playing it safe by not fixing two boats that ain't broke, while at the same time implicitly keeping his Olympic options open by promising Foster a shot at the four next season. A good result in St Catharines would secure a place for a boat on the Olympic start line in Sydney. If both four and eight were to qualify, as expected, Grobler would have a whole winter to play at who sits where.

Pinsent described the four's final on Martindale Pond in St Catharines as 'my best world championship race'. He said that it fulfilled the crew's twin aims of winning each race and improving their performance through the sequence. They led at every marker, pressed by Italy in the first half and Australia in the second. Meanwhile, the eight finished second to the Americans in a tremendous race that showed guts, grit and style. Foster, rowing in the number-seven seat, reported no twinges in his back. Together with the pair of Steve Williams and Simon Dennis, the four and the eight were sent directly to a camp on the Gold Coast in Queensland.

**

The squad entered its final year of preparation for the 2000 Sydney Olympics with uncertainty over seats. Had Foster done enough to regain his position in the four or would Coode hang in there after doing a superlative job in the previous season? In January Redgrave suffered a minor fracture of his arm when he fell off a medicine ball in the gym. As the trials and regatta season approached, the lead boat remained a coxless five, and consequently the make-up of the eight, and the future of the 'sixth' man, Greg Searle, remained in question.

Cracknell set the scene for the March 2000 long-distance trials in Boston, Lincolnshire, in his column for *Regatta* magazine. 'The importance of these trials for all of us trying to make the Olympic team whatever the boat was not underestimated by anyone taking part,' he wrote. 'At present, much of the focus is on the coxless five and until it becomes a coxless four, with the priority of boats decided, the picture for the rest of the team is not totally clear.'

The squad encountered gales on Henley Reach during the week running up to the trials on the bleak River Witham. The Boston course was reduced from 5 km to 3 km because of a fierce tailwind. Cracknell was partnered with Foster, and they were desperate to win. One obstacle was removed when Redgrave was absent suffering from a cold, and so Pinsent was paired with Simon Dennis from the eight's group. Foster's rival Ed Coode was rowing with Greg Searle. It was a gruelling time trial. Cracknell and Foster finished first ahead of Steve Trapmore and Bobbie Thatcher, with Searle and Coode third. Dennis and Pinsent finished ninth. The winning time was 8:29, and the tenth boat clocked 8:51.

The wait for a decision on the five seemed to go on interminably. The *Guardian* lunched separately with Redgrave, Pinsent and Cracknell and asked each their preference for the fourth seat. None expressed preference, and their indifference was genuine. In answer to the possibility of Redgrave being a casualty, Pinsent said he had never considered him not being in the boat, and Redgrave said that if he were to feel beneath scratch he would definitely resign before Jurgen had the chance to drop him.

At last, on 14 April, an impromptu press conference took place at Leander Club where Grobler announced that after a 'very competitive and fair' selection process, Foster would return to the four. 'It has not been easy having a coxless five for much of Olympic year. It has been a tough time for all of them, not least Ed and Tim.' The coach revealed that Ed and Tim had been required to share a room at all the training camps.

The announcement followed tough trials in pairs at Holme Pierrepont. The event, wrote Cracknell in his column, was not testosterone-filled. 'Ed and Tim are the two most laid-back men in the squad.' Grobler appeared unaffected by the men's frustration, too, said Cracknell. 'The top three pairs were expected to be from the Henley training centre, namely Coode and Searle, Cracknell and Foster, and the inexperienced pair of Redgrave and Pinsent... For Tim and I motivation was easy, with Tim aiming to secure his seat in the four and both of us realising that this was the last time Steve and Matt would be racing together, so we had to beat them now if we were ever going to.'

Cracknell and Foster led the final from start to finish, 'having one of those rows where you seem to get speed for nothing – very nice but very rare.' Searle and Coode chased them, while Redgrave and Pinsent clinched third place after lying fifth with 500 metres to go. Overall, twenty World and Olympic medallists were contesting for fourteen seats in the men's Olympic sweep-oared team.

'Tim was clearly in the driving seat,' Pinsent said at the press conference. 'There was no sharp intake of breath when Jurgen told us this morning.' Questioned on Redgrave's form, Grobler said: 'The four is not a gift shop. Many of the squad learned to win with Steve. I am very confident in having him in on performance.'

Cracknell pointed out that the crew announced on 14 April was the same as that announced in April 1997. 'Now, though, the route is set for Sydney. We know our crew and we are off. I get a shiver down my spine whenever I think about it. My life's ambition is so close and it is within our control to achieve it. If we don't win we will have failed. Our desire far outweighs any pressure that outside influences can place on us. The only drawback is that I am rooming with Tim again, and six months of Spandau Ballet and ABC beckon.'

Pinsent's take on the dominance of the four is that, from day one, the Redgrave–Pinsent legend was set aside, and there was never a hint that the boat was a vehicle for Redgrave to win a fifth consecutive Olympic gold. 'I know Jurgen won't take any risks with it,' he told the *Guardian*. 'If, say, Tim might make the four go quicker but Tim would also make the eight go quicker, the temptation is to put him in the eight and get two medals for the price of one. Jurgen's no dummy in this. I don't think he can afford to do that; you select the four best people and win by as much as you possibly can.'

Meanwhile, Coode's future hung between the pair with Searle or the eight, whose final line-up was yet far from settled.

* *

The four set their sights on racing to win and dominating their event in the world cup regattas leading up to Sydney. It began well on the Oberschleißheim course in Munich. Cracknell wrote that he looked forward to travelling there: 'Steve and Matt had to carry our bags, try our breakfast and call us "my lad" after losing to Tim and I on the golf course, where our hit-and-hope technique proved surprisingly effective.' On arrival in Munich, however, the omens were not good because the Union flag was flying upside down at the course, and the Brits were using a new, unfamiliar boat. Fortunately the final worked out well. After Slovenia led off the start, France and Britain moved up in the second quarter, and the British won. The crew's verdict on their performance was one of good and bad bits over their heat, semi-final and final. The understudy British four finished in fifth place.

The four won again at the Vienna world cup regatta, chased by New Zealand and the second British four, and then lined up against Australia in the final of the Stewards' Challenge Cup at Henley. In a storming race, Redgrave notched up his nineteenth Henley medal when the Leander-tagged crew crossed the line two-thirds of a length in front. Leander were warned for steering several times. They led by a canvas at the Barrier and a half-length at halfway. From there the Aussies never rated below forty strokes to the minute, and the Brits never dropped below thirty-eight. At the Mile Post the Aussies had closed the gap to two feet as a sudden shower drenched Henley Reach. Pinsent took the rating up to forty-three, and the finishing time was 6:50. He immediately made a twirling motion to request permission to take a lap of honour, and the umpire, Mike Sweeney, answered with a thumbs-up. The British crew turned and paddled past the enclosures to honour four years of being first at the line and their last race on home waters.

Searle and Coode won the Silver Goblets over Ramon di Clemente and Donovan Cech of South Africa. The British eight met the Australian crew they had beaten in Vienna in the Grand Challenge Cup, and went down by a length and a half.

Then, at the third and final world cup regatta in Lucerne – the last race before the Olympic regatta – disaster struck. The four's unbeaten record fell in the semi-final as they finished second, and their dominating confidence took a mighty dent when they plunged to fourth in the final, beaten by Italy, New Zealand and Australia.

Heads went down, or in Redgrave's case up as he gasped for breath. They had rowed eight races in three weeks, and the Lucerne final on 16 July showed them up. 'It is not a time to run around like a headless chicken,' Grobler told the *Guardian*. 'We get chased every time. The opposition expect us to win and win and win. This time the glycogen stores were a little empty.'

No sooner was the four on terra firma than Grobler ordered Cracknell into the eight as a last-minute sub for Louis Attrill, who was unwell. The eight won a brilliant final and Cracknell thus finished the day with a gold medal. This went almost unnoticed as the media spotlight focused inevitably onto the veteran Redgrave. Have eight races in three weeks drained your energy? Are you in as good a shape as you were in 1992 and 1996? 'No, I'm in better shape,' came the reply.

The acid test for Redgrave was the degree of confidence that his crew placed in him. The reactions of a 38-year-old body performing at such a level were largely uncharted, but age certainly increases the intervals between peak performances. 'What you find is that with Steve and myself, it takes bigger and bigger events to get us wound up,' Pinsent said. 'You're not going to win if you're not nervous. But in Sydney there'll be no trouble, no trouble to get nerves going. I just hope it doesn't take the others by surprise.' The main thing, he said, is that even though you could pick Redgrave off in training, he would produce consistent results.

Cracknell said that the result of the three days of monsoon on the Rotsee was hard to take. His analysis was that 'we're the best four athletes in the whole field. Out of all the crews we were racing, you wouldn't take anyone out of our boat. That's something I definitely draw on...' Boat speed is not an issue, he said. 'The crews that beat us we have beaten, and they have beaten each other, so now there are four crews who believe they can win in Sydney. We will have to remove their opinion that they can beat us in the Olympic heat and semi-final.'

He also sounded a warning: 'Stating Steve's age and questioning the possibility of five golds only winds him up, which is unwise.' It wound up the other three as well. 'We are very close.'

On 25 July at a crowded press conference at the River & Rowing Museum, David Tanner announced thirty-eight men and thirty-eight women for Sydney. Acknowledging the National Lottery's contribution of £8 million to rowing for the Olympiad, he claimed the British teams were in a strong position to bring back two medals – and the men's four was clearly earmarked for one of them. Grobler and his men were reticent to say what they had been doing since Lucerne, but they exuded confidence and smiles to the microphones and cameras. Unsurprisingly: their record thus far was three world titles, four wins at Henley, and three yellow jerseys in the world cup.

Ed Coode, named in the pair with Greg Searle, shared his coach's tips with *Regatta*'s readers: 'Eat lots. Focus on measurable. Introduce new ideas one at a time and measure them. Rig boats when it is sunny. Train hard in winter. Be extremely well organised. Have a bottomless toolbox. Remember people by ergo score, not name. Check everything one more time.'

They were ready.

**

From the first oar being dipped into Penrith Lake, the Sydney Olympic regatta was caught up in Redgrave fever. Everybody – even the supporters of rival crews – harboured a wish to see history made and to witness a phenomenal athlete crown his career with a fifth gold medal. The *Guardian* correspondent walked across the foot of the lake towards the press stand at 6.45 a.m. on 23 September, finals day, a strong sun was clearing the horizon in the east, and the flags hung limp. Suddenly a ripple of applause burst from the few dozen early fans on the bleachers. Cracknell, Redgrave, Foster and Pinsent glided across the finish line, turned, and paddled away up the lake into the sunrise. All the right people were in the boat, and God was in his heaven.

Much later the *Guardian* learned that Foster had woken the team physio, Mark Edgar, at 4 a.m. to work over his back. Foster hadn't told the others that he had experienced a twinge in the semi-final.

Half an hour before its scheduled time, the most anticipated race in rowing's history was almost derailed when the nations' flags began to flutter. Fair-minded FISA officials were fearful of postponing proceedings. But the cross-breeze wafted away, and the crews were lined up on the start at the appointed time of 10.30 a.m. It took the British four eight strokes to show their bow ball in front at the beginning of six minutes that will be etched onto their memories. Passing 500 metres they were 0.88 seconds ahead of the Australians who, like the British, were lifted by the roar from the crowd. At 1000 metres the Brits were 0.46 seconds ahead of the Italians who were now in second place. At 1500 metres they were 0.99 seconds ahead of the Italians who reduced the gap to 0.38 seconds at the line. The winning time was 5:56.24.

The British crew had had to raise their game twice in the final act of the drama that they began in the spring of 1997. At the end of the race the boat drifted to a standstill as Pinsent climbed over Foster to embrace Redgrave in the number-two seat before rolling into the water. No athlete in Britain, in rowing, in the Olympics or in an endurance sport had ever achieved five consecutive golds before. The crew progressed along the packed enclosures, and when it came to the medal ceremony the Princess Royal, president of the British Olympic Association, hung their medals round their necks before Juan Antonio Samaranch, president of the IOC, presented Redgrave with a gold Olympic pin.

Every reporter, and every photographer – and there were hundreds – gasped with the drama. 'That makes the 100 metres look tame,' summarised one. In the shadow of Redgrave was Pinsent with his third consecutive gold, and Cracknell and Foster with their first. And quietly in the background was Jurgen Grobler with a big smile on his face. He had just coached his seventh Olympic gold – his third with a British crew – won by less than four tenths of a second.

If the four made history, the pair of Ed Coode and Greg Searle reminded us of how misfortune turns. They led magnificently for three-quarters of their race, only to be overhauled by three crews in a scrambled finish. Less than a second separated them from the French winners, with the USA and Australia in between.

Complete dominance of Grobler's sweep crews thus eluded him, but honour was restored in the last event of the regatta when the eight won. A four-year campaign under Martin McElroy, much assisted by Harry Mahon, ended with sweet victory over the Australians in 5:33.08. Rowing a Vespoli boat with Carl Douglas's latest design of streamlined outriggers, they left the rest on the start, hitting a sustained rhythm instantly and delivering huge burns at 1000 metres and 1450 metres to clinch their piece of history – the first British gold medal in an eight since 1912.

Further cause for British celebration came when sisters Miriam and Guin Batten sculling with Gillian Lindsay and Katherine Grainger made another piece of history when their quad, coached by Mike Spracklen, won silver to become the first British women to secure an Olympic medal since women's events began in 1976.

Thus ended Grobler's most difficult season so far. For two years he had juggled half a dozen athletes around his lead boat at the mercy of injuries, while at Hammersmith twice as many men as available seats struggled to earn a berth in the eight. Like the Molesey group through the Barcelona and Atlanta Olympiads, Martin McElroy's fusiliers were often at arm's length from the chief coach who set the training schedule and was responsible for selection. Their roots were not at Leander, but at Imperial College, Nottinghamshire County, Oxford, and Cambridge. Despite the ARA's improving grip on its international programme, the squad system remained divided between the 'us' of Leander and 'them' of the universities. The golden lining was that both delivered on the day. Now there were sixteen Olympic champions – or fifteen, not counting Redgrave – who might make themselves available for Athens in 2004.

9

2004

The Athens Olympiad

'We can't have a weak year now that we have a huge amount of money. We can't buy the medals, we can't breed the guys, it's not a self-runner. Athletes are like gold dust. If I lose another athlete I am in trouble.'

— JURGEN GROBLER

After the Sydney Games, Steve Redgrave called a press conference and announced that he would start training on 1 November. Training, that is, to wind down. As a diabetic, he said, he must maintain fitness. This time he was definitely hanging up his oar. He would even refuse a seat in a Leander Grand eight for a shot at the only open Henley event that he had never won. 'I want more freedom and time to spend with my family,' he said, and thanked all his partners in boats for pulling him along, and the three outstanding coaches who shaped his career: Francis Smith, Mike Spracklen and Jurgen Grobler.

He did not say that he was satisfied, amazed, or wonderstruck that he won the world's only set of five gold medals in consecutive Olympiads in an endurance sport or that his career had not been equalled by anyone, ever. Nor in the many good things Redgrave has said of Grobler does he include the point that he is the only coach to match the record setting of his best-known charge. In Sydney a crew selected, trained and coached personally by Grobler from the moment of its genesis won gold for his fifth gold medal. That is to discount the five gold medals, out of a possible six, that his GDR women's squad won in Seoul in 1988.

Grobler said that coaching Redgrave was a 'ten-year partnership with respect and trust, something very special for a coach. Steve doesn't like special treatment, which is important. He is everyone's hero. Everyone can touch him. He's not snobbish.'

What of Matthew Pinsent? The man with three golds declared that 'the draw of Athens is strong, but so is the draw of the duvet.' So as the Athens Olympiad began, the crew makers of Grobler's squad were in doubt, even though the gold medal won by the eight in Sydney demonstrated the increase in depth of the British men's squad over ten years.

And what of Grobler himself? Thus far his career could be neatly divided into three segments. In the 1970s he took charge of the Magdeburg scullers, in the 1980s East Germany's women, and in the 1990s Britain's men. Was it now time for pastures new? In the March 2001 issue of *Regatta* magazine, Grobler revealed that he had signed a new contract in April 2000. 'I am very happy here,' he told the magazine. 'The recognition we have had is not just for the coxless four, but the whole men's team. Coming from a country where sport was important, I think it was great, absolutely great. I had lots of letters from people I never saw, just very nice letters. They explained their feelings and how they saw the races. People shook me by the hand in Waitrose and said how much they admired what we did. It's great, you know.' He was not going to run away, he said, citing prime minister Tony Blair's declared commitment to sport. 'For myself I would like to have four Olympic gold medals in a row. I have three now,' referring to those won by his British crews. 'My motivation is that I would really like to do it again, especially if Matt Pinsent carries on.'

Tim Foster had already announced that he was stopping. That spring Grobler faced the selection dilemma of having eight stroke-siders (including Pinsent and Cracknell) but only five bow-siders available from the Sydney veterans. So he announced that the four was dead and an eight would be the priority boat for 2001, while asking Cracknell to switch from stroke to bow side. If Cracknell could accomplish that, a pair with Pinsent was on the cards. But Grobler also pointed out that concentrating on an eight tends to kill off smaller boats: the Sydney eight had been pulled along by twice as many men over its three-year life before the final crew dominated Penrith Lake for gold. By contrast, the four and the pair had been together for a long time.

Grobler was also concerned by Britain's sculling. 'I still think so high ranking a sport can't be in just sweep. It has to be sculling as well. We can do a really professional job if we do not lose the opportunity to set up sculling in the same way as we have rowing. Of course I know it needs really new thinking and strong decisions to make it happen. We have to change a little bit the culture. It won't happen in four years' time.' He welcomed Henley regatta's introduction of a challenge cup for quadruple sculls. 'Henley is a big engine for development,' he said.

In addition, Grobler was critically aware that rowing had evolved in nineteenth-century Britain without a plan, whereas his German crews had been nurtured along a pathway that led as far as the rower wanted to take it. *Das Rudern* instructs all its readers in a single style whether they have ambitions for the Olympics or purely recreational rowing, which explains why *wanderrudern* or pleasure-rowing is bigger in Germany than anywhere else in the world. In Britain, however, you might start in a club in the Midlands as a 12-year-old cox and then, as you grow up, be given a chance to strain instead of steer. Or, like Pinsent, you could begin as a 13-year-old on the Rafts at Eton, where 700 boys have the privilege of a personal sculling boat and being taught their first skills by an older boy who knows nothing about teaching and as little about rowing. Bad habits are engrained from the start.

Usually the talented are identified by the ambitious coach and trained for whichever competition the coach thinks most likely to offer a win, as long as the talent stays in the club. Some like Ed Coode come through a good school programme, the junior national team and are directed along the Oxford and Cambridge route, which offers access to the highest standards of coaching and training but exclusion from the national squad. Because there are so many pathways crossing back and forth, there is bound to be talent lost – either through frustration or through the high chance of being in the wrong place at the wrong time. When athletes do reach the promised land, they find themselves in an authoritarian regime governed by the offer or withdrawal of funding and of survival by competing all day every day. It suits some.

As the East Germans discovered, crew sculling is the first requirement to make an impact as an international. It is achieved by training a number of bodies to a higher strength and skill level – performing each movement in absolute uniformity – than the average rowing medal-winner. But creating a quadruple scull from a British squad is almost impossible, drawing as it does from a dozen different sources arriving at various stages of personal development, with differences in style. Grobler's British rowing crews have won in every boat type almost continuously, whereas his scullers have rarely reached the podium. Male single scullers have popped up from time to time, but either as converted oarsmen with a maverick streak, like Greg Searle in 1997 or the equally idiosyncratic Alan Campbell for ten years through to Rio. In contrast, the British women – coached first by Mike Spracklen and later by Paul Thompson – have been winning world and Olympic sculling medals since their breakthrough in 2000. The difference is structural as well as cultural.

Cracknell's change of sides was tested on Mercer Lake in New Jersey. After he and Pinsent won the pairs at this first of four rounds of the 2001 world cup, Pinsent said that he thought they had the capability to be 'quicker than Steve and I ever were'.

In May 2001 a new four was set for Essen regatta comprising Ed Coode, Steve Williams, Toby Garbett and Greg Searle, but Searle resigned to become a grinder on an America's Cup yacht before his crew arrived in Germany. Phil Simmons was allotted the vacant bow seat, and they finished second to Romania. At the world cup in Seville the four, in a different seating order, finished second to Slovenia, while the pair won their second competition.

The third world cup round was held just before Henley. The fours event was scratched through lack of entries, but the British eight won and the pair came first again in their seventh consecutive win. Cracknell and Pinsent had established themselves as Britain's lead boat and the crew to beat on the world scene. They announced a sponsorship deal with Camelot, the contractors of the National Lottery, worth £1.4 million up to the Athens Games. At Henley they won the Silver Goblets easily against the lightweights Peter Haining and Nick Strange.

The four, now stroked by Richard Dunn at the expense of Simmons and coached by John West, won the Stewards' Challenge Cup by four lengths in a straight final over a Canadian crew. The eight did not put in an appearance. But all eyes were on the Queen Mother Challenge Cup for open quads, in which Sir Steve Redgrave – knighted for his services to rowing – sat in the number-two seat of Leander's boat. Leander won, giving the seventeen-stone oarsman his twentieth Henley medal.

And so to the fourth and final round of the world cup in Munich.

The eight finished third and the four were first, taking the lead immediately and covering each quarter in the shortest time. The pair did not attend because they were in training for a bold plan suggested by Cracknell and adopted by his coach and partner: to enter both coxed and coxless pairs at the forthcoming world championships in Lucerne.

* *

Doubling up at world and Olympic regattas was a tall order, and getting more difficult as standards generally improved. The last time that a British crew attempted it was in Seoul in 1988 when the coxed event had proved too much for Andy Holmes and Steve Redgrave after they had won the coxless event. Neil Chugani, the cox who joined Cracknell and Pinsent in Lucerne in the boat they called the Jumbo, described how Grobler told them that the principal challenge of doubling up was psychological rather than physical. To complicate matters, the coxed boat that was their second priority was scheduled to take place two hours *before* the coxless event.

Chugani had played his race endlessly in his mind before they arrived in Lucerne. They were confident that they could get very close to Grobler's predicted gold time. The challenge was to win efficiently and avoid being involved in a scramble for the line, which would manufacture a lot of lactate and cloud the chances in the coxless boat later. At the same time, Cracknell and Pinsent would need enough conviction to hit an effective rhythm in order to deal with the Italians Mattia Trombetta and Lorenzo Carboncini who, they knew, would harry them all the way.

They thrashed more than fifty strokes in the first minute. Even so, the start seemed to recede very slowly in the stroke man's field of vision. Chugani called for rhythm after a minute had passed and after 250 metres they were a canvas up on the Italians. The race was henceforth between the two. The rhythm call dropped the rate from thirty-nine to thirty-five and was intended to increase length of stroke and run of boat.

After 500 metres the Brits led by half a length. Here Chugani called for 'lock and legs' to get what Pinsent called 'the big guns' working. The focus was on a quick entry of the blade to the water with the body remaining rocked over at the catch, picking up the work through the legs and standing on the stretcher through the ninety-degree angle. This took them further into the lead, just as the race plan had forecast and as the cox had played out in his visualisation. The middle 1000 metres were long, solid and efficient, moving away from the Italians at a rating of thirty-four to thirty-five. They had a bit of clear water over the Italians as they moved into the last 500 metres, and Chugani could no longer see the other crew in his peripheral vision.

As they moved into the last 250 metres, said Chugani: 'I was counting the remaining buoys and telling James and Matt how far there was to go.' Then, with 150 metres remaining, Trombetta and Carboncini loomed back into his vision, an occurrence he had certainly not envisaged. He ordered a 'more power' squeeze and, with 50 metres left, a sprint. The Brits clocked 6:49.33 and the Italians 6:49.75. Economical or what?

Chugani had won gold, but he felt no elation at the line. The job was only half-done. He could only savour victory once he knew that it had not come at too high a price. They spun the boat round and headed towards Grobler on the pontoon. The coach wore a big grin and hugged Chugani, saying: 'Neil, you are a world champion. Now go and derig the boat.'

Cracknell and Pinsent took a cool-down walk, and the four men reconvened in the boathouse. While the oarsmen were given a massage, Grobler and Chugani wrote down rates from the cox box to analyse the coxed-race profile. Time seemed to pass quickly and soon the coach was delivering another pre-race chat. This time, he told them to go out and dominate from the start. 'The clear message was that there was no question in his mind that James and Matt would win.'

Chugani found a seat in the stand 100 metres short of the finish line and suffered the most nerve-wracking experience of his rowing career. He was not able to influence the outcome from the stands. The British pair were third after 500 metres, then fourth after 1500 metres and looking as if they would run out of course. But in the last quarter they began to reel back the leaders from Yugoslavia, Djordje Višacki and Nikola Stojić. Opposite Chugani they led by three feet when Cracknell hooked a buoy at the finish of a stroke and they lost all but the width of the bow-ball advantage. Somehow, Cracknell recovered, and they crossed the line in 6:27.57, two hundredths of a second ahead of Višacki and Stojić.

Chugani had a surge of emotion, and over the next twenty-four hours realised that he had been part of something very special. So had Cracknell, Pinsent and Grobler. The results show how close was their call. 'There's no way we're doing that again,' Cracknell, whose idea it had been, said. 'I want to go down as never having been beaten in a coxless pair. We'll stay unbeaten in the coxed pair because I don't want to do that again.' The others implicitly agreed.

Meanwhile, Garbett, Williams, Coode and Dunn also struck gold in Lucerne. 'This is something that the four of us created,' Coode said. 'It's the first time that I've done that and it means a hell of a lot to me.' The eight finished fifth.

*

When training recommenced after the double feat in Lucerne, Pinsent beat Cracknell at November's indoor rowing championships to remain top dog on the ergometer. The new competition season began in Duisburg, Germany, where Cracknell and Pinsent won on both days and the four of Josh West, Steve Williams, Toby Garbett and Richard Dunn also succeeded on the first day. On the second, Dunn crabbed and the crew lost to the Germans by a hundredth of a second. The pair and four both won again in Hazewinkel in June, and the pair won the Silver Goblets at Henley in a blustery race against the world bronze-medal winners, di Clemente and Cech of South Africa.

Henley was a dog's breakfast for the top British crews because a large number of team members suffered from gastroenteritis after dining at Leander on the evening before the finals. Cracknell and Pinsent's narrow win at first suggested that they, too, might have been among the affected. But the world champions' fast time of 7:35 tells a different story in the stormy conditions on the least-fancied Bucks station. The South Africans led for most of the first half before the British pair dropped their rating and powered awesomely ahead to hold off a sustained attack. The verdict was half a length, and this was their twenty-fifth unbeaten race.

As Cracknell and Pinsent crossed the Henley line, a new storm was gathering pace. An entry for their event in the Lucerne world cup on the next weekend caught their eye: a couple of Australians named James Tomkins and Drew Ginn, veterans of the Olympic-champion legendary four known as the Oarsome Foursome. Having no form as yet in 2002, the Aussies were a loose cannon, and they were drawn in the same preliminary heat as the Brits. Halfway down the course they overtook the British pair, bringing to an end not only Cracknell and Pinsent's winning streak but also putting the kybosh on any further notions of attempting more than one event.

The British pair were rattled. Pinsent was pragmatic and laid-back, while Cracknell was agitated and 'a lot more worried' according to coach Grobler, who remained a calm influence between his two men as they prepared for the final.

Tomkins was characteristically relaxed about his prospects. 'I'm old, and Drew had a crocked back,' he told the *Guardian*. 'If we knock 'em off, we knock 'em off.' And knock them off they did. Croatia and Germany led the final after 500 metres, and Croatia led at halfway. After 1300 metres the Aussies made their move, stretching away without raising their rate of strokes to claim a two-length lead, leaving the Brits struggling to beat Croatia.

This is how it came to pass on the Lucerne Rotsee that Cracknell and Pinsent learned to lose. 'We have a bigger engine than them but we are not using it,' Pinsent said. 'It's not fitness, it's not strength that's at fault, it's the way we are moving the boat that's not efficient.' The British pair would be scratched from the final world cup in Munich to prepare for the world championships in Seville on the safe waters of Henley Reach.

Their preparations clearly worked. After twenty-five strokes of the Seville final they were in front, and after 400 metres were nearly a length up. Pinsent took a look at the Aussies and heard Cracknell say: 'Bury them.' The Australians were struggling in the lane to the right of them, veering into the Brits' water. Cracknell shouted to them to move over. 'They must have been feeling our bounce,' he said. At halfway the British pair were ahead of the Croatian brothers Siniša and Nikša Skelin, and the Aussies were in fifth place. Cracknell and Pinsent recorded the fifth-slowest time from 1000 to 1500 metres and yet still ran out with their astonishing record. South Africa, Croatia and Australia followed them across the line, all within two seconds of one another.

'After today, I think we can go quicker than 6:14. Four boats came under the old world record,' said Pinsent, who had set the old record of 6:18.34 with Redgrave in 1994. The British pair qualified for a £40,000 bonus from their sponsors, Camelot. They had buried Ginn and Tomkins with honours, and rearranged the statistics of coxless pairs by lowering the world's best time by four seconds to 6:14.27 – which happened to be Grobler's prediction of the best possible time at the forthcoming Olympics. Pinsent had overtaken Redgrave's score of nine world titles and Cracknell had scored his sixth.

* *

At the halfway stage to the Athens Games, the men's team looked to be in good shape. The leading boat had recovered from the catastrophe vented upon it at the Lucerne regatta, and the rest of the squad had turned in good results at the Seville world championships. The coxless four of Williams, Josh West, Garbett and Dunn picked up a silver medal behind Germany, and the coxed four of Tom Stallard, Steve Trapmore, Luka Grubor and Kieran West – three of them eight-oared Sydney champions – won gold with cox Christian Cormack. The depleted eight, now coached by Steve Gunn after Martin McElroy moved on, reached their final.

As the year turned, the coxless four was looking safe and set. At the trials in Boston, Lincolnshire, early in the New Year, Williams and Garbett beat Cracknell and Pinsent, with Dunn and Josh West in third place. Yet the course of events in 2002 had also revealed how vulnerable circumstances could be. The squad had had to cope with a trail of setbacks: the pair's shock defeat, the four zapped by exam timetables, the quad disbanded by illness, the eight at sixes and sevens. In December three men were suffering back trouble, Coode was out for most of the coming season, Dunn was grounded for four weeks with groin strain, and Grubor announced his retirement.

Jurgen Grobler made clear in an interview with *Regatta* that doors remained open and that seats in neither pair nor four were safe: 'National Olympic selection is not over until just before the Olympics in 2004, especially if we qualify the team this year. Nobody should feel too young to challenge for a place in the senior team.'

It was a reminder that it was boats, not crews, who could qualify for the Games twelve months ahead at the world championships. It was also a reminder that, although Grobler's plight of being able to count the available major talent on one hand was now far behind him, he faced a dearth of talent discernible in the under-23 and junior squads. In addition, the coach was now prone to pressure he had experienced in East German days. 'We can't have a weak year now that we have a huge amount of money,' he told *Regatta*. 'We can't buy the medals, we can't breed the guys, it's not a self-runner. Athletes are like gold dust. If I lose another athlete I am in trouble.'

Cracknell and Pinsent did their bit by winning the British trials in Hazewinkel. Then they pulled into trouble. They finished third in the first round of the world cup in Milan, won the second round in Munich and won the Silver Goblets at Henley in a close race with Americans Jason Read and Bryan Volpenhein. They did not appear at the final round of the cup in Lucerne, but were on the starting line at their second appearance in Milan in 2003 – the world championships and qualifying regatta for next year's Olympics in Athens.

Six British crews won world medals in Milan. There were silvers for the coxed and coxless fours, the lightweight sculler Tom Kay and the lightweight women's pair of Julia Warren and Michelle Dollimore. There was bronze for the men's eight. But there was a seismic moment as James Cracknell and Matt Pinsent paddled away after their final while 'God Save the Queen' accompanied the Union flag being hoisted up the centre pole for Katherine Grainger and Cath Bishop, the champion women's pair. The men had been outpaced, outfaced and out-rowed in a complete reversal of their flier in Seville twelve months previously.

This Milan fixture marked the only appearance of the Aussies Drew Ginn and Jimmy Tomkins in Olympic qualifying year, and they took the race by the scruff of the neck, straight into the lead and clear water. 'We beat the Poms last year so they came back stronger. It's an escalation every year and we have to make sure we stay with it,' Ginn said. They stayed with it to slay their main rivals in a truly titanic race, coming home ahead of the Croatians, South Africans and Brits in that order.

Pinsent's take on the result was relief that the pressure of winning every time had been lifted. Until that point he had won a medal every year since 1988. 'The margins are quite small, and it's hard to turn a chase for a minor medal into something that you feel passionate about when your whole race and your whole day is about winning it, which is probably why it went so badly wrong in the last bit as it did.' Age was reducing the number of races that Cracknell and Pinsent could be expected to perform, as the Australian veterans had calculated by taking part in fewer regattas.

Grobler took a cautiously sober view: 'I think the men's team demonstrated progress, especially the eight, and holding our position in the coxless four. OK, it looks not so good, there's a big one missing from our top performers in the pair. Those things happen. We'll go home and decide what the next step is.'

Soon the crews would go to the British Olympic Association's training camp in Cyprus. Would the pair's race programme reduce? Would we see changes? Would Ed Coode's wish come true to win a seat in the 'four or the fastest boat'? With the four near the front and the pair trailing, would Grobler be burning midnight oil over his drawing board?

**

The squad that emerged over the winter following the Milan pair's catastrophe was entirely rearranged. Before Christmas, Grobler set out his strategy. 'The pair is our national selection tool,' he told *Regatta*. 'There is no ring fence round anybody, Matthew or James or any other guy. I think that is the key thing. For us there is still the opportunity for everybody. Our system has been that the pair is always important to the team. If you take the last Olympic cycle, always the fastest pair was in the four. The crunch point of who will be in which of the boats already qualified for Athens comes after the first world cup regatta in Poznań early in May. If the priority boat is to change, it will not change until then.'

The chief coach announced a camp where the top ten pairs were divided into two groups and partners switched in a version of musical chairs: 'We have to make all three crews strong, but of course the first thing is to make the pair as strong as possible. The pair should be the number-one boat, otherwise we send out the wrong message. We have to decide between the two boats that won medals last year, strengthening the four and the eight, and see if we still have a pair, so that there is no misunderstanding. We are not giving up on the pair. That's how I see it.'

He admitted his part in underestimating the challenge that faced Cracknell and Pinsent in Milan: 'We didn't push it mentally to make it the biggest year, and I am sure the Aussies pushed quite hard to make their comeback. I know now that we can definitely put something on top.' You can have a very good team, he said, but the key thing is how can we win gold medals? 'If you take the current four, they always have good races at the end but we haven't had that breakthrough. They haven't won anything since the world title in 2001, the year after the Olympics, and then in Milan we were beaten by someone else, the Canadians. We must change their race pattern. We have to look a bit deeper; it's not quite as we were thinking in Milan.'

The motivation for the whole squad is to go to the Olympics, he said. 'People have a real chance to get into the team. Of course they have to knock twice on the door. This can give me very hard decisions. But it gives me a good sleep in another way.'

The Olympic season began well at the first world cup regatta in Poznań with a win for a new lead boat – a four consisting of Coode (subbing for Cracknell, who had a fractured rib), Steve Williams, Alex Partridge (winner of the pairs trials with Andrew Triggs Hodge) and Pinsent. Coode laid down a lesson in crew making for David Tanner, who said: 'Ed Coode has shown what a class guy he really is. I'm totally impressed with the way that four rowed as well as raced. Ed was truly impressive in the bow seat.' The message got to their coach, too. 'I had a good feeling before the race,' Jurgen said. 'We have done some good things in training but you never actually know until you really see it. I was also really pleased with the technique I saw.'

But uncertainty remained in the air. Three weeks later Tom Stallard replaced Coode for a fifth place at the second world cup regatta, in Munich, and three weeks on – with Cracknell in the boat instead of Stallard – they finished third in Lucerne. This result was not what it seemed. The British crew and their chief rivals, the Canadians, were out in front, shadow boxing as they deliberated between bounding across the line first and holding back so as not to reveal a killer move reserved for Athens. While they were doing this, a rookie American four stole up the outside and grabbed the gold medal.

When Henley came around at the beginning of July, the line-up of Williams, Cracknell, Partridge and Pinsent was bedded in and had drawn a bye into the final of the Stewards' Challenge Cup, which would be the crew's only appearance in Britain before going to Athens. The whole men's team was among the Henley entries.

During the regatta, an episode of the popular TV series *Midsomer Murders* was being made, with actor John Nettles and the cast unravelling foul goings-on on and off the water. Meanwhile, the Olympic team produced a tragedy all of its own, with Grobler in the starring role without a script and with nowhere to hide from Leander Club's yard, where his crews assembled and around which members and guests swirled.

Grobler had scratched his eight from the Grand Challenge Cup before the regatta started because of illness in Lucerne. Illness also meant the double scullers were withdrawn, the quad took a substitute on board, and the flagship four had not been in one piece since Lucerne because Williams had a stomach upset and Partridge sore ribs. On the first day, Kieran West and Stallard were withdrawn from the Silver Goblets – officially because of Stallard's suspected tonsillitis, but actually to join the off-piste squad in training. The other squad pair in the Goblets ran into trouble when Garbett strained his back in the first round, resulting in James Livingston substituting with Rick Dunn all the way to the final, where they lost to the South Africans di Clemente and Cech.

On the second day of the regatta the four took to the water for the first time in ten days. On the third day the top sculler, Ian Lawson, caught a crab in the Diamond Challenge Sculls and lost to 20-year-old Colin Smith. The official commentary said: 'Lawson attacked the water whereas Smith sculled over it with great skill.'

After that series of tremors, the major quake erupted. On Friday evening, Grobler called Cracknell, Williams and Pinsent together and told them that Partridge has been grounded from rowing, flying, altitude training and the Olympics with a collapsed lung. 'This is not the time to be sentimental about what Partridge brought to the crew,' Grobler told the *Independent*. 'I am absolutely confident that it will be a good story in the end. You are already a loser if you give up on your goal.'

Partridge's condition was an extraordinary, unpredictable, freak accident according to Dr Richard Budgett, the chief medical officer at the British Olympic Medical Centre. It also meant that Ed Coode's wish came true: he was bounced into the number-three seat of the lead boat for the Stewards' Challenge Cup final and the Olympic Games. Pinsent greeted Coode's reappearance in a characteristically laid-back manner: 'It's not as if we just got him off the shelf at Tesco.'

The new crew, entered as Leander and Imperial, powered along the booms with defiant determination, covering the mile and 550 yards in 6:46 and beating the Australian combination from Melbourne and Queensland universities by two lengths.

With his sixteenth Henley medal round his neck, Pinsent described this as their easiest and hardest race rolled into one – easiest because Henley is a send-off to Athens, but hardest because none of them, not even the man himself, knew what was going on inside Partridge's chest, although they all knew what not going to the Olympics meant to Partridge.

'We have to make a clean start again,' Pinsent said. 'The opposition have not beaten the British four who are going to the Olympics. There's no point in chasing what might have been.' He took strength from previous experiences of illnesses, citing Steve Redgrave on a drip in hospital nine weeks before his gold medal in the pair at the 1992 Olympics.

Williams said he was not intimidated by the work they would have to do in the time they had to do it: 'All the crews I've been in under Jurgen Grobler have ramped up in the last six weeks. The support of the crowd was amazing, too. It is no secret that we've had a hard time, but it feels like they are getting behind us.'

**

The first time the final line-up of the British four of Williams, Cracknell, Coode and Pinsent raced together was in the final of the Stewards' Challenge Cup. Three further races on Athens' course at

Schiniás, close to the site of the Battle of Marathon, completed their short, glorious, undefeated reign.

At the end of his report on the close duel between the British and Canadian fours at the Lucerne regatta, the *Guardian* correspondent had written: 'Watch this space in Athens. If you blink, you might miss it.' At Schiniás, Canada, Britain and Australia won heats, with the Brits returning the fastest time. Canada and Britain won the semi-finals in almost identical splits. The Canadians – Cameron Baerg, Tom Herschmiller, Jake Wetzel and Barney Williams, coached by Mike Spracklen – were slender men compared with Grobler's giants. In the final, Pinsent leapt into the lead and showed a canvas advantage after 200 metres. After 500 metres the Brits led the Canadians by 0.41 seconds and after 1000 metres by 0.44. Then the Canadians moved ahead by 0.51 seconds at 1500 metres.

With forty strokes remaining, Pinsent looked across and decided to break them with a thirty-stroke burn. When he looked again after completing it, the Canadians were still ahead. 'And it just went longer and longer,' he said, 'and I was thinking: "Christ, we're not going to be able to shake these guys off," and at ten strokes to go I was like: "How are you still ahead of us?" I thought: "Well, it's going to be a close silver."'

Ten more big ones were required – the extra gear that crews stroked by Pinsent claim to have in reserve but are seldom required to engage. They engaged it, and crossed the line in 6:06.98. The Canadians clocked 6:07.01. Canadian blades were in the water and British blades were out. The gold had been shaved off the Canadian medals by three hundredths of a second.

Pinsent broke down in tears on the medal podium – tears that made Garry Herbert's in Barcelona seem like a whimper. He had won his fourth Olympic gold, was embraced by his Canadian-Greek wife Demetra and by a taciturn Sir Steve Redgrave, and given the most gracious compliment by Barney Williams, the stroke of the crew he had beaten: 'For me, Matthew Pinsent is the greatest sweep rower that I know, and I believe he has the ability to probably equal Steve's achievements. I have the utmost respect for him, very humble. He's a very quiet competitor, he doesn't style his hair in a Mohawk, he doesn't do anything rash and in your face, and yet he rows out and performs phenomenally well. To be beaten by him, there's no one else I would have accepted being beaten by.'

As for Grobler, he had coached his eighth Olympic gold – his fourth for Britain – by the skin of his teeth. The margin had shrunk during each Olympiad, at Schiniás dropping to three hundredths of a second. An Olympiad that had begun with such promise for Jurgen and his squad ran into sand at the hands of injury, illness and Aussies. His four achieved the only British men's medal by the narrowest of margins, while the women's team won three medals. Drew Ginn and James Tomkins, duly won their second Olympic gold medal in the Olympic pairs.

10

2008

The Beijing Olympiad

*'Performance is the key for selection. But I also love the challenge
and tradition of the Boat Race. I want every good athlete, and I am
sure we will find a way to integrate them.'*
— JURGEN GROBLER

A new coxless four emerged in 2005 and sailed through the season as
Grobler's lead boat. It won three world cup gold medals, the Stewards'
Challenge Cup at Henley and the world championships in Gifu,
Japan.

If Pinsent was the main man of the previous Olmypiad, Grobler
was looking for the crew maker for the next. Andrew Triggs Hodge
emerged that man. The Yorkshireman had taken up rowing at the
University of Staffordshire from where he graduated in environmen-
tal science in 2000. After enjoyable experiences competing against
full-time oarsmen, he decided to put his career on hold and joined
Molesey Boat Club. In January 2002 he went to an under-23 camp
in Seville where he rowed in a range of boats, including outings
with Pinsent and Cracknell, but knew he was still a long way from
the team: 'Jurgen sat down with the new guys, and I realised that
my experience was a long way behind everybody else. I was the kid

from Molesey. He was warm to us all. He welcomed us and told us to get on with it.'

Hodge recognised Grobler as the guy behind Pinsent and Cracknell. 'I got into it because I enjoyed it, and at each challenge I was able to step forward, so enjoyed it more. So I kept stepping forward until I found myself in the team. Never dreamed that I [could] follow Pinsent, the huge guy with the biggest lungs, or Redgrave the stone god. I just did it because I enjoyed it.'

Later that year he earned a seat in the British eight, coached by Steve Gunn, that reached the final of the world championships in Seville. Then he was in the 2003 eight that won bronze at the world championships in Milan. The eight was based in Hammersmith while Grobler was in Henley, so the group seldom, if ever, saw the chief coach. 'He never watched us train. We were not on his radar.'

In the spring of 2004 Hodge showed signs of becoming a 'maker' when he won the men's trials with Alex Partridge. It was Partridge, however, who was moved to the Athens four to join Pinsent, Cracknell and Williams, while Hodge stayed in the eight. Before the Olympics, Partridge was invalided out of the four and replaced by Ed Coode from the eight, leaving the latter boat weaker. Hodge seethed, but Grobler acquired what he was constantly looking for: a high-performance athlete with a grudge.

After the Athens Games, Hodge went to Oxford to do a Masters. He joined the Boat Race squad that was – like Cambridge's – filled with post-Olympic talent. Sean Bowden, the Oxford coach, put him at stroke with the 27-year-old hugely experienced US Olympian Jason Flickinger behind him at seven. Pete Reed, the naval officer who was to have an illustrious career with Hodge, was also in the Dark Blue boat, although barely more than a novice.

For the 2005 Boat Race both universities produced world-class crews. Cambridge made a poor start and Oxford took an early lead, but eccentric umpiring pushed Oxford out of the fast-flowing stream and Cambridge came back to level terms. This was a crew maker's moment, and Hodge rose to the occasion. Flickinger appeared to be hanging on by his fingernails, so hard and so prolonged was Hodge's attack. He sustained it for six minutes through the middle part of the race before Oxford were able to eke out a sufficient lead to be sure of victory. The physical cost to the whole crew was memorably extreme. Crew makers are defined as rowers whose actions in training and racing make a difference to the whole boat. They set the rhythm or change the pace. They shout the moves and combine the call with the decisive shift in power that lifts a crew from one gear to another. When they are good enough, they convert losses into wins. Hodge achieved this in his Boat Race, and it became his trademark. Grobler came to rely on it.

Hodge was paired with Reed at the national squad spring trials, and they won. This was Reed's entrée into Grobler's squad, although he had met his future coach twice before. The first time was when he was studying mechanical engineering at the University of the West of England, and much of his dissertation on the mechanics of rowing focused on the 2002 world championships where Cracknell and Pinsent broke the world record. Reed's university rowing coach, Fred Smallbone, had arranged for him to meet Grobler at Leander. Reed says: 'He was charming, and he talked me through my dissertation.'

Their second meeting came in 2004. Reed had finished sixth in the squad trials with David Livingston, making a mark. When Ed Coode fell ill later, Reed had a call asking him to turn out for training next day: 'When I got there it was me, Steve Williams, James Cracknell and Matt Pinsent. I was in the three seat and we did 20 km. I loved it. I would have done 50 km. I was there listening to the great man, rowing behind the great Matthew Pinsent, rowing with Stevie Williams for the first time.'

What followed was top place in the April trials in 2005 with Hodge. 'Next day at Leander, Jurgen called us into the office with Steve

Williams and Alex Partridge and said "you guys are the four, no more seat racing". That's when our relationship started. It's been eleven years since then, and I love the man.'

** **

The 2005 world cup began in May at Dorney, the new course at Eton. Selection of London to host the Olympics in 2012 was to bring additional funding for British rowing from the National Lottery, and attract the great and the good to turn out to see thirty-nine countries do battle in a world cup on the Olympic regatta site. The throng included Denis Oswald, president of FISA and the IOC member charged with ensuring that London met the Olympic requirements for the Games. He described Dorney as 'a wonderful new rowing facility', although that judgement felt a tad premature when the next day a fierce crosswind threatened fairness and provoked descriptions of the finals as 'a farce'.

The new British four – consisting of Hodge at stroke, Partridge at three, Reed at two and Olympic champion Williams in the bow – persevered under the conditions. Their win justified an announcement of a fresh round of sponsorship from Camelot and set them on course for an untroubled season. A British eight finished third, and namesakes Josh and Kieran West came fourth in the pairs.

At the second round of the cup in Munich, the four turned a clean start in the final into a length's lead in 200 metres, and they gained clear water long before reaching the 500-metre mark. They continued to move away from the field before easing off, finishing six seconds ahead of the next boat. They were now undefeated in five races. Williams said that they aimed: 'to do our thing well, and we are getting it quite effectively'. But he recognised that the year's hard race was yet to come.

Partridge, who had missed the Athens Olympics when he suffered a punctured lung, said: 'We have to be excellent. It's not enough to be good. It only takes one crew to challenge us, and there are more to come.'

Reed was euphoric, though. 'It really helps to be here right now beating the world's best,' he said. 'I really noticed the support of the GB system when our Saturday race was delayed. There were people to carry our boat, buns for hunger, massage. I felt spoilt. I've never had anything like that before.'

Their undefeated run continued at Henley, but the Stewards' Challenge Cup final was a disappointing spectacle after their Canadian opponents hit the booms and stopped. The Canadians recovered, but a deficit of one length had become four at a stroke. The British four had only to turn up for the Lucerne round of the cup three weeks later to retain the yellow jersey. Grobler announced that the approach would be to win by using technique and harmony to build confidence rather than going flat out. His strategy succeeded. They led all their races all the way, while remaining wary of the Canadians who were an unknown quantity but with individual pedigree, and the Dutch, all of whom were from the Olympic silver-medal eight of 2004.

In the final, the Dutch were a length behind at the line. 'They asked a few questions of us,' Williams said. 'It's been a luxury to be sitting four to five seconds up in a race, but we all know that that's not going to happen over four years. We still haven't shown our whole hand.'

That autumn, at the world championships in Gifu, Japan, Grobler's four gave a command performance. They were as awesome as the day was hot when they won the world title and completed an unbeaten season. They showed in front on the sound of the starter's buzzer and had clear water after 500 metres, able to survey the field behind them but not yet able to relax. Danger lay on both sides: Dutchmen to their left and a boatload of Olympic champion Americans to their right.

For Reed, the first half of this race was the most difficult 1000 metres in their career. 'At 500 metres at thirty-eight and a half it still felt a little bit funny, just not quite right, and then all of a sudden it clicked and everything felt fine as we went down to thirty-six. In a headwind, that's a good rate to be at. We're all very long and strong. We gradually increased the power and went faster. Hodgey did what he said he was going to do, take off as hard as he could.'

The tenacious Dutch refused to allow the British to move away, and at halfway the gap was narrowing. Williams, in the bow seat, bode his time before calling for a burn with about 800 metres remaining. The crew squeezed on immense power into the headwind, digging deep rather than raising their stroke rate, and ever so gradually opened their advantage to almost a length. The Dutch closed again, but ran out of water. With five strokes to go Reed thought: 'We're going to be world champions, and it's not long now.'

Grobler was proud of his men, and no doubt relieved to produce success again in a year when almost all his stars had retired. 'I think it was a brilliant race,' he said. 'I didn't quite expect we would win it so comfortably.'

Reed summarised his experience: 'It's been terrific from the start, and I remember the conversation I had with Hodgey four months ago at Oxford, to get together after the Boat Race and make a project of it. Ever since then we decided to really go for it, and we brought that attitude into the four. Alex and Steve didn't need any convincing at all, they were right there with us.'

* *

After the 2005 world championships, Grobler had a classy, champion four but little else to write home about going into the 2006 season. The eight – with Josh and Kieran West restored to it – had failed to win a medal in Gifu, and the pair and the quad had both failed to qualify for finals. The emergence of some promising scullers was hidden beneath the disappointing statistics.

The four continued its winning ways through the new season, beginning with a nail-biter at the Munich world cup regatta and continuing in Poznań, where they took to the water in a different seating order. Partridge was now at bow, Williams at two, and Reed at three behind Hodge at stroke. The new line-up was not pretty, but the boat didn't half move. The press judged that the crew had definitely stepped up since the close finish at Munich. 'It was refreshing to swap around,' Hodge told *Regatta*. 'Last year was like putting four blokes in a boat and seeing if it works. It did work, but now we are applying a lot of stuff that we are doing in training, and we have a better foundation.'

Grobler's men withdrew from Henley when Hodge was ill, but in Lucerne a week later they extended their unbeaten run to twenty-one consecutive races.

And so to the world championships on home water at Eton Dorney. The coach switched the order of seating back to the original one, with Williams in bow, Reed at two, Partridge at three and Hodge at stroke. Gone was the crudity of their first year together. In their second unbeaten season they had paid a lot of attention to how they rowed.

The Eton event had strong Dutch, German and American entries. But the Brits lead the final all the way and were fastest over the third quarter of the course. This shook off the Americans and gave enough leeway to answer the advancing Dutch and the phenomenal finishing speed of the Germans. 'Why the Germans don't press the throttle earlier is a mystery,' said *Regatta*, 'a mystery that the British crew is happy to leave unsolved.' Retaining a world title was a new experience for Reed, Partridge and Hodge, achieved in what Williams described as a top-class final. Grobler said: 'I think that was a big step in their lives. It was a great race, well under control.'

** **

There was no doubt that in 2006 – halfway through the Beijing Olympiad – the coxless four was the leading British boat. But there were other advances that year too. Alan Campbell emerged as an exciting sculler, winning out of the blue at the first world cup. In the course of doing so he beat the Olympic champion, Olaf Tufte of Norway, and reduced the world-fastest time set by Marcel Hacker of Germany. 'I haven't seen a win in a single scull in my time in Britain, fifteen years,' Grobler remarked.

The eight was also showing promise with Olympic champion Kieran West in the stroke seat and Toby Garbett at seven. But it encountered disaster in the Poznań final when the boat's rudder fell apart, and cox Acer Nethercott – incidentally, among the top Oxford philosophers of his year – had to steer with his arms. He managed to grab the yoke under the deck behind him but could not prevent blades chopping into China's water. Nethercott returned to his station, but lost his appeal against disqualification. The crew then lost Henley's Grand Challenge Cup to the Dutch.

At the world championships at Eton Dorney, the sculler Alan Campbell, the pair of Colin Smith and Tom James, and the eight took part in finals. All were set for better things. The coxed four and the lightweight four, the pair and quadruple scullers also reached the final round.

This being two years into the Beijing Olympiad, Grobler was interviewed about prospects for the British men's squad by *Rowing & Regatta*. 'Half way through the Olympiad it looks good, but we know from past experience that Olympic development moves on,' he said.

'In Athens 2004 we qualified six boats and won one gold medal, but the others did not reach the final. Two years later at Eton we had five Olympic boats in finals with one gold and a bronze for the double, but no quad. We were hoping for more. The same performance will not be good enough to get the same result in 2007. Our aim is to qualify in all six Olympic events, to defend our position in the coxless four and double scull, and to close the gap between our performance and the top crews in the other four events.

'In the three sweep events, the four will continue to be the lead boat, and we are keen to continue with the eight. We also want to qualify a pair. To take the mental pressure off the four after winning for two seasons, I am going to run a squad of six to give those guys different targets and challenges, so that [at the world championships] in Munich we end up with a pair as well as a four. In the "six" and the eight, our job is to help the best athletes to perform best in the interests of British rowing. The system currently motivates athletes towards the four – that's the boat they want to get into, so the pair will have no ranking. So for the sake of the eight we have to identify some more talent, new or old. We must fast track two or three more athletes.'

One change was that because National Lottery grants were restricted to full-time members of the national squad, those training in Oxford and Cambridge for the Boat Race were inaccessible to the coaches until their race was over, around Easter time. Thus Grobler had no call on Kieran West or Tom James until the spring trials were upon him.

'We want these guys in the team, but because they are on another programme I have no access to them. We also have to justify our action to others in the team – performance is the key for selection. But I also love the challenge and tradition of the Boat Race, and you can't change that. I want every good athlete, and I am sure we will find a way to integrate them.'

As the 2006 April trials in Hazewinkel approached, Matt Pinsent tried to read his old coach's mind in *The Times*:

'The two athletes who will have been the focus of much of the attention are Andrew Hodge and Peter Reed, two members of the four. The challenge is, does Grobler perform surgery to cleave the two best athletes out of a unit that is doing well?

'The British four's winning margin at the world championships in 2006 was less than a second. Which poses the question, if he was to exchange Reed and Hodge for two others, how much would the four slow down?

'It is a hard decision, but Grobler has taken them before. He was clinical in his treatment of the various boats before the Athens Games, first taking James Cracknell and me out of the coxless pair and building a new four only six months before the Games. At the time many people thought that it was a mistake, but he was right because we went on to win a gold medal. By eight hundredths of a second he was right.

'What is also clear, though, is that a shuffle now could be reversed in a few months' time, soon enough for the original four to regain their dominance before the Games in Beijing. Indeed, there are those who believe that this was only a rumour, deliberately started by Grobler to keep the men's group jousting and second-guessing on their way through the selection process. A complacent group may not perform to its utmost, but a nervous one will.

'But that has seldom been Grobler's tactics. I think he is after what could be his ultimate prize – two gold medals from his best six male athletes in one Olympic Games.'

What Grobler did was send his team, including his four and new pair, to the first world cup in the Austrian city of Linz – and then throw everything in the air for the following regatta.

In Linz the coxless four and the pair won. Little did the four know that three races which brought their unbeaten record to twenty-seven wins would earn them seats in an eight for the second round of the cup in Amsterdam. Nor could Colin Smith and Matt Langridge have foreseen the same fate after their spectacular burst upon the world pairs with a scything performance that took them from sixth to first in only their third race together.

Partridge was mindful of what their coach told them in Linz: 'As important as performing well is making mistakes so that you know where the boundaries are, and you know what still has to be done.' Reed had 'never felt so good on the morning of a race since we started. Being led in the semi was a new thing which we handled well.' And stroke-man Hodge brought the performance back to earth when he said: 'we'll never have the measure of the Dutch until the Olympic final. That's our focus; we'll never stop trying to improve until then. The final was a real big step forward from the semi-final.'

Smith and Langridge were an unlikely combination, dubbed the Laurel and Hardy of the men's team. Smith weighed about 20kg less than Langridge and was dwarfed in height by the solid mass of his stroke man and all who stood on the medal podium. Their partnership was a long shot by Grobler that paid off in dramatic fashion. Winning both heat and semi-final in Linz, their plan to lead a world-class final went awry when they found themselves in last place at halfway. But they moved steadily through the field, and after 1500 metres a surge took them past the Skelin brothers of Croatia, Olympic silver medallists, to win by a length.

Grobler's plan for the second world cup regatta in Amsterdam was to keep these crews fresh by giving them a run-out in a 'super eight', and to challenge the real eight – who had placed fifth in Linz – to find more speed. While Britain provided the drama on Amsterdam's Bosbaan – a recently refurbished course near the Amstel that was originally dug by hand to the plan of the architect Peter van Niftrik during the recession in the 1930s – the writing on the wall was in

Chinese characters. The 'super eight' stormed into a lead that they never lost and inspired the true British eight to hold second place until 300 metres from the finish line, where China claimed the silver medal. Less than two seconds separated the two British crews and gave renewed confidence to the chasers. The Chinese — hosts of the next year's Olympics — also took a gold in the women's quads, trouncing the British world champions.

Henley regatta, which followed Amsterdam, brought a fistful of minor and major disasters due to the outdoor nature of the sport of rowing. Rains during the weeks before the regatta turned the ground into a quagmire. The current was swift, winds played around and clouds emptied over the valley for the first three of the five-day event.

The troubles did not end with natural phenomena and waterlogged installations. Grobler did not enter an eight in the Grand Challenge Cup, and had to withdraw his pair from the Silver Goblets because Smith was ill. When he also announced that Partridge had a knee injury that would put him out of the four, the Henley chairman Mike Sweeney's face reflected the thunderclouds flying overhead.

Some recompense was made when the four took Tom James on board as a substitute and won the Stewards' Challenge Cup, and Alan Campbell had a dazzling Diamonds with a win that dreams are made of against his friend, the world champion Mahé Drysdale from New Zealand. Campbell hoisted his coach Bill Barry aloft, saying: 'I have the best sculling coach in the world. He told me what to do, and I did it. Now perhaps he'll get off my back.' Barry responded by announcing training as usual next day, 'but maybe in bed'.

The four beat the Australians and the Canadians to bring their record to twenty-nine wins. James stayed in it for the Lucerne world cup regatta, but saw their winning run come to an end at the hands of the Dutch, who pipped the British crew at the line of the final. Hodge put defeats by New Zealand in a semi-final and the

Netherlands in the final into wise perspective: 'I haven't done this sort of racing since before Athens in the eight, where every race is as hard as you can go. For me that's what's missing. We need that risk that you're not going to win, that you have to fight hard to get as close as you can.'

Next came the world championships – the Olympic qualifying regatta – on the Oberschleißheim course at Munich. How the mighty British fell. With Williams at bow, Partridge back in the number-three seat coupled with Reed at two on bow side, and stroked by Hodge, the four found themselves struggling for pace among a tight pack right across the course, and earned no place on the medal podium. Their run of world titles stopped at two.

There was some good news, however, as Smith and Langridge won bronze in the pairs. 'Next year I want to get into the top boat,' Smith said, little realising that he was *in* the top boat by default. The eight, too, rose to bronze after frightening the Germans for the silver slot behind the Canadians who had their name on gold from the first stroke. Tom James was back in the bow seat after Partridge was restored to the four.

Grobler went on record saying he was not very happy with fourth place for his lead boat: 'I have never been to a world championships where you have coxless fours where you could come first or last. But the heavyweight men's team has five boats qualified for the Olympics. No other nation has that. Now we have to look at the top end. I think we have space for improvement.'

Taken together, the British Olympic squads had moved on, with seven medals, including gold for the women's quad, taking them to the top of the table. Four crews qualified for the Paralympics. But rising standards were making the winning of medals harder.

* *

Grobler began the Olympic year by addressing the space for improvement. In February he told *Regatta* that, having lost important races
in Lucerne and the world championships, 'we now know why we
didn't get it right. We have the best pair – Hodge and Reed – in the
four.' He observed that the event was not that strong, and so 'the four
remains the lead boat'. He had nine bow-siders and eight stroke-siders
at his disposal – in reality fourteen men from whom to select a pair
and an eight, with a few more knocking at the door. Smith and James
were the second-fastest pair. Of the eight, he said that their medal at
the recent world championships was important in an event that was
a really tough regatta in 'every race, even C finals'. The eight was
overseen by a blend of the motivational coaching of John West and
Mark Banks's attention to style. Currently the third boat in the chief
coach's mind, it might come to take priority over the pair.

The winter began with a ruckus from a culture that Grobler was
relieved lay behind him. Nine Russian rowers were found guilty of
drug offences during a twelve-month period and were banned for two
years. All of Russia's current coaches and officials were banned from
international rowing federation events for a year, and the Russian
federation was fined heavily and threatened with a four-year ban.
Consequently the Russian national Olympic committee and sports
ministry agreed to set up a new federation by 31 March in order to
avoid exclusion of their one crew qualified for the Beijing Games.

Among the British squad musical chairs began straight away. Tom
James, Alex Partridge and Tom Lucy all took the bow seat at different
times with Williams, Reed and Hodge sitting tight. They let a Munich
headwind blow away the doubts when, with Lucy up, they won by
three lengths. Hodge articulated his feelings: 'It couldn't be better. It's
the best start of the season we've ever had. The technological commitments, the physiological commitments, it's all working. It's good
to believe in what we're doing again. I've had six or seven months

questioning myself, what am I missing, am I doing it right, is it good enough? That race just screams, "Keep going". I'm just loving it.'

By then Partridge had transferred to the eight and with Colin Smith at stroke it finished second as the men's sculling team – single, double and lightweight double – all won. It was an excellent start to the Olympic year.

However, by Lucerne, the four was derailed by a back injury to Hodge. Jurgen plucked Smith from the eight and with Lucy still at bow the crew slumped to second in the B final, or eighth overall. Alastair Heathcote came into the eight at stroke and led it to a silver medal.

The final cup regatta in Poznań saw the return of James and Hodge to the four for a silver medal when they could have done with gold. But the eight won with Smith back at stroke, and in doing so beat two German boats embroiled in a mutiny over Olympic selection. Robin Bourne-Taylor and Tom Solesbury now occupied the short-straw boat, the pair. They finished second in the B final and were resigned to be plugs for any holes that may appear. Grobler thus found himself in a dilemma as the pressure to name Olympic boats intensified. Should he tamper with a four that may be a bit wobbly or an eight that was on gold standard?

As the Olympic selection deadline approached, a rare breakdown of trust between athlete and chief coach manifested itself. A selection appeal was lodged less than a month before the Olympics opened. The case arose when a former world champion who performed well through the Olympiad was dropped from the squad on 4 June, seven weeks after he delivered the fastest overall time in April's seat racing matrix.

At the hearing on 7 July the appeal panel found that Grobler accepted that 'he may… have treated the appellant somewhat harshly' during a disagreement in October of the previous year, but that there was nothing to suggest that the appellant was treated unfairly up to the April test. The panel judged that the test results were not transparent. 'The conclusion that we draw is that the appellant was not treated fairly and properly in respect of the structure of the seat racing matrix trials or the analysis of the results... On the overall timings the appellant was the fastest.'

The judgment recommended that David Tanner as international manager 'should take reasonable steps to require that the appellant's suitability for inclusion in the Olympic squad be reassessed as a matter of urgency.'

The international manager's immediate response was to argue that time constraints ruled out further tests because the squad was already away at altitude camp, and the Olympic selection deadline was barely a week away (the Olympic team announcement is made by the British Olympic Association on the recommendation of what is now called British Rowing). But the threat of proceedings in the High Court changed his mind. He emphasised that Grobler fully accepted the findings of the panel, and announced that a time trial will take place in the Austrian Alps on the next two days, 12 and 13 July.

On 16 July Martin Cross reported in the *Guardian* that the appellant's pair 'finished just under a second over the challenging mark' in a 2000-metre time trial, thus releasing the coach from pressure to adjust his Olympic team by a hair's breadth.

This must have come as a relief in view of what the appellant learned before the hearing. A letter dated 4 July from his athletes' representative, offered support but stated that Grobler 'made it very clear to me that if you proceeded with an appeal, you would burn your bridges with him and the team and most likely stand no chance of getting back into the team.'

The proceedings cost time, anxiety, emotion, money and frustration for all parties, while in view of the above, Grobler's attitude may seem harsh as well as uncharacteristic. But by this stage in his career he had such a huge database of information about his men that he was well equipped to take the whole picture into account, and to regard an appeal against a selection decision as a consequence of a breakdown of trust within his squad.

Eventually Grobler changed neither boat. James, Williams, Reed and Hodge went to Beijing and won gold. Alex Partridge, Tom Stallard, Tom Lucy, Richard Egington, Josh West, Alastair Heathcote, Matt Langridge, Colin Smith and cox Acer Nethercott went to Beijing and won silver.

The spanking-new eight-lane tree-lined 2000-metre course in Beijing's Shunyi Olympic Park had grassy slopes leading to the lake. Wide avenues and an elegant bridge connected the boathouse, grandstand and finish tower, stylish modest edifices set in a beautiful space even if the mountainous backdrop was often lost in a heat or pollution haze. In readiness for this were floodlights fitted with sensors along both sides of the course. Mysteriously, a public call box sat at the 1750-metre mark.

Racing into a light headwind on sunny Shunyi, the British four did not take their customary lead from the first stroke, free to watch the other boats scrapping along behind. Instead, the Australians dug really deep and stole the show for three-quarters of the distance. When the British stroke Hodge looked round with 500 metres of the course left, he could just catch sight of the Aussies' stern. 'I said "Jesus", and we started to take the rate up and up, and at 250 to go it was all out from there,' he said. 'I wouldn't like to say that we planned to do that, but we really had to bring out our final gear. I'm glad to say that it worked. It shocked the hell out of me.'

From the grandstand this was a sublime moment as Hodge put his foot down and took Williams, James and Reed with him. Suddenly, eking forward became a leap and a bound and James, in the bow seat, passed his opposite number in the Aussie boat. 'It was like when you close your eyes just before a crash,' Hodge said. 'You close your eyes and hope for the best. I didn't see anything, just tried to keep the boat in a straight line.' The result was that Hodge's crew were three seconds quicker over the last 500 metres than the Australians – three seconds that nailed the Aussies to the silver slot. The victory by 1.28 seconds was huge for a last-500 turnover.

'We really paid for that with our souls,' said Williams, the only survivor of the 2004 boat. 'Athens was an epic journey, but I think we can possibly top that this year. We've all had back injuries in the last twelve months. Even a month ago we were having injuries. We've had some real low moments, but you carry each other through when you don't know if you're going to get on the start line.'

Overall, Britain finished top of the rowing medal table with six, one more than the British Olympic Association's target. The men's eight were persuaded that gold was in reach by their smouldering performance in the heats, but they got the final wrong. The mighty Canadians stole enough of a lead to answer whatever was thrown back at them. Alex Partridge, the bow man who four years previously had had the misfortune to lose his seat in the Athens coxless four and in the Beijing four just four months ago, said: 'I just rowed in the most enjoyable crew I ever rowed in, the best nine guys and the best two coaches.' Wells and Rowbotham followed the eight with a bronze in the double sculls after a near miss at silver.

On the Shunyi course Grobler maintained his record of coaching crews to gold medals at the Games since 1976. His score of golds for Britain now stood at five, the last three of which were in the coxless four. He told the *Independent* how his crew coped with taking a race to the last stroke, just as his Sydney four did and his Athens four did: 'I know exactly over the four years what they can do, what kind of character they have, how deep they can dig, and that's what you have to do on a day like today. The last 100 metres are in the brain. It is still sending the signal down when it gets a little bit dark. To still hold together and pull together is the main message.'

That message was still with him as the flame of Beijing's giant torch died in the Bird's Nest spectacular closing ceremony and the London Olympiad began.

11

2012

The London Olympiad

*'I stay enough away so that nobody thinks they can manipulate me.
One of my principles is that people must be able to trust me to make
decisions.'*

— JURGEN GROBLER

The British rowing team celebrated the start of the London Olympiad
with a burst of bling at the first round of the world cup in Banyoles,
Spain. Wildest dreams would not have forecast nine gold medals, one
silver and a bronze, spread across the Olympic rowing and sculling
events. Among the golds were the men's pair, four and double scullers
made up from the top end of Grobler's athletes, plus the sculler Alan
Campbell. The quadruple scullers – four men recruited by the World
Class Start scheme designed to find new Redgraves – finished with
a silver medal.

Grobler acknowledged the role of luck in an interview in the
American magazine *Rowing News* in February 2009. How, he was
asked, was he going to keep Britain on top after six medals in Beijing?

'Of course, we are lucky everything works for us. But we are
losing some top athletes, and that leaves quite a big gap. In a new
Olympiad, you can't rely just on the GB system. You need enough

people to challenge those who have been on the team and make it hard for them to get their seat back. We'll pick some young guys and push them forward and hope to close the gap. Looking to 2010, we slowly have to get into pole position to qualify for 2012 at the world championships in 2011. We have to be in contact with the medals. There's not a lot of time to develop those young guys.'

Asked how dependent he had been on outstanding athletes and figureheads, he replied: 'We need new figureheads to keep momentum and to make our sport attractive and give it identity. We had Cracknell after Redgrave, and now we have Zac Purchase, Hodge, Reed and Campbell. We also need journalists to be "helpful critical". Nobody is perfect, and I really enjoy having journalists around.'

He told *Rowing News* that the pair was likely to be the lead boat, but no final decision had been made: 'We wait and see what the best strategy is to develop athletes and keep that winning moment in the team, as well as mix and match the talent. Nobody spends the money we spend just for fun. A pair puts pressure on two guys straight away, fifty per cent on each, and you must have fun as well. Andy Hodge is a very competitive athlete, maybe a little bit like Steve Redgrave. He's quite a skilful athlete, good feeling for a boat.

'If I look in the last two years he's our most competitive and strong-est athlete. He likes to find out a little bit about himself, and that's what he's doing now. He won our sculling trials and is challenging Alan Campbell. Maybe we could try him in a double, or as stroke of an eight, but that's risky. Hodge has won our spring pairs title for the last five years. In the long term, we haven't got time to mess around, and I'm sure he will be our top sweep guy.'

When asked how he deals with black moments, such as sudden defeats or disruption caused by injury, Grobler replied: 'You can't have black moments. You can't run away. There are always some problems in the boat, and you try and solve it by not affecting all the other boats. Last year, for example, Tom James only had two races in the four before winning an Olympic gold medal. As chief coach you are accused of always taking the best people... I made it clear that the four was the leading boat, so we had to use a leading contender for the pair as a substitute when James was injured. All the coaches were behind it. I was not doing something just for myself. If the coach they're looking up to is panicking, what effect will it have on the athletes? So you have to stay cool and make the best of it.'

He described the balance between familiarity and remoteness: 'I stay enough away so that nobody thinks they can manipulate me. I like to have a partnership and I like to have fun as well, but to keep also enough distance to make my decisions and not feeling that I am binding myself in too much. One of my principles is that people must be able to trust me to make decisions.'

When it comes to selection, Grobler's policy in Britain was unchanged from his policy in East Germany: 'We have carried on using pairs and singles as the base line for selection, both of them Olympic events. The pair and the single give fair assessment opportunities, but it's not set in stone what we do. Every Olympics is different. I have to make selection in the best interests of British rowing, based on the performance level. That's my job, that's what I get the money for; I would never make it a personal thing.'

At the 2009 Banyoles world cup regatta, Grobler's strategy to return to the pair as the leading boat paid off when Reed and Hodge stepped into the shoes of past giants and commanded their event. The new four — the boat that Reed and Hodge sat in through the previous Olympiad — was coached by Mark Banks and also looked like a crew with a future. It contained Partridge in the bow seat, Richard Egington, Alex Gregory and Langridge. Gregory, from the World Class Start programme, was wide-eyed at the thrill of leading in a race, never having experienced such a thing before. The eight, coached by a new combination of Christian Felkel and John West and in which almost everyone had Tom or James as his given name, finished third in a feisty performance.

Such a stunning overall result – shared by the women's crews – was a keen indicator of new talent to replace the big names who retired after Beijing in 2008, and gave reason for optimistic excitement against the inevitable extra pressure of the home-based Games to come. But it was tempered by a small entry at this first regatta of the new Olympiad. The scene was to change at the second world cup regatta in Munich.

There, Reed and Hodge were brought down to earth by Eric Murray and Hamish Bond in the New Zealand pair. The new Kiwi combination clicked together immediately, and rumour had it that they were recording some remarkable times. In the final they had clear water by halfway and were destined to set a long unbeaten run. Meanwhile, Grobler's four were caught napping by two German boats knocking the hell out of each other and with their sights set on combining into an eight. The British eight finished third, the double and quadruple scullers finished fourth, and Campbell was defeated by his Kiwi friend and rival, Mahé Drysdale.

Murray and Bond came to Henley and dispatched Reed and Hodge – with Reed now in the stroke seat – from the Silver Goblets before winning the final against the holders Shaun Keeling and Ramon di Clemente of South Africa. The four and the eight won their events, while Campbell lost the Diamond Challenge Sculls to Drysdale. Matt Wells and Stephen Rowbotham lost the Double Sculls Challenge Cup to New Zealand's Matthew Trott and Nathan Cohen, and the quad lost narrowly to the Polish Olympic champions.

At the third world cup in Lucerne, Hodge and Reed showed that they were a class above everyone else – except for Murray and Bond, who were a class above Hodge and Reed. 'How fast they're going is astonishing,' Hodge said. But Grobler's four continued its Henley winning form while the quad finished second and the eight, with some seat changes, finished fourth.

The following month, true to prediction, the pairs final at the world championships on Malta Lake in Poznań was a two-horse race at the front and a four-horse race for the bronze medal at the back. Murray and Bond, with four notches for their victories over Reed and Hodge to date, wellied into a lead of three seconds at halfway. Grobler, who had changed his pre-race fire-up from 'you can beat them' to 'you will beat them', saw his crew respond, but they could not believe that the Kiwis were still 'taking inches off us' in Reed's words during the second 500 metres.

Reed and Hodge answered in the third 500, covering the distance in a second and a half less than Murray and Bond. With a couple of hundred metres to go, it was nail-biting stuff until the Kiwis won by a second and a half. The race whacked the stuffing out of all four men. Reed lay down in the boat, Hodge hung his head and said little for a long time after he had crawled ashore. Bond lay down also, and the interviews were conducted in breathless fragments. Nobody had puff enough for sentences.

Hodge deferred most questions to Reed, and Reed summoned up some eloquence with difficulty. 'Of course I'm disappointed, but I've loved rowing with Andy,' he said. 'The pair's been a lot of fun. The difference with last year is that there's no pressure on us because it's the year after the Olympics… nothing can top that for pressure. I'm pleased for them as well. It was a cracking race and it's just the start of this Olympiad. There are grounds to say we'd like to stay in the pair. I haven't spoken to Andy about it, or Jurgen…'

In the fours twelve months and twelve days earlier, a quartet of Australians had rowed a magnificent race for 1900 metres in Beijing, only to be destroyed by the most superlative charge that a Grobler

crew had ever put together. This had handed Britain its third successive Olympic fours gold medal. Now, in a spinning Poznań tailwind,
the same Australians were back to meet Mark Banks's new quartet.

Both came to the start line uncertain of the other's pedigree. Britain
had lost one round of the world cup to Germany and won two against
lesser opponents. Australia had been stewing in their Beijing runner-
up status for a year, unraced against international opponents while
lauded as the green-and-gold team's flagship boat. A rapid start
gave the Aussies the edge and for a few moments a race in the style
of Beijing was on the cards. But Partridge, Egington, Gregory and
Langridge had other plans. Langridge turned the screw and his crew
moved smoothly through and away.

Britain's eight, meanwhile, finished fifth, with the medals going to
Germany, Canada and Netherlands.

** **

The outcome of the 2009 season left Grobler in a cleft stick. His four
under Mark Banks were world champions while his best pair, Reed
and Hodge, were being flummoxed by Murray and Bond at each
meeting. But the London Olympics were still three years away, and
so he decided to maintain the status quo as the world cup regattas
approached.

When Henley came round in 2010, Murray and Bond had beaten
Reed and Hodge in Bled in May and in Munich in June. The British
pair took the lead in the final of the Silver Goblets in a blustery,
dancing wind. By halfway the boats had converged and received
warnings, after which the Kiwis tore away. Having matched them
stroke for stroke, the Brits were suddenly watching foam billowing
past their boat. The official verdict was 'easily', and *Rowing Voice*
put the margin – of two lengths rapidly stretching to six – down

to the wind, plus the smoother application of power by the New Zealanders. The score between these pairs was now nine to zero. Grobler shrugged: 'Lucerne is another day.'

The tenth title fight between the Kiwi and British pairs ended, predictably, in another victory for the men in black on Lucerne's Rotsee. Nobody else was within a country mile of these crews, but their similarities ended there. Murray and Bond had magic while Reed and Hodge were seeking a matrix to edge them closer.

The world championships were three and a half months ahead at Karapiro on the north island of New Zealand, which Grobler had last visited with the GDR team in 1978. Reed reflected on what needed to be done to catch the phenomenon that would have a home crowd behind it: 'We've been thinking hard about how to beat these guys. They are just two blokes with blood pumping round their veins same as us; they get tired the same as us. I can't believe they're *that* good. Of course they're better than us at the moment, but they *must* be a finished article. They must be varnished and race-tuned, while we're still building our engine in day-to-day training, and that paid off so much last season... I know we haven't done any of our race preparation, I know we haven't done any of our fine tuning, I know we're not the finished article, and if that all goes to plan over the next four months, then two people are going to be dynamite.'

Meanwhile, the coxless four, unchanged since winning the world title in Poznań, began its 2010 season where it left off, coming first in the Bled world cup. But in Munich three weeks later it lost to Australia and the USA. Injury to Langridge caused withdrawal of the crew from Henley, but they bounced back in Lucerne to take the gold medal and the world cup for their boat class. Gregory described this as 'amazing' and his 'best race for two years'. This, and the eight's bronze medal, was good news for Reed and Hodge while they were committed to the pair because it likely delayed the prospect of shuffling the pack.

Such a move can't have been far from the top of Grobler's thoughts. Reed and Hodge remained second-fastest pair in the world, and were closing on the Kiwis.

The showbiz element of the men's eights was Greg Searle's occupation of the number-six seat in the British boat. The younger of the brothers who had caught the Abbagnale brothers in the dying moments of the 1992 Barcelona Olympic coxed pairs, he had also rowed in the bronze-medal four at the Atlanta Olympics and finished fourth in the pairs at Sydney before turning to grinding on an America's Cup yacht. Now he was returning to rowing for a crack at a medal in London 2012 when he would be 40 years old.

Through his illustrious career as a racer, Searle had never won a medal on the Rotsee. His bronze with the eight was his first. 'We never had the system like we have now, so I used to find my way through the summer and then we'd go on the training camp. Now I feel that I've been near the peak all through the summer time. It's a much more productive way to race.'

No question, the eight was bubbling. Phelan Hill, the steersman, said: 'The guys were so hard in that second half, asked to put their hand in the fire for a little bit longer, and they delivered absolutely; it's really encouraging. We can now build momentum for the Olympics.'

Searle was deferential to his crew: 'I don't want to talk about myself without talking about this crew. It's on a road towards 2012, which started last year before I was in it, but I was standing on the bank watching it, and the boat was competitive last year and was reaching finals. Now we need to move it along to a boat which can win medals.'

* *

In November 2010 Reed and Hodge delivered an upper and a downer to Grobler at the world championships on Lake Karapiro. They came closer to Murray and Bond than in eleven previous races, but still lost the world title by 0.32 seconds. Grobler was delighted at the performance but disappointed that the fastest pair in Britain remained off the gold standard two short years before the London Olympics.

On the same day, the coxless four of Partridge, Egington, Gregory and Langridge lost the world title they had won the previous year. They were bounced out of the medals altogether in foul conditions. Sitting on the start, Gregory wondered if he should say something. 'The warm-up water was all waves, unrowable, but that was the same for everyone,' he said. 'There was not much shelter for the first 1000 metres, it was horrendously rough, and that was the same for everyone as well.' After halfway there was wind shadow – a patch of calmer water sheltered from the effects of wind – and the boat in lane one came first and lane six came sixth. The British boat was in lane four.

'Whatever happened happened,' Gregory said later. 'Our race was ruined by the wind. However anyone looks at it, we were the fastest boat out there. I wish I'd had the guts to put my hand up and say "you need to look at this", even if they told me to shut up, you're going to race anyway... it would have done something. We had quite a good start, a good lead at halfway. I looked across and the French were coming past us like a conveyor belt. We'd beaten them before, and there was nothing we could do about it.'

Grobler was furious. 'He thought we'd maybe gone off too fast. He was trying to find reasons other than the wind for us not winning. It was a bit of a shame. One of his philosophies is that you should be able to win in any conditions, any time of the day with your worst row. Unfortunately we didn't do that. No one outside our boat could know what it was like, but we felt that we'd let him down.'

The finals at Karapiro were spread over four days, the last day beginning with a sumptuous sunrise over the lake and ending with a paddle-past of Waka canoes and a Maori ceremonial farewell. There were plenty of highlights, including Katherine Grainger's fifth world gold in the double sculls with first-timer Anna Watkins; a sensational race between Britain and New Zealand in the men's double sculls when Matt Wells and Marcus Bateman led all the way until pipped by Kiwis Nathan Cohen and Joseph Sullivan; a similar gut-wrencher between Britain and Germany in the men's eights which the Germans just clinched at the line; a four-boat blanket finish in the men's light-weight fours won by Britain over Australia, China and Germany; and a comeback to first place by Zac Purchase and Mark Hunter, the Beijing Olympic champions in the lightweight double sculls.

The British four's fourth place and Reed and Hodge's second place were mollified by the eight's silver medal, but the results handed Grobler a cast-iron excuse to return to the drawing-board when his squad reassembled at the Caversham training centre at the end of the month.

'I'm very pleased how they performed,' he said after it was all over. 'I saw a really strong GB team, but for the one I'm responsible for, the men's side, I think there's a gold medal missing. But those crews racing here showed a lot of potential for the future. I am very pleased and of course I'm pleased because for the first time we have six boats in the final. We never had that before. That shows the basics are there. A little bit of cosmetic work has to be done. But I think the basics are there for improvement and that makes me really happy. I'm proud of what the guys did here.'

* *

After two years of finishing second, Pete Reed and Andy Hodge got to win the pairs at the first world cup regatta of 2011, held in Munich. However, Murray and Bond didn't attend. The four of Partridge, Egington, Gregory and Langridge also won, and the eight and double scullers finished with silver medals. Forty-six countries entered with nearly 800 athletes, including world medallists all over the shop. It was a well-contested meeting despite the absence of New Zealand and American, Australian and Canadian teams.

The second world cup regatta, in Hamburg, was disrupted by an outbreak of E. coli, causing Britain, France and the Netherlands to withdraw their crews. The All Blacks arrived to show that New Zealand rowing was far from the sickroom. The German hosts and New Zealand accounted for nine golds, six silvers and four bronzes, although if the absentees had taken part, this would have looked very different. Murray and Bond won the pairs with ease. As a venerable FISA observer put it: 'There are some very lucky people in Hamburg who should enjoy themselves very much, because never again will they take part in a world cup final.'

At Henley, balmy on the bank but steaming on the water, the British men's squad won five trophies in a splendid show of power in their last appearance at the royal regatta before the 2012 Olympics. Records fell thick and fast in twelve of the nineteen events, setting thirty-three new ones and leaving only one attributed to Sir Steve Redgrave standing. The sculler Alan Campbell, the pair of Reed and Hodge, the double scullers Wells and Batemen, the coxless four and the quadruple scullers all led the way against world-class opposition as records tumbled. Reed and Hodge equalled the record for the Silver Goblets set by Pinsent and Redgrave in 1995. The only blemish was that Murray and Bond, in company with the rest of New Zealand's crews, stayed away from Henley. Redheads Wells and Bateman, now known as the 'Red Express', had the satisfaction of beating the Olympic champions David Crawshay and Scott Brennan of Australia.

The four appeared with a new line-up and new seating order. Gregory was at stroke, Beijing Olympic champion James at three with his toe on the rudder, Egington at two and Langridge at bow, coached now by John West. They were on flying form against the American crew Chula Vista Training Center, lowering the course record by a second. If they continued to gain speed and consistency, wrote Rachel Quarrell in *Rowing Voice,* they would give Grobler a serious headache: 'He will have to decide whether or not to upset this combination and consider injecting the power of Pete Reed and Andy Hodge rather than risk them against New Zealand in an Olympic pairs final.'

The British eight was the exception to all this success, going down by a length to the German national crew in the Grand Challenge Cup after its appeal against being washed down by Hansa Dortmund crew was rejected by umpire Fred Smallbone. Greg Searle in the number-six seat said that the Germans pushed towards the middle of the course several times but each time responded to the umpire's warnings. Basically, the British crew was outmanoeuvred at the start and became a victim of classic match racing.

A week after Henley, British crews won ten medals in the final round of the world cup in Lucerne, including four golds, showing that the team was in great shape to qualify boats for the London Olympics at the forthcoming world championships in Bled.

Despite this, a Grobler shake-up remained on the cards before springtime of Olympic year after Reed and Hodge finished second to Murray and Bond for the thirteenth consecutive time. Reed and Hodge may have been the best pair in Britain, but they remained firmly the second-best pair in the world. Lucerne's meeting was the first between the crews in 2011. The British pair began slowly and went like a rocket in the final 500 metres, scything through Hungarians, Italians, Greeks and Canadians – but not the Kiwis. The result produced the same litany of analysis heard for two seasons: 'There's more in the tank; we have another gear; we can step up next race.' It had started to feel like an interminable wait.

Meanwhile, the four continued to make matters difficult for Grobler by winning with conviction. The eight was among the leaders of the pack, taking bronze behind the German crew who had beaten them in Henley a week beforehand. With the world championships in view, the men's coach had three medal-class boats, but only one on the gold standard.

Grobler's dilemma was confirmed in Slovenia in August 2011, where the world championships were held on the stunning lake at Bled set in a mountainous bowl surrounded by rocky escarpments and woodlands that have not changed in a thousand years. His four won the title while his eight followed Germany over the line and his pair once more came close, but not close enough, to Murray and Bond.

There remained no question that Murray and Bond were kings of the pairs, and likely to remain so at the London Olympics for which they had just qualified. Reed and Hodge once again hurled everything they had at them. Since the 2009 season the Brits had plumbed the depths of their rowing souls before facing the ordeal of another Olympics. In Bled they tried an extraordinary move. In the first quarter the New Zealanders led and the Greek Gkountoulas brothers edged Britain to third place. In the second quarter the Kiwis and Brits swept into clear water. Then Hodge began to build the rate, grinding back New Zealand's lead. Extraordinarily, he kept this suicidal charge for the line going, higher and harder than the surge he had engineered to achieve gold in the coxless four in Beijing three years earlier. But Murray and Bond engaged an elusive extra gear to hold onto the lead and finish 0.5 seconds short of the world's best time.

The verdict was three-quarters of a length, while Italy collected the bronze, two lengths back. The gold and silver medallists took a dip together from the medal pontoon and spent a few minutes cooling off before facing the massed press. Bond said of the Brits: 'They are great competitors. They keep on coming back at us.' The Kiwis had now chalked up twenty-eight international races (thirty-six if you count their Henley races) and three successive world titles.

At this point, everyone expected Grobler to cut his losses and move his pair into a bigger boat. Indeed, everyone wondered why he had stuck to the pair for so long. Reed attributes his and Hodge's longevity to themselves. 'I think Jurgen would have wanted to drop the pair earlier, but he asked us what we wanted to do and supported us,' he said. 'It made us better, and it was good for the whole team. We were going harder and harder, the four were doing more to stay in their line-up, and the eight was very, very strong. It was a strong team but not in the right order. But that doesn't matter in the middle of an Olympiad, because he had enough people to make choices.'

'In our boat,' says Gregory, stroke of the four, 'we were hoping it wasn't going to happen. We were waiting for them to catch the Kiwis. I finished the Bled championships after a faultless year at stroke, which gave me new impetus. I knew it was likely that Andy and Pete would come in. It felt like my Olympic seat was on the line. Going through a winter not knowing what Jurgen thinks of you is hard, it knocks the confidence very easily. But Jurgen pulled me aside in Bled and said he was impressed, I hadn't missed a day that season. It was a small comment that meant a lot to me and gave me confidence that I was doing the right things and sitting in the right position.'

Meanwhile, with the four safe on the gold standard and the eight winning silver behind the Germans – who claimed the title from the moment the start buzzer sounded, while the Brits fought off the others to end up exhausted on the medal pontoon – the most likely destination for mighty Reed and Hodge was the eight.

'I think we moved the boat as well as we could from start to finish,' Greg Searle said. 'Undoubtedly it's a bitter pill to swallow coming second, but in a way we'll be very motivated for eleven months.'

Partridge said: 'I think the difficulty was that the water out there was very tricky. The boat was moving all over the place. We weren't able to utilise what you'd ideally like to do to row. But that was the same for everyone...'

* *

Grobler's switch came about after the winter and spring trials. The Olympic qualification system only settles which boats take part in the Games but not who occupies the seats (with the exception of single scullers). At this point in the Olympiad, who sits where is the preoccupation of coaches round the world, and selection decisions involve analysis of likely opponents as well as the make-up and performance of their own crews.

The British pair that turned out in the first world cup regatta of the Olympic year in Belgrade was George Nash and Will Satch, placed second to a German pair in the absence of New Zealand.

The new four had a rough start. It took to the water first after the March trials with Tom James in the bow, Hodge at two (back in action after suffering from glandular fever during the previous October), Reed at three and Gregory at stroke. 'It was terrible, like going out at Evesham for the first time with three people who had never rowed before,' Gregory said. 'I think Jurgen's intention was to mix up the pairs. It just didn't work at camp in Varese. Everyone expected it to fly and it just didn't. We struggled in that combination for a few weeks to the first world cup in Belgrade.'

Then came a Jurgen moment. On the morning of the four's first heat in Belgrade the coach handed out spanners from his tool bag and directed his men to a completely different seating order. They rigged it with Gregory at bow, Reed at two, James at three and Hodge at stroke. In the race they flew, followed up with an easy win in the semi-final, and then won the final by two seconds after overhauling Belarus and leading Greece.

'We were gobsmacked,' Gregory said. 'At the time it felt like a risk. But it was a little stroke of genius. It was a public moment, the launch of a GB coxless four in Olympic year. We had to win.'

The eight's line-up for the first competition of the season was Nathaniel Reilly-O'Donnell, Partridge, Egington, Tom Ransley, Greg Searle, Moe Sbihi, James Foad, with Langridge at stroke and Phelan Hill coxing. They finished three seconds behind the Germans, having led for three-quarters of the race. The Netherlands came third. It was a good start to the season, but notable by the absence of several big guns.

The second world cup regatta took place in Lucerne, three weeks later at the end of May. The new four notched up its second win and registered the world's best time. On this occasion Australia formed the threat, keeping the Brits out of the lead until a characteristic Hodge burn did the trick in the last quarter of the race. Nash and Satch sank to fifth place in the pairs. The eight – with Marcus Bateman replacing Reilly-O'Donnell, and Foad in the stroke seat – came closer to the Germans than in Belgrade. Canada, always a force to be reckoned with, finished third.

The third cup regatta, the last competition before the Olympic world would gather at Dorney Lake, was in Munich in the middle of June. Here the four had a poor start and finished second behind the Aussies. Romania were the early leaders before fading to sixth place, while the Aussies took the lead after 500 metres and held it.

'Being beaten was the best thing for us,' Gregory said. 'I felt we hadn't really come together, the boat was not totally right, so it was the kick up the backside.' The experienced Hodge was also unfazed by defeat, and interpreted losing the last of the world cup series as part of Grobler's art of peaking at the right time: 'Most crews peak for the heat, and then cannot hold the speed they show early on. Whereas Jurgen peaks for the final' – by which he means the Olympic final.

The eight, unchanged from Lucerne, finished a disappointing third in a diminished line-up of four, with Poland first, Australia in second place and Ukraine fourth. Nathaniel Reilly-O'Donnell and Cameron Nichol finished third in the B final of the pairs. Campbell took bronze in the sculls, and the double and quadruple scullers finished fourth.

Going into the pre-Olympic training camps, the New Zealanders Murray and Bond continued to hold pole position in pairs, whereas Grobler's Reed and Hodge found themselves ahead of the pack but consistently trailing the Kiwi pair. The eight was firmly in the medal zone, and the wily British coach's reshuffle was looking like a better place to be than at the end of the 2011 season.

Henley 2012 achieved a record number of entries, but no crews preparing for the Olympics. They were all away at training camps, leaving the open events for the talents of those who had missed Olympic qualification, or for those preparing for the under-23 and world junior championships.

**

The London 2012 Olympics offered both an advantage and a disadvantage for the British team. A home Games generated massive and enthusiastic support but it also heightened expectations. In addition, nobody — athletes, coaches, officials — had experienced an Olympics at home. The Games of 1908 and 1948 were but a ghostly image, and 2012 represented a peak of pressure and prestige in the journey from the bleak Olympic days of 1996, when rowing had provided the British Olympic Association with its only gold medal.

David Tanner, British Rowing's performance director, secreted the team in Oakley Court, a Victorian luxury hotel on the Thames a mere mile and a half from the pedestrian entrance to Dorney Lake. Oakley Court was well known to generations of Etonian wet bobs as the set for *The Rocky Horror Picture Show* and Hammer horror films including *The Lady Craved Excitement*, neither of which could be regarded as suitable viewing the night before an Olympic final. Rowers were ferried by boat to a jetty at Windsor racecourse from where they could cross the river and enter the rowing site. When they heard about this, the Australian team management complained that the home team enjoyed an unfair advantage in avoiding the long bus ride from the Olympic Village in East London, but British Rowing defended the scheme by pointing out that the hotel was open to any competitors, and was indeed also home to the Russian canoe team. The Australians, meanwhile, occupied a house near Dorney's north entrance for use as a retreat for top crews during the regatta.

The regatta at Eton Dorney turned into a triumph. Some 35,000 people packed the stands every day from 28 July to 4 August, the sun shone, and the racing was superb. In particular, it was a triumph for the British team and its coaches, led by Grobler for the men and Paul Thompson for the women. 'To get four golds, two silvers and three bronzes is something special for a modern Olympic regatta,' said David Tanner. British crews were represented in thirteen finals of a possible fourteen events. Not since the Olympic regatta held at Henley in 1908 had British rowers performed so well.

The first gold medal to be won by Team GB at the London Games occurred on the fifth day of the regatta when Helen Glover and Heather Stanning stroked the water with miraculous efficiency in the pair. Grobler had to wait for his moment until the last day of rowing when his four – Gregory, Reed, James and Hodge – came to the start line. They had fought a spectacular semi-final two days before in a shifting crosswind, conditions that had caused angst among competitors when FISA chose not to move the fastest heat winners to the most advantageous lanes. The Brits were drawn in the same semi-final as their Australian rivals, and they brought the score of their duel to two victories each by surging through to first place in the last 500 metres.

The final of the coxless fours was thus set for a showdown between Grobler's Brits and Chris O'Brien's Aussies. As Martin Cross reported in *Rowing & Regatta*, there was no doubt that this race would set the tone for the day: 'Their semi-final victory had given Britain the coveted lane six and, though their Australian rivals had to settle for lane four, the presence of Drew Ginn, going for his fourth Olympic gold, meant that Hodge knew his crew had to do something special.'

Cross quoted Hodge's take before the race: 'We knew the steps we had to take from the semi. We knew deep down it was a risk. We knew we had to do something different.' That something, Cross said, was to neutralise the Australians' fast start and lead them through the first quarter. To do that required better length, power and rhythm than the British quartet had ever shown. It required engaging the clichéd bluff of having an extra gear in reserve. But the crew was confident. From the green light they led. They crossed the finish line 1.22 seconds ahead of the Australians in 6:03.97.

Hodge said afterwards: 'We executed our plan to the letter. We were in control right the way down. I can't tell you how perfect that race was.' The Australians chased in second place and Americans took the bronze medal, followed by Greece, Netherlands and Germany.

Grobler had coached his tenth Olympic gold medal, achieved by his fourth consecutive four. Once more he had surfed a huge burden of expectation, shared with his rowers, as Gregory told the press just before receiving his medal: 'The pressure on us has been incredible. We had to play it down and keep it cool but inside we've been desperate to win this. It would have been a nightmare if we didn't win.'

The other sweep-oared crews in Grobler's squad won bronze medals. George Nash and Will Satch were hoping to step into the pairs place vacated by Reed and Hodge a year earlier, but were duly pipped for the silver medal by the Frenchmen Germain Chardin and Dorian Mortelette – while Kiwis Murray and Bond continued their undefeated conquest of the universe. The eight took part in a tense final in which they put their nose ahead of reigning world champions Germany with 750 metres to go. The Dorney bleachers went wild as four crews closed up with 250 metres left. The Germans took gold and Canada squeezed ahead of Britain for the silver, while the United States missed the bronze medal by the width of a cigarette paper. Greg Searle thus won his third Olympic medal six Olympiads after his first in Barcelona.

The women's team snaffled three gold medals: Glover and Stanning in the pairs, the veteran Katherine Grainger and her partner Anna Watkins in the double sculls, and Katherine Copeland and Sophie Hosking in the lightweight double sculls.

Alan Campbell won the single-sculling bronze medal, and the men's lightweight crews added silver medals in the fours and Zac Purchase and Mark Hunter's double sculls to bring Britain's medal tally to nine.

Collectively, it was a fitting addition to Britain's Olympic record, and a daunting gauntlet thrown down for the Rio Olympics in 2016.

12

2016

The Rio Olympiad

*'When you graduate from Sierra Nevada to Silvretta, you are safe
in the knowledge that your coach knows where your edge lies – and
you know that you would not stop in an Olympic final.'*
— ALEX GREGORY

The Rio Olympiad began on a high. Britain had finished top of the
rowing table in London in 2012 with an unprecedented nine medals,
spread over men's, women's and lightweight boats – including gold
for Grobler's four.

Phelan Hill joined up for Rio with enthusiasm that winter. 'Nothing
is by chance for Jurgen,' he says. 'Four years out in 2013 he told us
that he wanted to win the fours and the eights in 2016. That was his
dream. That really made me excited and want to carry on. We would
never have won the eights if he hadn't had that commitment, and he
just instilled the process that he wanted to win the fours and wanted
to win the eights, it was a big thing to do.'

Britain had never won the eights world title, and Hill says they
didn't know how to: 'It was a big statement to us when he said that
all his top guys were going into the eight in 2013.' Grobler had never
coached an eight to medal success in his career. When he arrived

in Britain twenty years before, resources were meagre, with only a handful of outstanding athletes to rely on. Now there were more than a dozen of high potential, including several with the experience and achievement of winning gold medals.

From the beginning of the Olympiad, Hill developed a close relationship with his coach. During the London Olympiad he was merely a cox who was told what to do, but ever since Grobler's eight-oar declaration, Hill had established a level of trust between them. He reported to him every day, took timings on the finish line, related what happened during outings, discussed things together. 'He would identify the group he was going to coach through the winter and we would coach them together, so he would say things like: "we need to bring Will on, I see him as stroke of eight", and tell me about selection and strategy, what he was going to do, earlier than the athletes. I would share things with him — not like being a snitch or grass, but maintaining a difficult balance between being one of the guys or one of the coaches. I would tell Jurgen things which are not obvious to coaches, like an athlete in trouble and covering it up. I would pass on chats about worries of athletes; so-and-so needs reassurance.'

Hill says that the best way to describe Grobler building his project is as a chess player: 'He has a vision of what he wants, sitting there with all his chess pieces in front of him. He knows what he wants to achieve in four years' time. You watch other teams and their strategy is quite reactionary. They stumble on a combination that works.

'Jurgen's programme is really hard. Lots of weights, monitoring, big mileage, lots of testing. Some athletes can't manage it, get injured a lot and fall by the wayside. Some of the testing to get into the team is almost harder that the Olympics. If you can manage the four-year programme, you will put yourself in a brilliant place to go to the Olympics and stand on the podium.'

The first world cup regatta in March 2013 was in Sydney. Britain fielded five open men's crews and scored a gold medal for an eight that included Reed, Sbihi and Gregory and was stroked by Hodge. The quadruple scullers Bill Lucas, Graeme Thomas, Charles Cousins and Sam Townsend also won gold. The four – Scott Durant, Alan Sinclair, Matthew Tarrant, Nathaniel Reilly-O'Donnell – finished fourth, as did the pair of John Collins and Peter Lambert and the sculler Jonny Walton.

The second world cup was at Eton Dorney, where a different eight also came first and a four finished second. At Henley the eight was shuffled again and won the Grand Challenge Cup against the University of Washington, lowering the course record by three seconds. The squad chalked up other victories. Sinclair, Reilly-O'Donnell, Durant and Tarrant won the Stewards' Challenge Cup in a great race against the Olympic lightweight champions from South Africa. The quad of Walton, Townsend, Cousins and Lambert won the Queen Mother Challenge Cup and the double scullers Lucas and Langridge lost their final to Michael Arms and Robert Manson of New Zealand. There was, too, a message to be heeded in the Silver Goblets when the Olympic champions Murray and Bond staked their claim on another Olympiad of pair-oared pulling with an easy victory.

The eight's seating order changed again for the Lucerne round of the world cup that took place a week after Henley. Hodge was at stroke and his former pairs and fours partner Reed moved into the number-seven seat, but the result was a step backwards. The eight finished fourth behind the USA, Germany and Netherlands. The four finished in the B final, and the rest of the team achieved no medals.

The eight's seating was shuffled yet again for the world championships in Chungju, South Korea, the new order being Dan Ritchie, Ransley, Gregory, Reed, Sbihi, Hodge and Nash behind Satch at stroke and Hill in the coxswain's seat. It worked. They led at all the markers and fought off a late German charge at the end to take the gold medal – and become the first British eight to gain the world title. They had learned how to win. Germany was second and the USA third. The only other British result of note was the quad, which finished with a bronze medal, while the four came home in fifth place.

Thus closed the first year of the Rio Olympiad, with Grobler exploring combinations to test speed. Similar manoeuvres were going on in other countries, notably New Zealand where Noel Donaldson – coach of the Aussie Oarsome Foursome who had won the Olympics in 1992 and 1996 – had been lured from Australia, and in Russia, where Mike Spracklen had been hired to bring the men of the former Soviet state back to the podium.

**

In 2014 the first venture was for the European championships in Belgrade at the end of May. Here an eight with newcomers on board such as Oliver Cook and Philip Congdon finished third, while a powerful four with Gregory, Sbihi and Nash behind Hodge at stroke won gold. A world cup followed on Lac d'Aiguebelette, France, where Gregory, Sbihi, Nash and Hodge again finished first, and an eight with four changes and Henry Fieldman coxing finished second. The no-change quad won gold, and a new pair of Matt Gotrel and Paul Bennett took bronze.

The eight was shuffled again for Henley, with Satch continuing in the stroke seat and a returnee occupying the number-six seat – Constantine Louloudis, who had had time off from the squad in 2013 to continue his Oxford studies. The squad eight with Louloudis at six had the satisfaction of despatching Club France in the final of the Grand Challenge Cup by a length and a half. The four won the Stewards' and the quad won the Queen Mother Challenge Cup.

The eight's order was changed again for Lucerne's round of the world cup, with Sbihi coming in from the four to sub for Gotrel. They finished third behind Germany and Spracklen's Russians, while earlier in the day the four and the quad chalked up wins.

The world championships were held on the Bosbaan in Amsterdam. James Foad and Matt Langridge followed Murray and Bond across the line in the pairs, and the quad came second to Ukraine. Better than that, however, was the four winning gold – followed by the eight, with Gotrel back in the boat and Louloudis in the stroke seat. Louloudis brought a priceless ingredient to Grobler's boat: that of crew maker. While powerful and able, he was neither tallest nor heaviest, neither best lifter of weights nor top scorer on the rowing machine. But he could read a race, and he would make a boat go faster.

On the Bosbaan the eight beat Germany by 0.66 seconds. Louloudis treated the press conference to an analysis that compared their performance with the Olympic final of two years before: 'In 2012 we pushed at exactly 750 metres gone and the Germans responded, but this time we moved two strokes earlier and held the burn for a couple of strokes longer and held them off...' and so on down the course. The press felt that they were attending a classicist's tutorial on the Battle of Salamis.

The result in Amsterdam showed that, one way or another, the eight-oared gleam in Grobler's eye was now brighter than eighteen months earlier.

**

No men were sent to the first world cup in Bled in 2015. Competition commenced at the European championships in Poznań on 29 May, where a four consisting of Reilly-O'Donnell, Sinclair, Ransley and Durant finished first, while an eight containing three of the world-champion four finished second. Foad and Langridge won the pairs in the absence of Kiwis, and the quad came third.

Changes had been forced on Grobler by the significant absence of Hodge, who had stopped rowing in the previous October to recover from a recurrence of the glandular fever he had suffered in 2011. He attributed the cause to looking after his one-year-old son Sebastian after returning from training days in Caversham. Pre-Sebastian, he would have taken two hours' rest but this year he was laid off until the end of September, missing the competition season. Louloudis, who had won his fourth Boat Race, was pencilled in to stroke the eight but was also absent because his lumbar vertebrae were playing up.

At the Varese world cup, the Poznań four in a different seating order dropped to fifth, while an eight with three of the world-champion four on board – Gregory, Sbihi and Nash – beat Germany into second place. The quad finished first also.

For Henley's Grand Challenge Cup, Louloudis returned to the eight in the number-two seat and Satch was at stroke again for another victory over Germany. The four in a new seating order won the Stewards' against a Greek crew, and the quad won the Queen Mother Challenge Cup against a German crew. Foad and Langridge won the Silver Goblets and received a lecture from the umpire for not responding to a warning.

In Lucerne a week later, Foad and Langridge came second to Murray and Bond. The eight, with no changes, won again, while the four was dumped into the B final.

At the world championships in Aiguebelette, the eight continued its unbeaten season in a meeting that served as the qualification regatta for the 2016 Olympics in Rio. This completed a hat-trick of world titles for the big boat in the Rio Olympiad, and put Germany on the run.

Meanwhile, Foad and Langridge qualified as a pair in second place to Murray and Bond. The four, now with Stewart Innes replacing Reilly-O'Donnell at stroke, finished third, and the quad fourth. All of the men's team qualified their boats for Rio. And as the Rio Olympiad turned into its final year, all bets were off that a top-flight eight and a top-flight four still lay present in Grobler's squad. He had changed seats, strokes, spares and crews to breed flexibility into his oarsmen. Could he now find the combinations that would give him not one, but two lead boats?

**

The Olympic year began in earnest at the European championships in Brandenburg, in appallingly rough water. The four in its eventual Rio line-up of Gregory, Sbihi, Nash and Louloudis won gold, and an eight consisting of Gotrel, Durant, Ransley, Bennett, Reed, Hodge, Langridge, Satch and cox Phelan Hill finished behind Germany and Russia. Alan Sinclair and Stewart Innes, in the absence again of the defending Olympic champions Murray and Bond, came second in the pairs, the quad finished fifth and the double of Collins and Walton sixth.

Although Grobler claimed to be keeping his options open, commentators saw what they claimed to have known all along as soon as the team emerged from spring trials: that he had placed his eleventh gold-medal bet on a four stroked by Louloudis and backed by the top three in any form of trial. Few thought he would risk all on an eight when Germany, the United States and Russia were also treating it as their priority boat and there were so many moving parts to go wrong. He did not need to manipulate his data with subjective judgement. No one thought he should or could have selected differently.

The new four's win at the European championships in Brandenburg was tempered by most of the world's best fours being absent. In the Lucerne world cup three weeks later, Louloudis went down with a bug which had run through the team over the previous fortnight, and with Gregory at stroke and Callum McBrierty – the spare man from the bottom end of the men's rankings – they won, although the result was partly attributable to an Australian mistake in the last few strokes.

In a changed seating order and with Alan Sinclair subbing for Reed, the eight finished fourth behind the Netherlands, Germany and the USA. Reilly-O'Donnell and Tarrant were in third place in the pairs, won by – you guessed it – Kiwis Murray and Bond.

Up next was the final round of the world cup: the last regatta before the Olympics and the last opportunity for Grobler to test his two lead boats against the world's best. He was juggling two boats on the same training programme and, says Gregory, he managed it very well: 'I think we were quite an easy four to deal with. We were thinking and doing the same, and never felt sidelined because of the other project. We didn't want him to feel us needy.'

At 9.30 a.m. on the bright morning of 19 June by Malta Lake in Poznań, GB's head coach could be found adjusting and testing the rigging of his prize boat, the coxless four which was parked right-way-up on trestles close to the sparkling water. It would have been pointless to ask him anything requiring a coherent answer. He may have been adjusting or he may have been fiddling to control his nerves. His good manners responded to an innocuous question with a smile, but his mind was with his crew and the task in hand.

The crew had been out for its morning practice to get the bodies moving smoothly and feeling the water and the weather. Patchy clouds and sunshine persisted, and there was a variable, but discernible tailwind to push crews down the course. These were fast conditions, and in some races, when needs must, the top crews will break records.

At this point, most nations with big teams were still undecided about who would sit where in the big boats, and who at the margins would be selected to go to Rio. Grobler's four was set and certain, but his eight, by his own standards, remained a mess.

In the race, the four started at the same stroke rate and pace as the pack and gradually crept ahead with tiny, incremental, centimetres per stroke before Sbihi called for the switch into race pace. In contrast to the heat two days beforehand, rhythm was apparent immediately. The four men realised that they were rowing as one, their sense of rhythm and flow absorbing every tiny movement of the hull through the water while any minute peculiarity of movement by one was automatically compensated by another. They were fixed in the rhythm and the moment, with an intense feeling of interdependence rewarded by gradually drawing out from the other crews. With a quarter of the race gone, they had a lead of 1.72 seconds over Australia in second place. They might not have known their time for that 500 metres, but they did know that the rhythm was right and that the slow wastage of their overall resources was within a manageable limit.

Five minutes after crossing the line in that final, they were sitting in the shade, talking to the press. The compliments were flowing. Sbihi explained: 'Stan [Louloudis] was back and not only does he set a lovely rhythm and make it easy for us to follow, but you have to realise that he is bloody strong. Technically it was a much better first thousand and laid the foundation for the second half.'

Nash said it was 'the best race so far and was the real deal.' He explained that the crew changes pace in response to calls from Sbihi: 'After the start when the boat is up to race speed he calls a "settle" and we look to move down to the race pace as smoothly as possible. Apart from plain fitness training, changes of pace are the things we practice most.' There are 'opposition independent' moves and 'reactive' moves, he said.

In Poznań there was no need to reach for reactive moves. Although the Australians pressed in the first half and Italy moved fastest in the third quarter, the crew followed its race plan without cause to vary. As they crossed the line they knew that in their first top-level test in the entire Olympiad, they had complete confidence in their crewmates.

There were only five entries in the Poznań eights, and the British crew that finished second to archrivals Germany was the line-up that emerged from the permutations of four seasons to be named for the starting line in Rio. Hill was cox, Satch stroke, and numbering from the bow were Durant, Ransley, Hodge, Gotrel, Reed, Bennett and Langridge. They took an early lead and headed Germany, New Zealand, Belarus and Poland at the halfway mark. Then the Germans struck and were in the lead after 1500 metres, winning in 5:22.60 to Britain's 5:23.23. Not perfect, but good enough to be selected for Rio by the British Olympic Association at its press conference at the River & Rowing Museum in Henley.

Thus Grobler's die was cast. Two leading boats would go to Brazil in August: his four and, in association with squad coach Christian Felkel, his eight. All the other boats in the men's team fell under his mantle as head coach, but each had its own specified coach.

**

Meanwhile, all was not rosy in the city that would host the first Olympic Games in South America. When the Games were awarded to Rio de Janeiro, Brazil was enjoying a booming economy and a stable government. But by the spring of 2016, the economy was in trouble and President Dilma Rousseff had had her powers suspended, pending impeachment for alleged corruption. The country was hit by the mysterious, mosquito-borne Zika virus, the construction of infrastructure and Olympic sites was seriously behind schedule — when is it ever not? — and journalists were hounding the authorities over pollution of the rowing lake and sailing water. Ticket prices were high and sales disastrously low, and funding for the Paralympics, due shortly after the Olympics, was syphoned away. The population of the favelas and the poor of Brazilian society were left out of the party.

In addition to all this, a major crisis threw the IOC and the organising committee into chaos when WADA announced that the Russians were engaged in a state-run doping programme. The IOC left the international sports federations with the problem of what to do about it, and hundreds of Russian athletes were consequently banned from all competitions, including some from the Olympic Games. Members of Spracklen's Russian eight were affected, removing one of the serious challengers to Britain's boat.

Some of the claims about pollution and the environment turned out to be untrue. At rowing's trial event, the world junior championships in 2015, the water at the Rodrigo de Freitas Lagoon was declared clean by FISA. Fish were jumping, and continued to leap during the Olympic regatta.

For the chosen athletes, the prospect of an Olympic experience in a magical city set between beaches and jungle-clad mountains could not be bettered. Warm, sunny and pulsating with the beat of samba and bossa nova, Rio boasted the fabulous Sugar Loaf mountain, miles of white-gold sand by the rolling breakers of the South Atlantic, and a rowing venue lying under the gaze of Corcovado mountain's Christ the Redeemer. In the lead-up to the Games, David Tanner – Sir David by this point – visited Rio on numerous occasions, and in 2014 he took thirty-six athletes to a camp in Rio so that they could get over the 'wow factor' and encounter the thrill of the Olympic city. Part of the excitement was that it wouldn't be what they had imagined. After all, half of them knew only a home Olympics, and a quarter of them knew no Olympics at all.

'Perception and fact are not the same,' Tanner said. 'It won't be the same as going to Madrid where the Metro works. Does it matter? Only if you let it. I rest my case.' He asked his guide if Rio will be finished in time. No, of course not, came the reply, but Rio will be ready!

**

While romantic Rio awaited, and expectations were building, one last obstacle remained for Grobler's crews: his final altitude camp on the Austrian melt-water lake at Silvretta. For all the athletes in the team, this was the last hurdle before the Games, and for those who would be hanging up their oars after Rio it was the last time they would ever be required to plough up and down in chilling mountain air on cold water at 2000 metres above sea level. It was the last time their every breath and movement would be monitored by the all-seeing scrutiny of the head coach ensconced on his promontory above the lake.

At least the Silvretta stay does not have the dread of the camp in the Sierra Nevada, Spain. There, almost twelve years ago, Jurgen tested each man's bottom line. Alex Gregory recalls that Sierra Nevada almost broke him:

'You're always pushing, trying to get that little bit more out of yourself, trying to find "the edge". With the Olympics only a year away there's even more desire to push. The line is always thin, at altitude, up there in the Spanish mountains, it's hair thin. It's all land-based, all ergos and weights, and it is the one the guys dread more than any. It's the psychological training as much as the physical. I can't even explain how long an hour on an ergo feels. From the first stroke you just want to be off. You think "I'd do anything", it hurts so much. Three, four times a day for the best part of two weeks. We all hate it when we're there.

'We're indoors the whole time, we barely step outside. Bedroom to dinner hall to ergo room to weights room… Come the end of it, we are clawing the walls to get out of there. As you get down the hill, you can feel your body regenerating. I'm not sure anybody in the world does a camp like it.

'I have been broken by it. You are thinking about everything in your life and you realise it has only been ten seconds. It's not an option to stop – that is looked upon very unfavourably. What is there to say you would not stop in an Olympic final?

'When you graduate from Sierra Nevada to Silvretta, you are safe in the knowledge that your coach knows where your edge lies – and you know that you would not stop in an Olympic final.'

13

Rodrigo de Freitas

'You are going to go into the darkness and come through a very uncomfortable area, but you'll get through it. The most important thing is to trust each other and trust the rhythm.'

— JURGEN GROBLER

On the evening of Thursday 11 August Britain's coxless four and their coach Jurgen Grobler gathered on the top floor of the Ipanema Inn. It was the evening before their Olympic final, and they were twitchy, nervous, and excited as Grobler told them there was no one out there who could beat them. 'Sometimes when he says that I haven't believed him,' Alex Gregory, the bow man, says, 'but this time I knew he believed what he was saying. I believed it; we all did.' After all, they had won their heat and won their semi-final, each from the front. They were the fastest semi-finalists for three-quarters of the course before easing off ahead of Canada and the Netherlands. The qualifiers from the other semi-final, irritatingly faster, were Australia, South Africa and Italy.

Gregory could remember feeling uncertainty after a hard semi-final four years before in London, but in Rio Grobler was really confident and relaxed – a mood that he passed across to the crew. 'He is really good at not putting pressure on us for the biggest race, the most important thing in our lives. He'll motivate by saying "you race hard, you're so powerful, so good in the bow seat, Alex", or whatever. He never puts pressure on us because he knows that we won't race well if we're tense. Being a little bit relaxed works for us. We're confident in knowing we have done his programme every day for four years, and that's a huge advantage for us.'

Afterwards they went to their rooms – Gregory sharing with stroke Louloudis, while Sbihi shared with Nash. They got their kit ready for tomorrow and chatted. It was no big deal, Gregory says: 'We don't want a climax on the evening before. It's just another race – a trial at Caversham or a world cup.'

Gregory slept well but woke up nervous. Before six o'clock the next morning he and Louloudis were at the Ipanema's breakfast buffet, eating fruit and granola. Sbihi was already there; Nash stumbled out of the lift, last as usual. 'One of the things I like about us is that you don't have to do anything special at Olympics. There is no special diet. You live your life normally. A normal breakfast takes pressure off unnecessary worries, and simplifies sport.'

At 6.02 a.m. they took the minibus shuttle and at 6.40 a.m. passed through the security check at the Rodrigo de Freitas Lagoon. Grobler was waiting by the boat, a spanner in his backpack, arms folded, serious, a bit tense but not afraid to give someone a smile or crack a joke. At seven o'clock they lifted the boat onto the water and Grobler pushed them off for their pre-paddle. For the last four years this had been an 8-km warm-up, but this morning he surprised them by cutting it to 4 km.

Gregory said good morning to the little bird nesting by the landing stage, as he always did. It was a nice day and there were lots of fish in the lake. The waters had been very, very tricky, always different, throughout the week, and the crew's heat and semi-final had both been unsettlingly postponed because of weather, but throughout the emergency Grobler had kept really calm. Indeed, he had been calm through the whole Games.

At 7.45 a.m. they disembarked, put the boat on trestles and returned to the hotel, leaving the coach in his own thoughts to fiddle with the rigging.

After a second breakfast, the men dispersed, each to his own preparation. 'We weren't talking much at that point,' Gregory says. By 9.30 a.m., two hours before their race, they were back in the bus and headed for the stretching room when they arrived at the course. Grobler was waiting for them at the beginning of an hour and a half of sitting around in kit, stretching and wishing it were all over. A bit tense, wanting to get it right. With an hour to go, the coach began his final chat by asking them: 'Any thoughts from the previous evening?' The plan, he said, was to do what they knew they could do, do their own race, eyes in the boat, not worrying about the opposition as no one could beat them out there. He said: 'Moe, you read the race, you tell the guys… Alex, if you feel something, say it to the guys, it will help.'

They had a loose plan, entailing Sbihi making calls at the 500- and 1000-metre marks and with 500 metres to go. It was very simple; all the complicated stuff had already been done. 'We are the best crew out there,' Grobler told them, before spending a couple of minutes reiterating his belief in them.

Although he was really wary of the Aussies, Gregory *believed* his coach. Crew and coach were as confident as they could be before an Olympic final. Gregory thought of Grobler and his record of four straight wins with British fours since Sydney 2000. It played heavily on his mind. He could negate his nerves by telling himself that he already had a gold medal at home. Instead he told himself that there was no proof that anyone could beat them. Grobler needed them to win this, and they wanted to win it for him almost as much as they wanted to win it for themselves. They didn't want to be the crew to break his record. It just wasn't an option not to win.

For fifteen minutes they went off to fill water bottles and do whatever they had to do before Grobler pushed them away with Gregory's blade. He picked up their shoes and took them to the landing stage. Maybe he said 'have a good row', but his crew would already have been paddling away towards the one race in their lives that mattered.

At 11.25 a.m. the starting clog was cradling the bow of their boat.

The buzzer sounded, and the race was flawless. The Italians in lane one made a rapid start, but the British boat in lane three showed its bow ball almost immediately. They clocked 1:27.36 for the first 500 metres. The Aussies in the neighbouring lane were quickest over the next 500, passing the halfway mark a fifth of a second behind the Brits, possibly even nudging ahead, although it never felt like they did, and the Brits responded to Sbihi's call by imperceptibly squeezing on the pressure to eek their bow ball ahead by a full second at the 1500 marker. The boat was creaming through the water. They covered the last 500 metres in 1:28.52 – not as quick as the third-placed Italians, but safely over the line for the gold medal.

'I wouldn't change a single stroke,' Gregory says. 'We did everything Jurgen suggested we do, everything we had been practising. It always felt we were in control, and that is something Jurgen always talks about. You don't have to be ahead to be in control of a race. For someone like him who hasn't raced much, that's quite an insight. It could have looked out of control, but it wasn't. We were waiting for Moe's call. We had the measure of those Aussies from stroke one. I wouldn't change a stroke. It was my perfect race.'

The crew were all on the same page. For stroke Louloudis the race was a picture of composure. 'Four years' work distilled into six minutes,' was his pithy summary. Sbihi, the seat-two man, describes feeding off the energy: 'It's a big responsibility to keep an eye on what's going on. I waited a long time to say Go!' Nash says that Gregory pulled them round at the start: 'If he does that, we know we're on for it. We do the basics well, connect well, we drive the boat together. The rest is the cherry on the top.'

Their win brought Britain's medal count to two golds and one silver – and they had delivered coach Grobler's eleventh Olympic gold, his seventh for Britain and his fifth consecutive title with a coxless four. They also increased the pressure on the eight who trained alongside them and who were due on the start twenty-four hours later.

* *

The eight-day Olympic regatta ran into trouble on its second day when varying winds caused postponement of racing. It did so again on the fourth day, and had FISA officials tearing their hair out as they tried to square the predictions of four forecasting agencies and adjust the timetable accordingly. Beneath skies that varied from clear azure to threatening black, the wind was prone to shift suddenly, first gusting off the ocean, then off the nearby peaks and back again. Crews training in the early morning became waterlogged, including a dramatic floundering of Grobler's boats when the eight rushed to the assistance of the four.

The main problems arose on the first 1000 metres, where a headwind whipped up white caps and piled water against the concrete wall behind the start pontoons. On the second day this was complicated by drag of the cables that anchor the lane-marker buoys, an incident that required a couple of hours to fix.

Despite rowers twice waking up expecting to race only to be disappointed, there was no complaint about unfair conditions. Nor, for that matter, about polluted water rumoured by the press, nor of biting mosquitos.

The first medal for a British crew came on the sixth day, 11 August, when Katherine Grainger and Vicky Thornley won silver in the double sculls. This was a fifth Olympic medal in five sequential Games for Grainger, who had taken two years off after winning gold in London in 2012. The duo burned off like a rocket and held the leading position until the Poles Magdalena Fularczyk-Kozlowska and Natalia Madaj caught them in the last 200 metres. On recent form it had been touch and go whether Grainger and Thornley would reach the medal zone, and so when they did they were ecstatic. They took the positive view that they had won silver, not that they had lost gold.

They were followed by Helen Glover and Heather Stanning, who retained their London Olympic pairs title in a beautifully measured race they controlled from the front. Never defeated, they were coached for their second Olympiad by Robin Williams who was recovering from cancer while guiding them. 'Job done,' he said as they faced the cameras after receiving their medals. 'Get control early, preferably from the first stroke. We rowed down the Danes in the heat, the only time we've had to do it in that part of the race. If you go out, someone has to come at you, and it's the last-chance card in the last 250 metres. We have a good sprint finish in reserve. We have got those gears to go. We are difficult to beat if all phases are covered.' And all phases were, indeed, covered.

Williams reflected Grobler's pearls of wisdom next day to the magazine *Row 360*: 'Losers train harder, so we have to be prepared that the people we beat in the last three years will train harder, no question. They don't win because I say so. I'm not the one sitting in the boat.'

The women's double and pair apart, the regatta was going pear-shaped for other British crews. New Zealand's Murray and Bond duly retained their pairs title, while Alan Sinclair and Stewart Innes, who were thought to have a chance of silver or bronze, finished fourth.

The men's double of Jonny Wells and John Collins and the quadruple scullers both finished fifth. The quad was probably suffering from the last-minute substitution of Jack Beaumont when Graeme Thomas was taken ill. The lightweight men's four and double scullers both won B finals for a ranking of seven, while Charlotte Taylor and Kat Copeland, fancied for the golden zone, plummeted to the C final where they ranked fourteenth in the lightweight double sculls. The sculler Alan Campbell rowed his semi-final under the weather and withdrew from the B final. His Tideway Scullers club mate Mahé Drysdale of New Zealand retained his title in a sensational photo finish with the Croatian Damir Martin, sculling into a light headwind and knocking three seconds off the Olympic best time.

** **

On Friday night Grobler, his co-coach Felkel, eight oarsmen and cox Hill were all seated in the lounge at the inn for their last ever briefing. The guys were quite relaxed and buzzy as Grobler talked about technical aspects of the boat, length in the water, big strokes, the catch. He spoke in simple, mundane phrases that together they had refined during the last few weeks – about making the boat go faster, the difference between performances at Lucerne and Poznań regattas, about taking fewer big strokes and more lesser strokes. A lot of what he said was calculated to give confidence, reminding them that they had already done the work to enable them to feel confident of winning when they went out to row next day. The atmosphere was quite geed up, but not loaded with adrenaline.

'A few of the guys said a few things, but it wasn't as if we were going straight out to race there and then,' says Hodge, the veteran in the number-three seat. 'The next thing to do is try and have a good night's sleep.'

For Phelan Hill, this was the end of four years serving as Grobler's right arm. His remembers the Athens Olympiad as fragmented and difficult, an 'us and them' situation between Grobler's four and Steve Gunn's eight group. During the London Olympiad there remained a division between the rowers and scullers in the men's squad. But in this Olympiad there had been a real effort to get the team together. 'There was much more mix in the Rio cycle,' Hill says. 'In 2014 Jurgen took the best athletes and put them in pairs with the newest through the winter months. That was all about bringing on the bottom end and making it stronger, letting the new guys learn from the experienced and spreading the winning mentality across the board. He had all the biomechanics data. He knew who were the biggest pullers on each side of the boat, who were the big boat movers.'

Hill notes that the coach had run all aspects of training camps, including who roomed with whom: 'The room combinations one year indicated the pairs next year. He's thinking that these two are going to be in same boat in the future. He sees them as foundations for the eight later. All this was planned by Jurgen. Brilliant!'

Similar attention was drawn to the equipment. Grobler maintains a close relationship with the German Empacher brothers at the cutting edge of racing-boat manufacture and design. The Empacher craft used in 2012 and 2016 were modified from the firm's standard 1986 mould. The process would happen about two years into the Olympiad with chats between coach and cox. For example, after his experience in 2012 Hill wanted four speakers fitted to the boat and their positioning changed. The London eight had no lip round its sides, running the risk of water splashing in a crosswind. The Rio boat added a small lip with wedge-shaped streamlining under it, aerodynamically designed to cover up the bolts that secure the riggers to the hull. Modifications were discussed with the manufacturer and with FISA by Maurice

Hayes, British Rowing's equipment manager, to ensure that no rules were violated.

When it comes to technical coaching, Hill says that Grobler often seems to do little. But the cox notices plenty going on behind the scenes: 'He sets a vision of what he wants — for example: "we need to pick the boat up better." He gives a structure to each session and leaves the athletes to work out how to deliver. In the eight he's the broad brush and occasionally gets involved in details, but it's up to me to decide how it's to be done.'

Hill also notes that Grobler never misses a session: 'On a 20-km outing he'll say nothing until the break at 12 km, when he'll say: "OK, that is good, fulfilling my expectations." But he always thinks long term. He has a long-term strategy.'

In the gym Grobler's approach is similar: 'Never at any point does he say you need to hit these scores, nor would he ever say "More power!" The way he gets people to work harder is to appeal to their competitive nature. The ergo scores are transparent, and there's a lot of banter over the scores and what everybody's pulling. It's the guys who talk about it. If anything, Jurgen will tell people to back off. He'll walk round the ergo room and then just look at someone, gain eye contact and gesture to slow down. He never tells people to work harder. He'll sometimes shorten an ergo session. He has sensitivity of knowing when to push people and when not to. He's always managing things.'

His skill, Hill says, is on recognising breaking point. There will be discussion and he'll adjust the programme because he doesn't want to break people. 'I think of him as a fatherly figure. You always wanted a little pat on the back. He seems to breathe that 'thing' — everyone wants his approval, wants to do well for him. That's part of it.'

The British rowing team has a consultant psychologist, but Grobler relies on his own instincts and knowledge for the mental wellbeing of his charges. 'There is no real direct psychology. If you do Jurgen's programme and it's been successful, you know you're going to be strong,' Hill says. 'He will indicate that at wash-up meetings at camp. He shows them his test results for, say, a 5-km ergo. Personal bests will be indicated in yellow, so all can see. He will comment that so-and-so is back to where he was before injury, good. It's reinforcement that we are really strong as a group. He doesn't say so, he just shows you the scores that show it.'

In pursuit of his dream to produce a champion eight as well as a four, Grobler set himself a particularly gruelling regime for the Rio Olympiad. At camps he would be in the launch for full water sessions – 20-km back-to-back sessions for the four and the eight – with before and after briefings for both, as well as wash-up meetings in the evenings. All the way through the camp. He was always punctual; usually the first present. At camps he often wore pristine retro kit from a past Games – wearing his experience on his sleeve, so to speak.

In Rio he kept up the pace by conducting a briefing before and after every session of the four and eight, plus occasional evening meetings and daily coaches' debriefs to cover the programme that he had laid down for the whole men's team.

'He never stopped,' Hill said. 'I don't know how he does it. He was nervous as well. He must have been flat-out knackered by the end of it.'

This particular race day holds two final chances of medals for the British team: the women's eights in the penultimate race of the Olympic regatta, and the grand finale, the men's eights. David Tanner knows that his target of six medals is not going to be met. So far he has three: golds by the women's pair and men's four, and silver by the women's double scullers. It is not only the number of medals that matters, but also the colour of the metal. Generous funding from the National Lottery has been behind the glittering rowing programme since it was set up in 1996. In 2016, conditions for athletes, coaching, equipment, lifestyle, support services in all the squads – men, women, lightweights, senior, under-23 and junior, Olympic and Paralympic – are unrecognisable to the 1990s generation, and unparalleled by other teams. But generous funding will diminish unless gold is struck on this day in Rio. British Rowing and the British Olympic Association have drilled the message into the athletes. Their press conference mantra is to praise the Lottery. As coxswain Hill says, one gold is better than three silvers: 'That's what it's judged by.'

At the appointed time on the morning of the eight's final, Grobler walks with them to the boat. It has just gone 11 o'clock, twenty-five minutes before the race is due to start. As soon as Hill orders hands on, everyone is totally focused. They collect their oars, laid out ready by Reed who has brought them from the boathouse, climb aboard, lock feet into clogs and oars into swivel gates, while Felkel collects their shoes. Grobler offers a last bit of confidence, a gee-up, a calming 'This is your moment' or 'Be cool'. It could be anything to anybody. His accent is noticeably more German than usual, but there are no surprises in the repertoire.

When they are ready, Grobler grasps a blade and pushes them off. It is very quiet, only the chop of stabbing strokes to get the boat moving, perfectly steady. The chopping strokes morph into a whoosh of blades in water followed by the swish of wheels on slide runners. He stands, serious, impervious, watching his eight embark for the last time.

The crew does one final tune-up before reaching the start line, so that 'everyone knows he can take himself into the locker from the first stroke' in Hodge's words. Hill uses the Drysdale race to remind them that the last stroke counts, to keep their eyes in the boat so as not to risk giving it away on the line by looking across.

Meanwhile, Grobler makes his way to the finish area where he will watch the race, invisible, calm of visage and nervous as hell.

Whilst the eight paddles smartly to the start for the last time, the women's eights are sent on their way. Every punter plus the *New York Times* is expecting a runaway win for the invincible Americans who have dominated the event at world and Olympic regattas for ten years. The Americans, notwithstanding some rolling heads and heaving shoulders, duly deliver. The race, however, turns out to be a gripping tactical struggle. The eventual medal winners hang back while the eventual tailenders charge ahead – no doubt unintentional, but etching intrigue into the race. At halfway the Brits and Romanians are placed sixth and fifth respectively, allowing the Canadians, New Zealanders and Dutch to burst their boilers. The Americans bludgeon their way into the lead in the second half, and the British cox Zoe de Toledo spurs her crew into action for a terrific sprint for the line, delivering a first Olympic medal for a British eight-oared crew. After a terrible start, their silver has been executed brilliantly and matches the most optimistic expectation. The Romanians take the bronze while the first-half leaders bring up the rear.

Fran Houghton is the only member of the British crew to have reached an Olympic podium before, having sculled in silver quads in 2004 and 2008. 'It was an incredible row. The heart and passion, the soul that people put into that race was phenomenal,' she says.

Tanner's pot now contained two golds and two silvers, with one chance still to come.

At 11.27 a.m. six eights wait, tense and quiet, for the light to turn green and the clogs to release. There is hardly a ripple on the surface. The dancing winds from the rainforested mountains and the billowing breeze from the South Atlantic that together ruffled the regatta earlier in the week are blown out. Fish are jumping, and from his perch on Corcovado, Christ the Redeemer stretches his arms toward the sunbathed lake. At the far end, while the women's medal-winners await their ceremony, thousands of anxious eyes turn to the big screen to watch the race unfold. The large and vocal British contingent is enveloped in a maelstrom of red, white and blue, and the press stand is crammed.

A moment later the light goes green and the clog falls away from the bow of the boat. Eight oars emblazoned with Union flags lock into the clear water of Rodrigo de Freitas Lagoon and fire the yellow Empacher into a bounding leap for freedom as eight lions leap from their cage and spring cox Hill into the race of his life. His opponents are locked out from the first stroke. Four years of every aspect of preparedness comes together during the next five and a half minutes. Four years of lifting weights, gym circuits, ergometer splits, strength tests, altitude camps, oxygen uptake and lactate production merge. The hours on water, the steady-state and speed work, the personal bests and three world-championship titles, assessments and nurturing – all compress into a perfect flight into the Rio Roar in the approximate direction of Ipanema beach. The statistics in Grobler's notebooks, the motivation and psychology in his head, the selection mantra, the rowing technique and physical and mental strength of the anointed men – all come together. The minutiae of the sleek shell's hydrodynamics and aerodynamics, refinement of boat, oar and outrigger are called into service.

In fifteen strokes, bow man Scott Durant is swept alongside the German bow ball on his magic carpet. They pass the 500-metre mark first in 1:20.39. The Germans are less than a second behind, but the New Zealand boat unsettles them by harassing them through the second quarter. As the Brits flow past the halfway point with a lead of half a length, Hill comes level with the German bow ball and they reduce their rate of strokes knowing that, now, the gold medal is theirs to lose. They are bullet-proof, empowered by Jurgen Grobler, partaking of their journey's climax. They pass the 1500-metre mark in 4:06.37, still two seconds ahead of the suffering Germans and comfortably leading the Netherlanders and the Poles. They streak ahead through a fusion of time-was, time-is and time-will-be. Trailing crews are burning to catch up, but the Brits don't need to raise the ante to stay ahead. The Germans are quickest over the last quarter, but Grobler's men have peaked masterfully, on the right day, to a fraction of time. They cross the line more than a second in front in 5:29.63. The Germans take the silver by a second over the Dutch.

Amid the cacophony of the stands, Hodge at three and Reed at five have won their third Olympic gold medal, and the rest – Durant at bow, Ransley at two, Gotrel at four, Bennett at six, Langridge at seven and Satch at stroke, not forgetting cox Hill – have won their first. They have benefitted from Grobler's skills and experience accumulated since he entered college in Leipzig half a century ago. They have peaked at the right moment of the right hour on the right day in the right place. They are the first British eight to win an Olympic title since Sydney 2000. They have presented their coach with his eighth British Olympic gold medal, raising his total of individual Olympic gold medallists to twenty-nine with forty-eight medals between them, and raising British Rowing's Rio total to three golds plus two silvers.

In the mayhem round the medal ceremony, the crew is talking to cameras, microphones, recorders, embracing parents and partners, posing for selfies, high-fiving fans and hugging teammates. Moisture in his eyes gives way to the wide, rare, sunny smile that breaks onto Jurgen's handsome, weathered, 70-year-old face, and his German accent softens again as he is glad-handed all over the arena. His coaching of twelve Olympic gold medals across ten Games – eight of them British – is unsurpassed.

The eight's win, Hodge says later, is completely down to Grobler: 'Having the nerve and ability to hold back and know when to do the important stuff is one of the skills that Jurgen has in spades... We know he has wanted this for a long time. His whole strategy for the last four years has been building up to this. He knew the talent and depth he had in the team. This is not a flash-in-the-pan idea. There was no fluke. It's a genius at work, defying the odds consistently, and that's Jurgen Grobler.'

EPILOGUE

SUNDAY 1 OCTOBER 2017

Florida

'In his constant search for the perfect, efficient stroke, Jurgen has found a way of imparting his knowledge to more athletes in more generations than any before him.'

The end of September 2017 at the world championships in Sarasota, Florida, marked the close of the first year of the Tokyo Olympiad. Historically Grobler has made his decision to continue in his post to the next Games while gold medals are being hung round his crew's necks on the Olympic podium. It was no different when his four and his eight struck gold in Rio. He spent this first Tokyo year waiting patiently to see who among his latest crop of medallists would return to the squad, and experimenting with crew line-ups through the world-cup season. In Sarasota a four led by Moe Sbihi from the Rio four and Will Satch from the Rio eight, accompanied by two from the typing pool, Matthew Tarrant and Matthew Rossiter emerged as the best shot.

The water was usually fair, and when the wind blew it behaved no worse than any of the courses where Grobler sends his crews to race. The regatta and the racing conditions were good, but there turned out to be a shortage of good news for the British managers.

In the final of the fours, the Britons watching at home had the disadvantage of a deliriously partisan television commentariat with absurd expectations that were dashed before their eyes. The boat with Grobler's name and reputation on it and with the lead athlete of this Olympiad – Sbihi in the number-two seat – finished third. Even before the crew landed in the USA it had the normal problems of blending two outstanding champions, Sbihi and Satch, with two relative newcomers, Tarrant and Rossiter, but at the Lucerne regatta it had looked really commanding, with the *whoomph* of Sbihi's rhythm putting the whole crew on a conveyor belt to the gold. Yet in Sarasota the four was far from settled. Satch was ill one day then better the next, and hot-desking the stroke seat with Oliver Wynne-Griffith. Wynne-Griffith was on the crew list declared on the morning of the final, but when the camera focused on the boat sitting on the start line, Satch was holding the stroke oar. They raced well, but not as well as Australia and Italy.

The eight, meanwhile, never looked comfortable at high speed in Sarasota. There was just one survivor from Grobler's Rio crew: 32-year-old Tom Ransley. Film of Ransley in 2016 and 2017 showed the same athlete rowing the same style, but the strain of going more slowly in Sarasota was visible in the shoulders and even the grip on his blade. The scrubby beard did not hide the stress on his face. In the repechage for places in the final, the crew was there or thereabouts through the entire race, but unable to summon a change of pace when it mattered. After the race Oliver Cook was taken out sick and replaced for the B final for places seven to twelve.

The *schadenfreude* of other nations pleased to see the Brits cast down will be short-lived. There was nothing in that performance which could not be sorted. It was far from a 'thin red line' with gaps appearing after heavy action. Instead, as Cook fell, Cameron Buchan stepped into a seat he had occupied on and off throughout the season, and the crew dominated the B final.

Grobler was not happy, though. He is as competitive now as at any time in the last fifty years, and he knows better than anyone what has to be done to turn this competent but dull group into winners. He will develop their confidence in his ability to improve their performance incrementally, and in his knowing exactly how fast they will have to be to win in Tokyo. They might not be good enough now, but they will be as good as those bodies can possibly be. And they will have had the best platform in the world to spring from.

In the sculling squad the story was the same. There were mid-regatta substitutions, unreliable gossip in the press tent and oscillating expectations in every event. The quadruple scull had a strong sequence of warm-up races and several interchangeable scullers. It reached Florida with a reasonable chance of gold but – with Peter Lambert's back seizing up while the crew went to the start of the final – Graeme Thomas from the double scull was plucked from the stands where he was sitting with his mum, driven to the start and dropped into the stroke seat. No practice, no rehearsal. Off they went to take up second place, with the Dutch as improbable leaders. Entering the last quarter of the race, the crews were in line across the course with the Netherlands, Britain and Lithuania level. Lithuania had the greater change of pace and won. The Brits were hugely relieved with silver, but dismayed that Lambert had missed out.

The depth of the squad was revealed, however, when the 23-year-old spare man was entered in the single sculls to keep him busy. In his heat Tom Barras beat the find of the season and holder of the world-best time, Robert Manson of New Zealand. Manson was rumoured to be sick, but he stayed in the competition. Barras needed a top-three finish in the quarter-final and was drawn with four-time world champion Ondřej Synek. Instead of settling for a place in the semi-final, which he had secured after 500 metres, Barras stuck to Synek and, although there was little chance of an upset, finished with his bow ball level with Synek's backside. Point made. That earned him a start in the easier semi-final, which he won. In three races he had gone from spare man having fun to contender for a medal.

In the moment it was easy to see why. Like the rest of the team, he is built on the right scale and has come up through the junior squad where he had little real success but was coached assiduously. In Saratoga he looked easy in his work, kept the length of his stroke and, most importantly, was not intimidated by the great man in the next lane. Indeed, Barras used Synek as a pacemaker. In the final he made a novice's bodge of the start and was last after ten strokes, but he stuck close to the Czech, and although Synek skinned him in the last 500 metres, he held off the late charge of the Rio dead-heater, Damir Martin, to win the bronze medal. A hero from zero – even if he did look a bit of a squirt on the podium beside Angel Fournier Rodriguez of Cuba when they lifted Synek onto their shoulders in the traditional salute of the champion.

The revelation of this tale is that the scullers, like the rowers, are constantly refreshing a squad that is large and filled with bodies possessing the necessary physical qualities. Those short of the right stuff soon find their own way to the exit. For those who survive, Grobler and Paul Thompson offer the best (and possibly the hardest) pathway to the podium. The only country equally well set up is New Zealand, with Australia not far behind. All the rest are deficient in one quality or another. China spends large sums but is too large and has too many regions to concentrate talent into an Olympic funnel. It also has a poor record with WADA. Germany runs a really good men's eight group but nothing much behind that, and so on across the world. Italy waxes and wanes but was looking strong in Sarasota, finishing at the top of the medals table with Britain in eighth place. But strip out the Olympic events from the world-championship programme, and New Zealand goes top.

The conclusion of the Sarasota championships for Grobler and British Rowing was that the result for each boat could be analysed, and causes for success and failure identified in good time for solutions to be found. Anyone betting against Grobler finding answers to the struggles encountered in Sarasota would be betting against his lifetime in the top flight. But Grobler's post-Olympic rebuilding season was a struggle. The excessive highs of Rio were matched by lows as his journeymen rowers one by one switched off the alarm and opted out of the 6 a.m. start on the water. Careers now match the durability of the East German team of the Seventies: a junior medal followed a couple of years later by an under-23 medal before entering the senior squad for the next Olympiad. Some who win a world title but don't make the Olympic team – like Matthew Tarrant – carry on. Others – like Paul Bennett on whom the Rio sun shone most brightly and who took gold in the number-six seat of the eight – think twice before testing Darwin's least magnanimous theory for four more years.

This is a danger of a centralised system without club loyalties. People sign on for the medal, endure the hardships, take their due, discover that ambition is fulfilled, and move on. It is noticeable that Molesey club members like Hodge, Reed, Sbihi, and Greg Searle had extended careers in the modern era. It is also noticeable that as nations such as Australia move to a centralised model – with the men in Canberra and the women at the 2000 Olympic venue at Penrith – their results took a leap up in Sarasota. The price in longevity will not be known until 2021.

* *

The unavoidable conclusion of watching Grobler's triumphant progress through the last fifty years of rowing development is that while he has not changed his methodology of 'observe, analyse, change and improve', with science as the basis of each decision, the way his crews are prepared and the way they move their boats is changing constantly.

At the Olympic regatta in Rio, his two crews were the cynosure of every eye. It was known that there was the good chance of a win both for the four – the boat class won by his crews at every Olympics since 2000 – and for the eight, which was his only declared unfulfilled dream. Both crews had lane three, which the FISA selection system gives to the fastest qualifier through the heats and repechages. The cameras and the commentators could not get enough of either.

In the frenzy of the start, the styles and even the colours of the crews in line abreast were merged in one kaleidoscopic blur. But, in both races, the British crews emerged from the pack as they passed the 500-metre marker, and it was possible to put a critical eye on their style of moving the boat and the effort required to take and hold the lead.

If he had cast his mind back to his first Olympic golds in 1976, Grobler would have been able to mark every change in style from the heyday of East German orthodoxy to his crews gradually turning the screw on rivals in Rio. Klaus Filter recalls that many years ago he and Grobler identified that the crucial moment which defines boat speed is the catch, when the blade grips the water and is drawn past the fulcrum by the athlete pulling the oar and pushing his legs against the foot stretcher. The boat moves faster when the blades are clear of the water and body weight is moving toward the stern. Filter, Grobler and Peter Schwanitz set up a measuring frame and calculated for each athlete the moment that power was pushing the stretcher down and slowing the boat and the moment when they were pulling back on the blade and moving the boat in the right direction. Ninety-nine per cent of athletes had a negative peak at the catch and stopped the boat before they moved it. Only one in Filter's experience had no negative reaction. She was the weakest in the East German team, but she could make a contra action in the middle of her body, catch the water and move the boat without negative push on the stretcher. He named her as Christine Scheiblich, Olympic single-sculls champion in 1976 and 1980.

In 2017 Paul Thompson, speaking of Constantine Louloudis, stroke of Grobler's 2016 four, said he 'has perfect timing'. When pressed on this point, Thompson said much the same as Filter about the application of power being timed perfectly to the thrust of the boat through the water.

Examining his eight as they stretched into a lead in Rio, Grobler will have seen that their exceptional boat speed came from a relatively long slide. Although the bodies are curved to allow a good reach at the catch, they remain close to constant in position over the hips. The arms take the catch at full stretch and only break to add to the draw after the legs are driven almost to flat. The catch was slightly less emphatic in the eight than in the four, presumably because the faster-moving boat could be tapped along by a crew working perfectly together to apply the maximum power when their oars were at right angles to the hull. The impulse is wholly directed towards pushing the boat forward, without slippage. The four had a slightly sharper catch to pick up the greater weight of the boat relative to the number of rowers to pull it along.

What is undoubtedly true is that Grobler, marrying the sciences that he has practised all his life in a constant search for the perfect, efficient stroke, has found a way of imparting his knowledge to more athletes in more generations than any before him. His men and women are fitter and stronger than all but the best of the others, and their success comes from the most intricate and precise instruction on using that fitness to move boats. He may not be a genius, but he has trained himself and others to win in a way unprecedented in the history of sport.

He has played his life game with extreme guile, courage and effort, and has reaped the highest rewards. His first good decision was to choose sport as his profession and put himself in the place where his countrymen were going to push the most resources. What he and his fellow top coaches asked for they got – not for themselves, but for their sport. In Grobler's case this comprised equipment, training facilities at home and abroad, and the material benefits that would keep the athletes straining for success. They also had what very few in the whole country shared, which was that they could criticise the quality or quantity of services the state offered and expect to see improvement. What is taken for granted in a western consumer society – the right to complain and demand better – was not a concept enjoyed by East Germans, except for the few top coaches. A major part of Grobler's rise was that he had the perfect combination of working within the confines of a rigid system and the wit to choose the moments when he could exercise flair and judgment to step outside the system in search of greater success.

Perhaps the one factor the state could not control, though, was luck. And Grobler had luck that he was reaching for promotion in the one place that had taken sport to a new plane, and was continuously pouring resources into the medal table. Later, when he had come without a blink through the trauma of the disintegration of his homeland and the fall of the principles by which he had lived, he landed in the country that had the two best physically equipped oarsmen of their generation. As their careers faded, he was the reigning champion when the monetisation of medals caused the word 'sport' to get smaller as the word 'business' grew bigger in the games people play. For the first four Olympics that he attended, East Germany spent the most money and won the most medals, and for the last five Olympics Britain has paid the highest cash price per medal. It may be luck or good management, but Jurgen Grobler has certainly been in the right place at the right time with the best banker. Twice.

He also had luck that when the time came to switch from the regime that stopped at nothing to win to a regime that played more closely to the rules, no one in an official position thought to ask him the direct question about his past involvement in artificial testosterone. It shows a remarkable lack of curiosity among the rowing managers at Leander and later the ARA (now British Rowing) not to ask anything at all on the point which their many silver-medal winners were vocally grumpy. It was top of the agenda in the debate as East Germany was integrated into the West, but no one in Britain thought it mattered enough to ask.

* *

The other personal characteristic remarked on about Grobler is his discretion. All the interviews woven into this story confirm that he has never broken down or even let his guard down, with anyone, for a minute. He has sometimes drunk a little too much but never let that unlock his tongue or temper. He lives on his nerves but does not allow them to push him to the boil. When he told the authors that he would not collaborate with this book, he followed up – in the next breath – with an invitation to have a drink with him in the bar downstairs. In spite of a combined seventy years in sports journalism, we were both a little hesitant about drinking through the afternoon, but we swallowed our prejudices and several pints.

As usual, Grobler was great company and we spoke easily for two or three hours about our only subject. He was witty, relaxed and informative while never saying anything that put us ill at ease. He calculated like any conversationalist speaking in his second language, but he never backtracked or redirected a sentence. Each of his public utterances is weighed for its effect. When he chooses to tell his own tale from the inside looking out, it will follow the chronology of these pages but will differ in reasoning. One thing that will undoubtedly be the same in both tellings is the impact he has had on his athletes – the belief he has instilled in them and the effort that has produced.

Matt Langridge rowed in Grobler's squad for seventeen years and won Olympic silver in Beijing and bronze in London. After the eight's last pre-Rio race when they lost to Germany by half a length, he was asked if he thought he could still win in Rio. He replied: 'Oh, we will win in Rio. We have six weeks, and we go to altitude at Silvretta tomorrow and he has the genius of bringing a crew on and closing that gap. We will work on it, until it is certain.'

As the pull to Tokyo progresses and toughens, as the pressure builds on a coach in his seventies with an impeccable golden record to which the most recent podium statistic has added two further Olympic-champion boats to his total, there are thirty-odd Olympic champions who, like Langridge, owe thanks to Jurgen Grobler. If he keeps his nerve – and there is no reason to suppose that he won't – there will be more.

Acknowledgements

In collecting a lifetime's worth of quotations and information to tell Jurgen's story the authors have striven for accuracy, and we bear sole responsibility for any mistakes that may come to light. While written sources are outlined in the Bibliography, we would like to thank the many athletes, coaches, officials and journalists who have talked to us and given us valuable information. In particular, More Power is a better book for the assistance of Astrid Ayling with German matters and contributions from the following:

Mark Banks, Brigitte Berendonk, John Boultbee, Ed Coode, Martin Cross, Klaus Filter, Prof. Werner Franke, Tim Foster, Brendan Gallaher, Toby Garbett, Alex Gregory, Garry Herbert, Phelan Hill, Andrew Triggs Hodge, Tom James, Bob Janousek, Ivor Lloyd, Constantine Louloudis, John Pilgrim-Morris, Lord Moynihan, Birgit Peter, Sir Matthew Pinsent, Sir Steve Redgrave, Pete Reed, Moe Sbihi, Peter Schwanitz, Greg Searle, Jonny Searle, Catherine Shakespeare, Matt Smith, Jana Sorgers, Peter Spurrier, Sir David Tanner, Paul Thompson, Andy Trotman, Ian Wilson, Arnie and Roswitha Zarach.

From the inception of More Power, the authors invited Jurgen to take part in interviews and accompany us on his journey. After much deliberation he decided not to be involved officially with a biography or autobiography until he has finished coaching – a position he has consistently maintained for a decade or more. To Jurgen's great credit we have enjoyed informal discussions on several occasions while this book was in preparation and relations between the book's subject and its writers have remained as cordial as they have been since Jurgen's arrival in Britain in 1991.

We would also like to thank Nick Bates for his enthusiastic support as publisher at HQ/Harper Collins, Charlotte Atyeo, our meticulous editor, and our indefatigable agent Charlie Campbell of Kingsford Campbell.

Hugh Matheson and Christopher Dodd

The Stasi papers

Stasi records revealing the contents of personal files compiled by informers for the East German secret police became available in 1998. Their publication triggered press inquiries to sports bodies and employers of former East German coaches. *Regatta* magazine offered Jurgen Grobler the opportunity to tell his story in his own words. Grobler declined, but during the next few weeks he was forced to break his silence, particularly in answer to a sustained campaign of insinuations made by the *Mail on Sunday*. Some sections from those articles demonstrating the order of events are outlined here:

Ian Pocock and James Toney, *Mail on Sunday*, 15 February:

> *Steve Redgrave, Britain's greatest Olympian, is being coached by a man, now alleged to have been a key figure in East Germany's reviled programme of drug cheats. Evidence from Professor Werner Franke – the foremost authority on sports doping under the old Communist regime – is claimed to link the coach Jürgen Grobler to the use of drugs to boost East German sports men and women. Franke alleges Grobler forced the testosterone-based drug, Clomiphen, on aspiring international rowers during his time as East German rowing coach. 'Grobler was instrumental in the decision-making of doping', said Franke.*

On the 16th February the ARA responded in a statement with 'full confidence' in their appointment:

> *'Recent speculation, whilst not to be treated lightly, is rumour and comment that has surfaced from time to time over recent months. However, given our own certainty of being a clean sport, and the success we have achieved under his coaching guidance the ARA expresses full confidence in Jürgen Grobler as its men's chief coach.'*

Grobler himself subsequently appeared on BBC *Newsnight* (albeit by telephone) with reporter Adam Mynott, 19 February:

> *I have to live with what went on in East Germany. I was born in the wrong place. It was difficult to have the strength to say no. That is difficult for me. All I can say is that no one was forced. They could walk away. I look in the mirror and see myself. I had to live with a system that I knew was wrong.*

Wilfried Hofmann, former president of the East German rowing association, former chairman of FISA's junior commission and former manager of Dynamo Berlin (the police sports club), spoke to *Newsnight*, on the 19th February to assert *'We did not rely on anabolic agents or any other drugs.'*

Michelle Verroka, director of ethics and anti-doping, UK Sports Council, on *Newsnight*, on the 19 February stated

> *'Evidence is only just emerging in the last eighteen months of the effects of what happened in the GDR. Coaches could have been forced to take part in the system also.'*

Other key UK sporting personnel went on record such as Howard Wells, chief executive of the UK Sports Council, 20 February:

'In the UK we have an entirely different approach to the achievement of excellence in sport than in the former Eastern Germany. Individual cases must be seen in the context of a state-controlled doping regime whereby coaches and athletes may all have been victims.'

As well as the UK Sports Council, who stated on the 20 February:

In the light of ongoing investigations and prosecutions in Germany, the UK Sports Council has invited governing bodies to examine their recruitment procedures for coaches and officials.

Michelle Verroka, director of ethics and anti-doping, UK Sports Council, 20 February:

Governing bodies need to be confident that coaches will uphold their policies on conduct, particularly on doping issues.

The Mail on Sunday continued to look hard at Grobler's role in the GDR system and what the implications for that may mean.

Ian Pocock and James Toney, *Mail on Sunday*, 22 February:

It is now almost certain that Grobler, 51, will face criminal prosecution for his alleged role… Grobler is likely to be accused as a result of the side effects of Clomiphen and Oral-Turinabol steroids it is alleged that he helped to administer… The ARA's support could be overturned by rowing's international governing body, FISA. Matt Smith, FISA chief executive [sic] said: 'we have a life ban for first offences and we take it very seriously. We do whatever we think best for rowing. We want to appear tough when we do find something.'[1]

---

1   FISA has not threatened to overthrow the ARA's support for Grobler, even if it were in FISA's power to do so.

FISA will meet in a fortnight's time to decide on the future of Grobler and other international coaches from the former East Germany.[2] After the meeting Grobler will be called to FISA headquarters in Lausanne to give his account of events during his 18-year spell on the East German state coaching staff from 1972 to 1990.[3]

British rowing, meanwhile, could lose its £1.5 million Lottery grant in the light of allegations against Grobler... The Sports Council, who have been expressing doubt over the ARA's handling of the affair, could withhold funding if they do not get reassurances from rowing chiefs.[4]

Press Association/Sporting Life news service on the internet, 22 February:

The fate of Jurgen Grobler as chief [sic] coach of the British men's rowing team lies in the hands of Steve Redgrave and other leading British oarsmen. 'We are going to have an in-house meeting with athletes and other officers of the association and base any decisions on their views,' said ARA chairman [sic] Martin Brandon-Bravo. Rowing's international governing body, FISA, will meet in a fortnight to discuss Grobler's future.

Duncan Mackay, *The Observer*, 22 February:

Grobler is a graduate of Leipzig's College for Physical Culture, the nerve centre for East German sport... which has earned itself a

---

2 FISA did indeed meet a fortnight later at its annual joint commissions meeting in Zagreb, a meeting scheduled a year previously at which neither doping nor Grobler was on the agenda.

3 No such summons took place or was ever mooted.

4 No such threat has been issued nor has any Sports Council expressed doubts about the ARA's conduct of its affairs.

reputation as a leader in hormone-doping research long before the official evidence came to light... 'I had to live with a system I knew was wrong,' Grobler has said... It is far too simplistic for those of us who have never lived under a totalitarian regime to say people like Grobler should have simply walked away. While the rewards for the successful coaches were huge... the repercussions for those brave enough to stand up to the system were dire... It also brought the unwanted attention of the Stasi, the feared East German secret police... Leipzig was more than a drugs factory; it also made a vast investment to ensure it produced the best-qualified, most knowledge-able coaches whose expertise ranges from physiology to psychology.

Interest extended to the point of letters in *The Times* as here from James Palmer, 23 February:

Sir – when I was an oarsman in the late 1970s, neither I, nor my teammates nor our coaches had any doubt that our East German opponents used drugs to enhance their performances. Nor did we have any doubt that our opponents and their coaches were deprived of the freedom of will that we all took for granted.

The essence of a good coach to us was, and is, the ability to impart exceptional sporting technique and to inspire outstanding mental and physical performance.

Should we now revisit a happily distant era in sporting history and condone an attack on a man undoubtedly as much a victim of an oppressive political regime as its own unfortunate athletes? Should we now deprive a victim of that system of an honourable and respectable rehabilitation, our own athletes of his abilities, and ourselves of a national pride in their performance?

On 28 February the ARA Council issued a statement setting out the association's position:

Our sport, this association, and its officers past and present have been in the forefront internationally in unequivocal opposition to drug taking. That opposition is undiminished.

The ARA stressed that rowing in Great Britain was clean, and expressed concern over the allegations of drug use emerging from the Eastern Bloc as well as for the shadow cast over professional coaches worldwide who may have been part of that social structure and approach to sporting success.

'We neither approve nor condone what may or may not have happened under the political regime in the GDR', stated the ARA' but we believe that we should approach these matters with understanding', reiterating their formal statement of the 20 February 1998.

The ARA did, however, caveat this in regards to Grobler at this time stating, *'he accepts that our support cannot be unconditional, for whilst we have no reason to believe any actions being considered in the new Federal German Republic involve him, should that change and a legal process begin our officers would take immediate and appropriate action.'*

Wilf Paish, athletics coach, on BBC TV's *Heart of the Matter*:
We should see drug taking as an acceptable way of enhancing performance in sport. The rules simply do not work and should be scrapped.

Ian Pocock and James Toney, *Mail on Sunday*, 8 March:
Britain's men's rowing coach, Jurgen Grobler, is facing a life ban from the sport over drug-cheat claims. As more evidence of his alleged involvement in the East German sports-doping programme became public, the sport's governing body, FISA, met in Zagreb yesterday and decided to launch their own investigation. Next week FISA

members will travel to Germany to meet officials of the national
federation as well as police investigators. 'We have to be tough,'
said FISA chief executive [sic] Matt Smith. 'Doping in rowing is
the most serious of allegations and a life ban is usually the only
available penalty'... These are very serious allegations and it's our
duty to carry out our own extensive inquiry.'

FISA commissions and executive met in Zagreb but did not 'launch
an investigation'. What Smith actually told Pocock on the telephone
was that allegations on a single sheet of fax paper was not grounds
for any investigation, but that FISA would monitor the situation.
The meeting in Germany referred to was an inspection of the 1998
world-championship facilities in Cologne arranged weeks before,
and did not involve 'police investigators'.

FISA Council guidelines issued 8 March:
FISA is following the ongoing official investigation in Germany with
close attention. It is in contact with the German sports authorities
and trying to obtain all possible information on these cases. FISA
will take any appropriate decisions as soon as all pertinent elements
have been established and are available for careful and detailed
investigation.

Derek Hunter, *Mail on Sunday*, 15 March:
Britain's rowing chiefs will review the position of coach Jurgen
Grobler if he is formally charged for alleged doping offences...
'What people have to understand is that this is a whole culture
we are talking about and it affects hundreds of people. We are not
prepared to hang out one man to dry when it was the system'... a
delegation from FISA's Swiss headquarters has now established a
dialogue with the German attorney general's office.

In April the *Mail on Sunday* sent Michael Calvin to the British training camp in Hazewinkel, Belgium. His story, although by-lined 'with Ian Pocock and James Toney', put an entirely different twist on the trail of misinformation published by the paper and the Press Association hitherto. Here are some extracts:

Mail on Sunday, 19 April:

The faceless men haunted Jurgen Grobler for 15 years. They preyed on his fears, held his family hostage and forced him to compromise his principles... As ever, perception is more powerful than reality. His personal Stasi file might summon the stereotypes of John Le Carré, but in essence, his 15 years reporting to the Ministry of State Security, from July 1974, was an exercise in bureaucratic mundanity that would have done Sir Humphrey proud.

Grobler to Calvin: 'Some things that were going on at that time might not have been correct, but I can look everybody in the eye and not feel guilty. I am not a doping coach. I am not a chemist... It was my job to bring in gold medals, but to do that I had to be a diplomat in a GDR tracksuit. You must understand that hundreds of thousands of people were contacted... The most insidious informers within rowing were the coxes, who tended to be specially trained secret policemen.

'I wanted to leave Germany because I wanted to prove I could succeed in a different system... I love it here. People in Britain have been really great. I've had letters, faxes, phone calls from people I don't know. They tell me: 'Stay here, be strong. We are with you.'

Olympic gold medallists coached by Jurgen Grobler

Montreal 1976

GDR M2+ Harald Jährling, Frieddrich-Wilhelm Ulrich, cox Georg Spohr

M4x Wolfgang Gueldenpfennig, Rudiger Reiche, Karl-Heinz Bussert, Michael Wolfgramm

Moscow 1980

GDR M2+ Harald Jährling, Frieddrich-Wilhelm Ulrich, cox Georg Spohr

(Los Angeles 1984 boycotted by GDR)

Seoul 1988

GDR W2x Birgit Peter, Martina Schröter

Supervised by Grobler as chief coach for GDR women

Barcelona 1992

GBR M2- Steve Redgrave, Matthew Pinsent

Atlanta 1996

GBR M2- Steve Redgrave, Matthew Pinsent

Sydney 2000

GBR M4- James Cracknell, Steve Redgrave, Tim Foster, Matthew Pinsent

Athens 2004

GBR M4- Steve Williams, James Cracknell, Ed Coode, Matthew Pinsent

Beijing 2008

GBR M4- Tom James, Steve Williams, Pete Reed, Andrew Triggs Hodge

London 2012

GBR M4- Alex Gregory, Tom James, Pete Reed, Andrew Triggs Hodge

Rio de Janeiro 2016

GBR M4- Alex Gregory, Moe Sbihi, George Nash, Constantine Louloudis
M8+ Scott Durant, Tom Ransley, Andrew Triggs Hodge, Matt Gotrel, Pete Reed, Paul Bennett, Matt Langridge, William Satch, cox Phelan Hill

Bibliography

One of the extraordinary things about rowing is the stream of writing devoted to it. Here we list a handful of volumes that involve coaching and Jurgen Grobler, and some that unravel the history of the two countries where he has spent his professional life.

Among them, Leander Club's history of its first 200 years contains Grobler's account of his arrival at his first coaching berth in Britain. *The Sport of Rowing* makes copious references to coaching and coaches, Grobler included. *Rudern* is the official East German coaching manual, and *Doping* is a comprehensive study of substances and their use.

The Story of World Rowing, written shortly after the fall of the Berlin Wall, covers the history of competitive rowing in the two Germanys and Britain. *Olympic Obsession* is an account of taking on East Germans, while *Four Men in a Boat* describes the passage to Olympic gold from a seat in a Grobler-coached crew.

Books

Berendonk, Brigitte, *Doping: Von der Forschung zum Betrug* (Rowohlt Taschenbuch, 1992)

Burnell, Richard and Page, Geoffrey *The Brilliants: A History of the Leander Club* (Leander Club, 1997)

Cross, Martin, *Olympic Obsession* (Breedon Books, 2001)

Dodd, Christopher, *The Story of World Rowing* (Hutchinson, 1992)

Foster, Tim with Rory Ross, *Four Men in a Boat: The Inside Story of the Sydney 2000 Coxless Four* (Weidenfeld & Nicolson, 2004)

Herberger, Ernst (tr. Peter Klavora), *Rowing Rudern: The GDR Text of Oarsmanship* (Sport Book Publisher, 1987)

Mallory, Peter, *The Sport of Rowing: Two Centuries of Competition* (River & Rowing Museum, 2011)

Trotman, Andy (Ed), *Leander Club, the First 200 Years 1818-2018*, Vision Sports Publishing, 2018.

Unknown, *Physical Culture and Sport in the GDR: Information, Facts, Figures* (Panorama DDR, 1978)

There are many books on the conditions and way of life in East Germany, of which the following are readable:

Funder, Anna, *Stasiland: Stories from Behind the Berlin Wall* (Granta 2003)

Kuczynski, Rita (tr. Anthony J. Steinhoff), *Wall Flower: A Life on the German Border* (University of Toronto Press, 2015)

Schneider, Peter (tr. Leigh Hafrey), *The Wall Jumper* (Penguin Classics, 2005)

Steele, Jonathan, *Socialism with a German Face: The State that Came in from the Cold* (Jonathan Cape, 1977)

Vaizey, Hester, *Born in the GDR: Living in the Shadow of the Wall* (OUP, 2014)

There are many more on the collapse of the Wall, of which the following are good:

Sarotte, Mary Elise, *The Collapse: The Accidental Opening of the Berlin Wall* (Basic Books, 2014)

Sebestyen, Victor, *Revolution 1989: The Fall of the Soviet Empire* (Weidenfeld & Nicolson, 2009)

And this is excellent on the conditions of war and politics which led to the formation of East Germany:

Bessel, Richard, *Germany 1945: From War to Peace* (Simon & Schuster, 2009)

Magazines

Regatta

Row 360

Rowing & Regatta

Rowing News

Internet

www.biorow.com

https://heartheboatsing.com

www.row2k.com

https://rowingvoice.wordpress.com

Credits

Quotations.

Page 19, *Das Rudern* English edition, Herberger, Ernst (tr Peter Klavora), Sport Book Publisher, 1987; Page 22, *The Independent*, 2012, Michael Calvin; Page 30, *Das Rudern* English edition, Herberger, Ernst (tr Peter Klavora) Sport Book publisher 1987; Page 31, *Das Rudern*, English Edition, Hernerger, Ernst (tr Peter Klavora) Sport Book Publisher 1987; Page 74, *The Guardian*, Jan 9 1991, Christopher Dodd; Page 76, *The Guardian*, April 19 1991, Christopher Dodd; Page 80, *The Guardian*, August 1992, Christopher Dodd; Page 81, *The Guardian*, August 1992, Frank Keating; Page 82, *The Guardian*, 28 March 1990, Christopher Dodd; Page 90, *Regatta*, October 1991, Christopher Dodd; Page 92, *The Times*, March 1992, Mike Rosewell; Page 96, *The Guardian*, 26 June 1992, Christopher Dodd; Page 97, *The Guardian*, 26 June 1992, Christopher Dodd; Page 99, *The Guardian*, 3 August 1992, Christopher Dodd; Page 102, *Regatta*, July 1995, Christopher Dodd; Page 108, *The Guardian*, July 1995, Christopher Dodd; Page 108, *Regatta*, July 1995, Christopher Dodd; Page 110, *Regatta*, September 1996, Christopher Dodd; Page 111, *Regatta*, September 1996, Christopher Dodd; Page 116, *Regatta*, February 1997, Christopher Dodd, Page 120, *The Mail* on Sunday, 19 April, Michael Calvin; Page 121, *Regatta*,

CREDITS

May 1998, Various; Page 121/122, *Regatta*, April 1998, Martin Cross; Page 123, *Regatta*, July 1998; Page 124/125, *Regatta*, August/September 1998, Christopher Dodd; Page 126, *Regatta*, March 1999, James Cracknell; Page 128, *Regatta*, May 1999, James Cracknell; Page 129, *Regatta*, August/ September 1999, Christopher Dodd; Page 130, *Regatta*, March 2000, James Cracknell; Page 131, *Regatta*, May 2000, Mike Rosewell; Page 132, *Regatta*, May 2000, James Cracknell; Page 133, *The Guardian*, April 2000, Christopher Dodd; Page 134, *The Guardian*, July 2000, Christopher Dodd; Page 135, *Regatta* August/September 2000, Matthew Pinsent; Page 135, *Regatta* August/September 2000, James Cracknell; Page 136, *Regatta* August/September 2000, Ed Coode; Page 139, *Regatta*, February/ March 2003, Christopher Dodd; Page 140, *Regatta*, November 2000 No, Christopher Dodd; Page 140/141, *Regatta*, March 2001, Christopher Dodd; Page 145/146, *Regatta*, October 2001, Neil Chugani; Page 146, *Regatta*, October 2001, Christopher Dodd; Page 148, [The Guardian, 13 July 2002, Christopher Dodd; Page 149, *Regatta*, February/March 2003, Christopher Dodd; Page 151, *Regatta*, September 2003, Christopher Dodd; Page 151, *The Independent*, 1 September 2003, Christopher Dodd; Page 152, *Regatta*, December 2003 – January 2004, Christopher Dodd; Page 153, Regatta, June 2004, Christopher Dodd; Page 154, *The Independent*, 4 July, Christopher Dodd; Page 164, *Regatta*, August 2006, Christopher Dodd; Page 164, *Regatta*, October 2006, Christopher Dodd; Page 165/166, Rowing & Regatta, December 2006/January 2007, Christopher Dodd; Page 167, *The Times*, April 2006, Matthew Pinsent; Page 171, *Regatta*, February 2008, Christopher Dodd; Page 173, *The Guardian*, 16 July 2008, Martin Cross; Page 175, *The Independent*, 20 August 2008, Christopher Dodd; Page 177, *Rowing News*, May 2009, Christopher Dodd; Page 184, *Rowing Voice*, 12 July 2010, Christopher Dodd; Page 188, *Rowing Voice*, August 2011, Rachel Quarrell; Page 196, *Rowing & Regatta*, August 2012, Martin Cross; Page 215, *Row 360*, issue 13, Autumn 2016, Rachel Quarrell

Appendix

Image Credits

D0%B9%D0%BB:Bundesarchiv_Bild_183-G0920-0021-001,_Berlin,_11._
DDR-Staatsratsitzung.jpg. Used under Creative Commons license CC
BY-SA 3.0 / (include details of any alterations eg. contrast increased
from original). Grobler with DDR womens squad © Getty / ullstein
bild. Day 1 at Leander © Catherine Shakespeare Lane. Atlanta '96 M2-©
Peter Spurrier/Intersport Images. Sydney 2000 M4- © Peter Spurrier/
Intersport Images. Athens 2004 M4- © Peter Spurrier/Intersport Images.
London 2012 M4- © Peter Spurrier/Intersport Images. Rio 2016 M4- ©
Peter Spurrier/Intersport Images. Erg duel © Peter Spurrier/Intersport
Images. Rio 2016 with M8+© Peter Spurrier/Intersport Images. Grobler
with Lady Redgrave and Mrs Grobler © Peter Spurrier/Intersport Images.
Grobler and Redgrave Sydney 2000 © Getty Images Sport / Mike Hewitt.

Every effort has been made to trace the copyright holders and obtain permission to reproduce material within this book. Please do get in touch with any enquiries or information concerning copyright.

Index